STE
Test Prep

MW01168359

CLEP

Introductory Sociology

Essential Content

3rd edition

Customer Satisfaction Guarantee

Your feedback is important because we strive to provide the highest quality educational materials. Email us comments or suggestions.

info@sterling–prep.com

We reply to emails – check your spam folder

3   2   1

ISBN-13: 979-8-8855728-6-6

Sterling Test Prep materials are available at quantity discounts.

Contact info@sterling–prep.com

Sterling Test Prep
6 Liberty Square #11
Boston, MA 02109

© 2025 Sterling Test Prep

Published by Sterling Education

 Printed in the U.S.A.

STERLING
Test Prep

Thousands of students use our study aids to achieve high test scores!

Scoring high on CLEP Introductory Sociology is essential for earning a sociology college credit. Understanding the material, extracting and analyzing information, and distinguishing between similar answer choices are more effective than mere memorization. This book helps you master CLEP Introductory Sociology topics and develop the ability to apply your knowledge to quickly choose the correct answers on the test.

This study guide provides thorough coverage of topics tested on CLEP Introductory Sociology. It explains important principles and relationships and how they apply to exam questions. The material is clearly presented and systematically organized to provide targeted and comprehensive test preparation.

From the early theories on human societies to modern interdisciplinary perspectives, you will develop a better understanding of all major sociology theories, principles and approaches that elucidate multidimensional concepts of groups, communities, institutions, and social behavior. Learn about social psychology, social culture, demography, social inequalities, and research methods, as well as historically significant sociologists who contributed to these knowledge areas. The book also describes concepts of personality, self-presentation, and other aspects of social behavior and how they affect social networks and interactions.

Experienced sociology instructors and researchers analyzed test content and developed the material that builds knowledge and skills crucial for success. Our editorial team reviewed and systematized the content for targeted preparation.

Using this book you will significantly improve your test score!

240704akp

Featured on

If you benefited from this book, we would appreciate if you left a review on Amazon, so others can learn from your input. Reviews help us understand our customers' needs and experiences while keeping our commitment to quality.

CLEP study aids by Sterling Test Prep

Biology Review

Biology Practice Questions

Chemistry Review

Chemistry Practice Questions

Introductory Psychology

Introductory Sociology

American Government

History of the United States I

History of the United States II

Western Civilization I

Western Civilization II

Visit our Amazon store

Page intentionally left blank

Table of Contents

Table of Contents (*continued*)

Table of Contents (*continued*)

Table of Contents (*continued*)

CHAPTER 4: SOCIAL CULTURE & BEHAVIOR (*continued*)

Table of Contents (*continued*)

CHAPTER 4: SOCIAL CULTURE & BEHAVIOR (*continued*)

Table of Contents (*continued*)

Table of Contents (*continued*)

Table of Contents (*continued*)

Table of Contents (*continued*)

Table of Contents (*continued*)

CHAPTER 7: RESEARCH METHODS (*continued*)

Table of Contents (*continued*)

Page intentionally left blank

CHAPTER 1

Introduction to Sociology

Sociologists research social institutions and socially connected individuals in communities. They use scientific analysis to examine social issues and how they relate to and impact communities.

Sociology researchers study human behavior's origins, evolution, and aspects, including its development, interactions, and collective behavioral patterns in social groups. They investigate the causes of human behavioral change over time and identify the various factors contributing to behavior change.

Sociology Discipline

Sociology – a study of human society

Sociology is the study of human social behavior, including patterns of interaction among individuals and in groups, forms of organization of social groups, and their influence on individual action. While its origins can be traced back to the Enlightenment in the 18th century and Immanuel Kant (1724–1804), the first to use the term was Auguste Comte (1778–1857), who is considered the founding father of sociology, along with Émile Durkheim (1858–1917), Karl Marx (1818–1883), and Max Weber (1864–1920).

Sociology was developed in the 18th and 19th centuries when Western Europe underwent several economic, technological, and social changes that significantly impacted the social order.

Sociologists specialize in social problems, social psychology, social statistics, industrial sociology, sociology of work, occupations and professions, and other topics. Race, gender, sex, cultural diversity, labor and industrial relations, personnel management, and business relations are areas of specialization.

Sociology is not an intangible idea. Sociologists study collective group behaviors (e.g., people living in the same area and being influenced by the same social forces). Sociologists identify and assess these factors. We encounter numerous examples that sociologists study in daily life and our interactions.

Sociologists are social scientists focused on society's institutions, interactions, and growth.

Sociologists research social structures, including groups, organizations, and processes of interpersonal interaction.

Sociologists examine how people behave, interact, and work together. They monitor social, religious, political, and affinity groups, organizations, and institutions. They examine how social factors, such as institutions and organizations, impact people and groups.

Sociologists offer insight into how interpersonal environments influence behavior. They analyze human *social interactions*, *group dynamics*, and *social processes*.

Sociological imagination is when sociologists conclude interactions and societal structure data.

Sociologists use *qualitative* and *quantitative* methods to collect data about social questions.

Sociology views the world from the perspective of communities and cultures.

Sociology uses *analysis, problem-solving, critical thinking, creativity*, and *innovation* to test hypotheses (i.e., *untested questions*) about social issues.

Sociologists collaborate with interdisciplinary research projects assessing education, religion, family, and public safety.

Sociological focuses

Sociologists study human behavior, interactions, and organizations in various contexts. Health, families, crime, gender, poverty, education, aging, racial and ethnic issues, and population are a few social topics.

Sociologists gather data through surveys, interviews, or observations and then analyze the data to conclude. They write scholarly articles and reports, present research, and identify policies.

Sociologists study social influences and how they impact individuals or groups. Sociologists track the development and beginning of these interactions and groups. For example, the impact of a policy on a specific demographic.

Sociologists frequently research using statistical analysis software, numerical measurements, and qualitative techniques.

Organizations that create and conduct research in the humanities and social sciences are large employers, followed by educational institutions, federal and local governments, and research organizations.

Sociological relationships

People build relationships and eventually a culture when interacting, forming a group, or collaborating. Sociologists investigate how groups interact, how human behavior evolves, and what factors influence the success or failure of cultures and organizations.

To test their theories about how people interact with one another, sociologists gather survey data, make observations, and conduct interviews.

Researchers examine data and present their conclusions in presentations or written reports.

These social scientists might work with and guide groups looking for solutions to sociological problems, other social scientists, or policymakers.

Sociologists can concentrate their research and study efforts on social issues, such as gender, poverty, crime, aging, labor markets, families, racial and ethnic relations, health, and education.

Sociologists often work in offices and might travel to conduct research or give conference presentations of their findings.

Branches of sociology

There are many branches within the discipline of sociology. Each branch of sociology assists with different aspects of society and areas of function. Some major branches of sociology include social psychology, applied sociology, political sociology, urban sociology, environmental sociology, social physiology, and human ecology, among others.

Social psychology studies how the presence of humans or other stimuli influences someone's behavioral, emotional, or thoughts. A social psychologist may study a specific group's dynamics and interactions, such as those within a prison or school.

Applied sociology is using sociology in practice. Practitioners will use different sociology theories to work with their clients. This type of sociology may look at ways to improve a program or system.

Political sociology analyzes the relationships among individuals, societies, and political powers—all of which can be influenced by factors like race, ethnicity, class, and gender. Researchers explore political movements, community action, and organization and how power is gained, maintained, and wielded through political institutions.

Urban sociology studies social structures in urban areas, as well as the events, dynamics, and challenges that are present there. If you are interested in the subfield of urban sociology, you may want to look at institutions set in urban areas that would allow you to study the subfield in an urban environment.

Environmental sociology seeks to comprehend how we interact with environments and how those interactions affect us personally, nationally, and internationally.

Social physiology looks to understand the interactions between society and physical functioning. This branch of sociology can include the study of law and religion.

Human ecology is the study of human and non-human interactions. This area of sociology would include areas of biology, anthropology, and economics. Human ecologists may look at how society is impacting the local environment.

Sociology education

A bachelor's degree in sociology can be used to get more entry-level jobs in related industries like social services, education, or public policy.

Sociologists seeking a master's or doctoral degree follow degree pathways.

Conventional sociology programs prepare students to pursue a Ph.D. afterward. Alternatively, a master's degree in an applied, clinical, or professional field prepares graduates for work.

Courses frequently impart the analytical skills to conduct quantitative and qualitative research. Statistics and research methodology courses are essential.

Programs provide internship opportunities. Before entering this career, internships expand your educational training while gaining professional experience.

Strong communication, analytical, writing, and critical thinking abilities are expected. These abilities are required when working with colleagues, research participants, and other academics.

A master's or doctorate is required for most jobs. Master's degree programs in applied, clinical, and professional studies train graduates to conduct sociological research in a workplace environment.

Many sociology Ph.D. graduates teach college-level courses while others conduct research for businesses, governments, or nonprofits.

Perspectives in Sociology

Microsociology *vs.* macrosociology

Microsociology is concerned with everyday, small-scale human social interactions and agency. It is associated with phenomenology and not supported by statistical or empirical observations.

Micro-level sociologists concentrate on face-to-face small-group interactions, often with in-person interactions. For example, group discourse norms (e.g., teenagers *vs.* executives).

Microsociology relies on *interpretative analysis*.

Interpretative analysis may include *symbolic interactionism* and *ethnomethodology*.

Ethnomethodology spawned subdivisions and studies, such as *microlinguistical* research.

Macrosociology broadly examines populations and social systems, often drawing conclusions and analyzing research using necessarily prominent levels of theoretical abstraction. It examines individuals, families, and constituent aspects of society, focusing on relationships to an extensive social system.

Large collectivities, such as the church or education system, are studied in macrosociology.

Macro-level sociologists look at patterns within and between groups and societies. They research past, present, and future significant societal events. For example, how language use has changed over time and with social media.

Macrosociology examines patterns and social systems

Human populations are considered societies to the degree that they are politically autonomous, and members engage in cooperative activities. For example, French people are a society, but every person worldwide who speaks French is not a member of that society.

Macrosociology analyzes societal and global trends, including war, poverty, and environmental deprivation. It focuses on the specific outcomes of those trends, such as the role of women, the nature of the family, and immigration.

Macrosociology includes paradigms or theoretical frameworks, such as structural functionalism and conflict theory.

Functionalism

Structural functionalism (or *functionalism*) is a main theoretical perspective in sociology. It is a macrosociological analysis focusing on society's role in promoting *solidarity*, *functionality*, and *stability* as a complex system of working parts.

Functionalism approaches society from a macro-level orientation, looking broadly at social structures and functions that shape society. Elements within society that functionalism focuses on are norms, customs, traditions, and institutions.

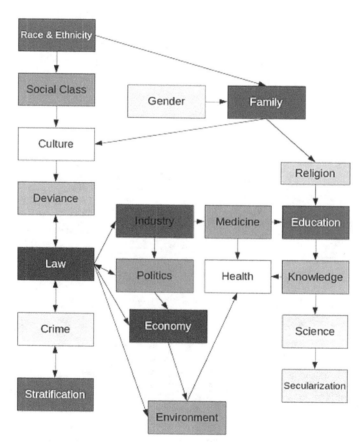

Interrelationships of structural functionalism

English sociologist Herbert Spencer (1820–1903) represented society as like the human body. Constituent parts of society are "organs" that work toward properly functioning the "body" as a whole.

American sociologist Talcott Parsons (1927–1973) distinguished structural functionalism as less of a specific school of thought and more a stage in the methodological development of social science.

Conflict theory

Conflict theory is a central perspective of sociology and a macrosociological theory used to examine society. It emphasizes and deconstructs a social group's social, political, or material inequality and critiques the broad socio-political system.

It is fundamentally at odds with *structural functionalism* and *ideological conservativism*.

Generally, conflict theory contrasts historically-dominant ideologies by explicitly drawing attention to power differentials. Social conflict theory stresses the role of coercion and power in producing social order.

Conflict theory operates on the notion that social order is established by the exerted dominance of those in the society with the greatest political, economic, or social resources. Often, a conflict theory approach highlights ideological aspects inherent in traditional thought.

There are varied types of conflict theories, and many of them may be similar in certain aspects, but conflict theory cannot be considered a single, cohesive school of thought.

Karl Marx (1818–1883) was a revolutionary German philosopher and sociologist who founded social conflict theory. Marxism asserts that the various institutions of society, such as the legal and political systems, serve to further the *domination and interests of the ruling class*.

Karl Marx, German philosopher and socialist

According to Marx, Western society evolved through four principal epochs:

primitive communism → ancient society → feudal society → capitalist society

Prehistoric societies constituted classless societies with a primitive kind of communism. Since then, societies have been divided into one of two major classes.

In ancient societies, there were *enslavers* and *enslaved people*. In feudal societies, there were *lords* and *serfs*. In capitalist societies, there were *capitalists* and *wage laborers*.

Max Weber (1864–1920), a German sociologist and one of the founders of sociology, disagreed with Marx in categorizing class in economic terms.

Weber believed that classes develop in *market economies* where individuals co mpete for economic gain. To Weber, a class or a group of individuals was determined by the similar position of those individuals in a market economy.

Because of a commonplace in the market, these individuals received similar economic rewards. An individual's class could be thought of as their market situation.

The number of opportunities available to an individual was shared with others in a similar class.

Within each class, a corresponding *economic position* directly affected the likelihood of the individuals in that class obtaining the things deemed "*desirable*" by their society.

Symbolic interactionism

Symbolic interactionism is a central theoretical sociology perspective and is particularly influential regarding *microsociology* and *social psychology*.

Symbolic interactionism draws strongly on American pragmatism (the value of an idea is the function of its practical outcome) and specifically on the work of American pragmatist philosopher George Herbert Mead (1863–1931).

Mead's work was extensively studied and interpreted by his student, Herbert Blumer (1900–1987), who coined the term "*symbolic interactionism*" and wrote what is still considered the most straightforward theoretical summary of *symbolic interactionism*.

The *interactionist perspective* operates from the essential idea that people act toward objects based on the *meaning they ascribe to those objects*, which are first derived from *social interaction* and modified through *interpretation*.

Symbolic interactionism as *sociological framework* seeks to understand human behavior by examining the meanings people acquire and construct throughout their lives. In society, various things, motions, actions, and occurrences could signify various things.

For example, emojis are common in mobile communication, with various meanings to different audiences. Emojis with a smile may express happiness or passive-aggression.

George Herbert Mead, American philosopher

Sociologists working in the tradition of social interactionism have conducted wide-ranging research using various research methods. The most common are qualitative research methods, such as participant observation, in which an investigator attains entrance and acceptance into a foreign society to understand its internal structure. These research methods focus on studying aspects of social interaction or people's relationship with themselves.

In Blumer's summary, he established three core principles of interactionism:

that people act toward things, including each other, *based on the meanings they have for them*; that these meanings are derived through *social interaction* with others; and that these meanings are managed and transformed through an *interpretive process* that people use to make sense of and handle the objects that constitute their social worlds.

Framing perspective

David Snow, professor of Sociology at the University of California, in a continuation and broadening of Blumer's principles, developed a *"framing perspective"* with four principles.

   human agency,

   interactive determination,

   symbolization, and

   emergence.

Snow states that these four principles are the basis for discussing social movements.

Human agency, the ability to act independently and of one's own free will, emphasizes humans' active, willful, goal-oriented character. The emphasis on agency is *observing* actions, events, and moments in social life, which require asserting agency.

Interactive determination means that individuals, society, and groups of people do not exist only with each other and, therefore, can be fully understood only in terms of their interactions. This specifies the necessary understanding of objects of analysis, whether they are identities, roles, practices, or social movements.

Symbolization is when any aspect of an environment, including events, conditions, objects, or people, becomes meaningful based on a prescribed orientation. It is essential because human behavior is contingent upon what this prescribed orientation symbolizes (or means) to an individual, group, or society.

Emergence is the processual, routinized, and habitual side of social life. It does not purely look at the organization of societies but at the meaning of practices and feelings of individuals engaged in these practices. This principle includes shifts and developments in functioning social systems and the possibility of new forms of social existence and organization.

Social constructionism

Social constructionism is a sociological perspective operating on the premise that ideas about the world are constructed in coordination with other human beings.

Individuals' perception of aspects of their environment does not develop significance or meaning separately within them; their perception is developed in contingency with others.

Social constructionism is based on the assumptions that humans process experiences by creating a perception of the social world and how it functions, and that language is the essential system through which humans construct reality.

Social constructionism approaches social constructs as the cumulative, organic, and amorphous result of countless human choices rather than strict codes designated by human reason.

Social constructionism opposes *essentialism*, which sees phenomena (cultural occurrences) as inherent, timeless essences or truths independent of human reason.

Social constructionism attempts to decipher how individuals and groups participate in the construction of their perceived social reality. This analysis examines how humans create, accept, routinize, and make social phenomena and behaviors into customs.

Social construction of reality is an ongoing, dynamic process that is (and must be) reproduced by people acting on their unique interpretations and knowledge. Societies and individuals that comprise them must constantly maintain and re-affirm perceived social constructs for them to persist because social constructs *do not inherently exist in nature*.

This process of participation allows for the possibility of change. Answers to the questions of what human rights are and who deserves them, as well as other questions, shape the reality of a social construct and have evolved immensely with time due to a change in human perception and resulting social phenomena.

Social exchange and rational choice theories

Social exchange theory was pioneered by sociologist George Homas in 1961 and posits that human relationships are formed and broken by using subjective cost-benefit analysis and the comparison of alternatives.

Social exchange theory draws on economic principles observed in business and assumptions founded in *rational choice theory* and *structuralism*. The development of social stability between parties engaged in a *mutually beneficial* relationship underlies social exchange theory.

During the 1960s and 1970s, Peter Blau, James Coleman, and Karen Cook expanded Homas's original framework. They developed it into a modern model of *rational choice*, which, over the years, became increasingly mathematical.

Rational choice theory is that aggregate social behavior results from the behavior of individual actors, each of whom makes decisions. It assumes that an individual has preferences among available choices, which allows them to state their preferences.

The concept of rationality in theory is different from the common usage of the word "rational," which typically means "sensible," "predictable," or "thoughtful."

Rational choice theory uses a narrow definition of rationality, whereby the behavior is rational if it is *goal-oriented*, *reflective* (evaluative), and *consistent* (across time and situations).

Rational behavior *differs* from random, impulsive, conditioned, or adopted by blind imitation.

Intersectionality

Intersectionality is a perspective in sociology that investigates how intersecting power relations influence social relations across diverse societies as well as individual experiences in everyday life.

Intersectional theory views the categories of intersecting relations such as race, gender, social class, sexuality, ability, and age as interrelated and mutually shaping one another. Taking these intersecting factors into consideration paves the way for understanding and explaining complexity in individuals, the world, and the human experience.

As a concept, intersectional theory contrasts *monism*, which is the idea that each factor of an individual (e.g., race and gender) can be adequately understood or investigated separately from one another as a single dimension.

Intersectional theory believes that speaking of these factors as separate entities is inaccurate as there is no such thing as gender issues being apart from class, and there is no such thing as sexuality being apart from race.

Intersectionality aims to increase the understanding that humans are shaped by the interaction of different factors and that these interactions occur within a context of connected systems and structures of power. Some of these power structures include laws, policies, governments, religious institutions, and media. Through this, people can be privileged and oppressed in many ways, such as through racism, homophobia, transphobia, sexism, and ableism.

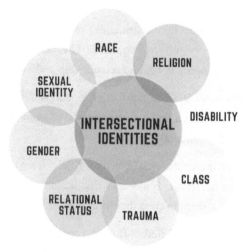

Overlapping areas show various intersectional identities

Relationship matrix

Notes for active learning

CHAPTER 2

Personality

Self refers to the thoughts and beliefs individuals have about themselves. The concept of *self* is complex and multifaceted; it includes gender, racial, and ethnic identities, and beliefs about the individual's ability to accomplish tasks and control different situations.

The concept of *self* develops over time and is shaped by factors, including society, culture, individuals and groups, and unique experiences. How people view themselves influences their perception of others and, by extension, their interactions with them.

Self-Concept, Self-Identity and Social Identity

Self-concept

Psychologists Carl Rogers and Abraham Maslow first identified *self-concept* and *self-identity*.

Self-concept and *self-identity* refer to beliefs people hold about *themselves* and their *abilities*.

Beliefs in three domains significantly influence a person's overall self-concept:

self-esteem,

self-efficacy, and

locus of control.

Self-esteem

Self-esteem is the level of worth a person believes they possess.

High self-esteem people see themselves as valuable and are accepting of themselves. They are typically *confident* and *optimistic* about the future.

Low self-esteem persons view themselves negatively. They tend to be *highly self-critical* and *sensitive to criticisms* from others. They typically have *low self-confidence* and are *pessimistic*.

Self-efficacy

Self-efficacy refers to one's belief in their ability to reach a goal. It concerns the level of competence a person believes they possess for a particular task.

For example, someone who believes they can quit smoking possesses high self-efficacy, while someone who believes they will never be able to quit possesses low self-efficacy.

Research shows that the level of self-efficacy a person has about a given task influences both their level of success on that task and the likelihood that they will start the task.

High self-efficacy people are more likely to take risks than those with low self-efficacy and can recover more quickly from setbacks.

Low self-efficacy people avoid challenging tasks and lose confidence in their abilities when faced with a setback.

Locus of control

Locus of control is a person's beliefs about how much they can control events affecting them.

Individuals with an *internal locus of control* feel they can control many of the events affecting them. They are more likely to *take responsibility for their actions* and circumstances than those with an external locus of control.

Individuals with an *external locus of control* blame outside forces (e.g., luck or chance) for their circumstances. This often leads to feeling hopeless when faced with challenges.

Locus of control lies on a *continuum*; most people fall between an internal and external locus.

Locus of control has become more internal with *age* and varies by *culture*.

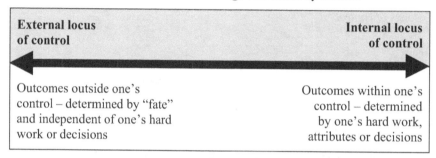

Social identities and ethnicity

Social identity refers to their psychological relationship to particular social categories. It is primarily based on groups that an individual belongs to.

Research suggests that a person's social identity is influenced by race or ethnicity, gender, age, sexual orientation, and class, factors interacting to form a person's self-identity.

Intersectionality is when an individual simultaneously belongs to two or more social groups.

Ethnicity refers to distinctions based on national origin and culture, including language, relation, and place of origin. A person's racial and ethnic background can influence how they perceive themselves. Racial and ethnic identities are passed on from earlier generations.

Ethnic identity is believed to develop during adolescence. Jean Phinney proposed a model for adolescent ethnic identity development that breaks up this process into three stages.

In the first stage of ethnic identity development, an adolescent's ethnic identity is unexamined. Many theorists believe that adolescents from a dominant culture stay in this stage and do not form a sense of ethnic identity.

During the second stage, *moratorium*, adolescents search for the meaning of their ethnicity.

In the third stage of ethnic identity development, adolescents feel secure about their sense of ethnic identity; their identity becomes an integral part of their self-identity.

Racial identity

Race refers to physical distinctions (e.g., skin color and eye shape) and a social construction.

Psychologist William Cross proposed a model for *racial identity development*, particularly Black identity development, which comprises four identity statuses.

Pre-encounter is the first stage of *racial identity development* when individuals are unaware of their race and the effects their race has on others.

Encounter stage is when a person has an encounter that leads to examining their racial identity.

Immersion stage follows the encounter stage, where individuals explore their racial identity, through interaction with individuals of the same race.

Internalization and commitment are the final stages of racial identity development when individuals have formed a secure sense of racial identity and can form positive relationships with individuals who share their racial identity and those who do not.

Gender and sexual orientation

Gender is a social category that refers to attitudes and behaviors a culture associates with a particular biological sex.

Gender identity refers to a person's subjective experience of their gender, typically as male or female. When an individual's gender identity and biological sex are incongruent, they may identify as transsexual or transgender.

Sexual orientation is a person's sexual identity about the *gender to which they are attracted.*

Sexual orientation includes *heterosexuality*, *homosexuality*, *bisexuality*, and *asexuality*.

Stigma may be associated with homosexuality, bisexuality, and asexuality.

Sexual identity is how individuals think of themselves regarding who they are sexually attracted to and may or may not align with sexual orientation. Contemporary models of sexual identity acknowledged its formation occurs in both sexual minorities and majorities.

Age identity

Age identity refers to a person's inner experiences of age and aging.

Research on age identity has found that older individuals tend not to feel old. Researchers have suggested that this is due to self-continuity and self-enhancement.

Self-continuity is the desire to remain the same over time.

Self-enhancement refers to maintaining a positive self-image.

In the United States, people with *older identities* report *lower life satisfaction* levels.

Societies often associate aging with decline; older individuals may wish to identify as younger. Thus, age and age identity differences are less pronounced in Asian cultures, where age is less associated with decline.

Older individuals tend not to feel old due to self-continuity and self-enhancement

Social class identities

Social class refers to social divisions in which individuals are classified by *wealth*, *education*, and *occupation*.

Social classes are typically *lower*, *middle*, and *upper class*. Social class has wide-ranging effects and may become a part of a person's identity.

Individuals from the upper class are typically able to send their children to better schools, while those from the lower class may believe that getting a good education is beyond the means of their class.

Being in a lower social class also has *negative health consequences*. Lower-class people often receive poorer quality healthcare than the upper classes.

Influence of Social Factors on Identity Development

Gender development

Gender is a social construct that forms over time.

Gender identity development begins at an early age, between the ages of three and six.

Some theories of gender development break the formation of gender into three stages.

First stage of gender development is when toddlers learn about the socialized traits of gender.

Second stage of gender development is when gender consolidates and becomes rigid, typically between the ages of five and seven.

Third stage is when socially defined gender roles become relaxed for the individual.

Sandra Bem developed *gender schema theory* as a cognitive theory for gender development.

Gender schemas are sets of gender-related beliefs an individual holds that influence behavior. Bem proposed these schemas form by children's observing males and females within society.

Bem proposes that gender identity is formed primarily from being *sex-typed* at an early age. *Sex-typed* refers to the acquisition of sex-appropriate preferences and behaviors.

Social-learning theory approach to *gender development* focuses on the role of parents and caregivers in an individual's acquisition of gender identity. Walter Mischel proposed that parents reward their children for engaging in gender-appropriate behavior.

For example, a boy might be praised for being interested in fixing cars, and a young girl might be praised for wearing a dress.

Influence of individuals

Imitation is a form of social behavior that refers to copying another person's behaviors.

Imitation occurs even in young infants, suggesting that people have an innate ability to imitate others. One area of research within this field concerns mirror neurons.

Mirror neurons are neurons that are activated when an individual engages in a task and when an individual observes another person engaging in the same task.

Mirror neurons may be responsible for the propensity to imitate others.

Expectations of others influence identity formation. Individuals within a family or group tend to take on a specific role. The influence of this role formation is closely related to social norms; we adapt to the expectations of others.

Roles in one setting (e.g., family) can carry over into another (e.g., peer group). Individuals can internalize these roles and view them as parts of themselves. For example, a girl who takes on a mothering role to her brother may act in a nurturing manner within her friend group and subsequently view herself as a nurturer.

Looking-glass self is a social psychological concept that a person's identity grows out of the perceptions of others. Accordingly, people form their self-identity by combining how others view them.

Three components of the *looking-glass theory*:

> 1) imagine how they appear to others.

> 2) imagine others' judgments about how they appear.

> 3) develop a sense of self through the judgments of others.

Looking-glass self states that a person's identity grows out of the perceptions of others, imagining how others view and judge them.

Reference groups

Social groups are collections of people who share similarities and interact with one another.

Social groups can function as powerful influencers of behaviors.

Reference groups are groups that the individual uses to compare themselves to.

Three reference groups:

*Aspirational reference group*s have people that an individual wishes to be more like.

Associative reference groups have individuals with similar interests to themselves.

Dissociative reference groups (or *out-groups*) have unfavorable individuals to whom the person does not want to belong.

People typically adopt the social norms of aspirational and associative reference groups while actively disdaining the norms of dissociative reference groups.

Primary and secondary groups

Social groups are divided into *primary* and *secondary groups*.

Primary groups are groups in which individuals intimately interact with one another.

Primary groups typically exert a great deal of emphasis. They commonly include families, fraternities, sororities, classmates, and friends.

Secondary groups are groups individuals belong to but do not interact with often.

Relationships within a secondary group are typically brief. They do not exert as much influence on the individuals belonging to them as primary groups.

Influence of culture and socialization on identity formation

How people view themselves is heavily influenced by their childhood culture and socialization. This occurs through the social roles that individuals learn through socialization. When individuals internalize these roles, they become a part of their identity.

Individuals form their identities by comparing themselves to others they interact with.

People compare themselves to the *ideals and expectations* of their culture. Individuals who do not meet these cultural expectations may develop poor self-esteem.

Culture has been found to influence the *locus of control* of individuals.

For example, individuals from the United States typically have a more *internal locus of control* than individuals from Japan.

In the U.S., African Americans tend to have a more *external locus of control* than whites.

Notes for active learning

Self-Presentation and Interacting with Others

Expressing and detecting emotion

Individuals vary in how they express their emotions and detect the emotions of others. Researchers are increasingly concerned with the factors that influence these processes.

Emotional intelligence is the ability to express one's emotions and detect the emotions of others.

People with *high emotional intelligence* have social support and avoid interpersonal conflicts.

Individuals with high emotional intelligence are *less likely* to abuse drugs and alcohol.

Gender and *culture* have been found to shape how individuals express and detect emotions.

Gender in the expression and detection of emotion

Researchers have found differences between how men and women express and detect emotions. Women can typically read verbal and visual emotional reactions better than men.

Women *experience emotions* more intensely than men and are likelier to *display emotions*.

Women are more likely to experience disgust, shame, and guilt, while men are more likely to experience anger.

Men are typically able to tolerate *distressing emotions* more than women.

Research has found that *women score higher* on emotional intelligence tests than men.

However, men with high emotional intelligence are typically more successful than men with low emotional intelligence.

There is much debate on why these sex differences exist.

Some researchers point to *biological factors* (e.g., hormone levels) for these differences.

Some theorize that *cultural stereotypes and socialization* are responsible for gender differences. For example, the parents of a young boy might express disapproval when he cries, while a young girl's parents might comfort her.

A combination of biological factors and socialization likely contribute to gender differences.

Role of culture in the expression and detection of emotion

While emotions are universal, how emotions are perceived and regulated differs across cultures. Research by Paul Ekman has found that cultures share the same facial expressions of emotions.

These expressions, however, occur at different frequencies depending on the culture.

Display rules are the cultural expectations of the expression of emotions.

Norms dictate which emotions are acceptable for people to display in the presence of others.

Display rules differ across cultures; for example, individuals in the Utku Eskimo population rarely express anger and face ostracism when they do.

In the U.S., expressing emotions is encouraged; repressing emotions is considered insincere.

For example, Americans prefer excited smiles over calm smiles. In contrast, Japanese culture discourages the expression of emotions; suppressing emotions is viewed as mature.

Impression management

Impression management is engaging in behaviors to influence the perception of others. It can be conscious or subconscious.

Common strategies in impression management include *flattery*, *ingratiation*, and *intimidation*.

Impression management contributes to an individual's social identity, which refers to how individuals are regarded in social situations. It is goal-directed, meaning that the individual engaging in impression management wants the person they are interacting with to perceive something in a specific way.

Individuals often engage in impression management to increase their self-esteem. Thus, they may highlight their accomplishments and positives while downplaying their failures.

People may change their behavior to adapt to the person they are interacting with.

For example, an individual might put on their "*best self*" when interacting with their boss but joke around with a coworker.

Impression management is used for self-presentation and when an individual wants something or someone else to be perceived in a certain way.

For example, a person might tell his parents good things about his significant other while leaving out information that puts his significant other in a negative light.

Front stage *vs.* backstage self

Dramaturgy is a sociological perspective on social interactions proposed by Erving Goffman.

Dramaturgy uses theater as a metaphor for presenting oneself in social situations; thus, how an individual presents himself is considered their "performance." This approach emphasizes the *context* in which social behavior occurs.

According to Goffman, people's actions are influenced by those around them.

Erving Goffman, Canadian-American sociologist and writer

Goffman identified three stages in which people "perform."

Front stage is when the individual knows they are being observed and behaves according to the audience's expectations.

Backstage is when performers are present, but their usual audience is not. Thus, performers can act "out of character" but still act to fit in with their fellow performers.

Off-stage is the place where individuals are not involved in any performance.

For example, a server is front stage when waiting tables and interacting with customers, backstage in the kitchen with fellow servers, and off-stage driving to work.

Verbal and nonverbal communication

Interpersonal communication involves both verbal and nonverbal communication. Verbal communication is explicit communication, whereas nonverbal communication is implicit communication. Nonverbal communication includes body movements, posture, eye contact, and facial expressions. Verbal and nonverbal communication interact to form a complete idea. Therefore, isolating nonverbal communication and analyzing individual gestures is not typically helpful.

Posture includes *open* and *closed postures.*

Open posture is a body position that conveys openness, typically sitting or standing with arms and legs uncrossed.

Closed posture conveys disinterest or discomfort with arms and legs crossed.

Mirroring is an important aspect of posture. Individuals who mirror another reflect body movements and position. Mirroring indicates interest in the other person.

Researchers typically categorize nonverbal communication by the functions that they serve.

Emblems are gestures that can be roughly translated into words. For example, a handshake can be roughly translated into a greeting.

Illustrators serve to emphasize spoken language. For example, an individual might point somewhere while giving directions to someone.

Affect displays are gestures that show the other person how someone feels. For example, someone feeling sad might frown to let the person they are talking to know how they feel.

Regulators are social gestures used to give another person feedback during a conversation. For example, someone might nod to indicate they are listening and encourage the speaker to continue talking.

Adaptors are gestures that satisfy a physical need (e.g., adjusting a leg after it falls asleep).

Attitudes

Outside actors

Generally, people believe they form opinions or attitudes about people, objects, and ideas.

However, psychologists have found that groups around us influence these attitudes more than most realize or are willing to admit.

Social psychologists have studied this phenomenon and recognize how vital *outside actors* are in forming our attitudes and opinions.

Components of attitudes

To understand how attitudes are influenced, attitudes must be defined.

Attitude is a set of beliefs (either favorable or unfavorable) toward a person, place, or object.

Attitudes have *cognitive*, *affective*, and *behavioral components* interacting to form attitudes.

> *Cognitive component* is what the person thinks about the topic. For example, "My boss always forgets what I tell him. He is a real jerk."

> *Affective component* of the attitude is the feeling or emotion associated with the attitude. For example, "Every time I see my boss, I feel angry."

> *Behavioral component* of the attitude is the action taken. For example, "I'm currently applying for other jobs within my company to get a different boss. I also try to avoid my boss as much as possible."

These components of the attitude result in an overall perspective toward the object or person.

Behavior influences attitudes

Attitudes and behavior are connected. In the above example, the attitude toward the boss is causing the individual to apply for new jobs and avoid the boss. However, what would happen if the individual spent more time with their boss? Might the attitude change?

After spending time with the boss, the person may discover that the boss is a single father and incredibly overworked and overwhelmed. Their attitude might change upon learning this because they understand why he forgets what they tell him. Thus, the attitude changed due to the behavior change (i.e., instead of avoiding their boss, they spent more time around him and learned something that made them feel differently about him). This is one example of how *behaviors may influence attitudes*.

However, there are other ways behavior influences attitudes.

One process is the *foot-in-the-door* phenomenon, named after door-to-door salespeople who believed that if they could get one foot in the door, the homeowner would be unable to turn them away. The foot-in-the-door phenomenon states that you should first ask for a simple request, and once this has been agreed to, you should follow up with a more substantial request.

For example, outside of the voting location, someone might ask a person to sign a petition so that a candidate may run for a particular office. Once you sign it, you may be asked to volunteer several hours to help this candidate's campaign.

Door-in-the-face technique is the opposite. With this technique, you start by asking for a substantial request, and when it is rejected, you follow up with a simple request that is likely to be accepted. For example, one might ask their neighbor to watch their 9-month-old baby for the weekend while they take a trip. When the neighbor says no, they may ask the neighbor to watch the baby for 2 hours while going to the grocery store. The idea is that the neighbor is so relieved about not being pressed to undertake a demanding task that they will help with a simpler one.

Role-playing is a process where behavior influences attitude. This was famously observed in Philip Zimbardo's *Stanford Prison Study*. In this study, a group of men were randomly assigned to be either correctional officers or prisoners in a mock prison set up by Dr. Zimbardo in the basement of a building at Stanford University. Local police arrested the "prisoners" and "booked" into the prison. The "guards" were given uniforms and free rein to run the prison.

After approximately one day, some of the "guards" began acting brutally toward the "prisoners." The study, which was supposed to last 2 weeks, was ended after only 6 days due to the sadistic behavior of the "guards" and the extreme distress of the "prisoners."

Stanford Prison Study is cited when discussing how role-playing affects attitudes. The participants in this study were average, emotionally stable, law-abiding American males, and it was due to the flip of a coin that one was assigned to be a prisoner or a guard. The result of playing these roles over a matter of days caused a severe shift in behavior in both the guards and prisoners. The guards' attitude was to perceive the prisoners as inferior, and the prisoners' attitude was to believe that they were inferior. Thus, the *role-playing* significantly influenced the attitude of the guards, prompting acts of sadism, and influenced the attitude of the prisoners, prompting submissiveness.

Self-presentation is another case where attitude can appear to change, though it usually does not. In this scenario, an individual will profess attitudes that match his or her actions to avoid feeling foolish. There is usually awareness that a discrepancy exists between the presented and true attitudes. However, contrary to the true attitude, the behavior is assumed to help one appear consistent.

Attitudes influence behavior

It is reasonable to assume that attitudes consistently predict behavior. Richard LaPierre demonstrated that this is not always true. In 1934, LaPierre drove the U.S. with a Chinese couple and stopped at over 250 restaurants and hotels. They were only refused service once.

Sometime later, LaPierre surveyed the owners of the restaurants and hotels about their attitudes toward Chinese people, explicitly asking if they would serve Chinese people in their business. Ninety-two percent stated that they would not serve Chinese people.

In this study, the attitude did not influence actual behavior. Most owners admitted to racial bias (i.e., attitude's cognitive and affective components). However, they did not act when confronted with serving the Chinese couple (i.e., the behavioral component of attitude).

Subsequent studies have focused on determining the circumstances when attitude predicts behavior. One of the biggest problems with attitudes predicting behaviors is that often, people are not honest about their attitudes, especially if there is a negative social consequence for holding a given attitude. For example, an individual may have a negative attitude toward a specific racial group; however, expressing this negative attitude may be socially unacceptable. Thus, the individual may try to hide their genuine attitude.

To minimize this, social psychologists have created the *bogus pipeline paradigm*, where a person is connected to wires and electrodes and told that the apparatus measures whether they are telling the truth. The wires and electrodes are not measuring anything. Still, this increases the probability that the subjects will be honest in their attitudes, making predicting behavior more accurate.

Bogus pipeline paradigm was created to simulate a lie detector

Asking about specific attitudes rather than general ones helps predict specific behavior. For example, if someone generally asks about a religious attitude, it is unlikely to predict whether they will attend church next weekend (a particular behavior). However, the attitude could predict the total number of religious behaviors over time (general behaviors). The more specificity with an attitude is identified, the higher the predictive value.

External factors (or conditions) impact whether attitudes affect behavior. One's attitude is more likely to affect behavior if no other external factors are involved. For example, an individual may not want to volunteer at a food bank because they believe people should find gainful employment if they want to eat. However, if that person's close friends volunteer at a food bank as a group, the individual may engage in the volunteering behavior. The external force of *peer pressure* influenced the behavior, not the attitude.

Desire to conform to a particular group's behavior is closely related. In one study, a group read about a proposed law to pay unemployment benefits. Half of the group was told it was a Democratic-backed proposal, while the other half were told it was a Republican one. Among those who were told it was Democrat-backed, those who identified as conservative said the proposal was too expensive, while liberals supported it.

However, among those who were told the proposal was Republican-backed, conservatives approved of the proposal, while liberals said the pay was not high enough. In this study, the participants demonstrated behavior (i.e., deciding whether to support the proposal) based on the political party of their preference and not the proposal's content itself. This is an example of how belonging to a group influences attitude and, thus, behavior.

Similar findings occur in the "real world" if two conditions are met. First, the individual must identify with the group. For example, someone with few ties to or no opinion on politics is unlikely to have a strong attitude about a politically charged topic.

The second condition is that the issue needs to be ambiguous. For example, people usually have strong feelings about abortion, but how much government assistance one should receive each month is more ambiguous.

Theory of reasoned action

Theory of reasoned action is a model used to predict behavior from attitude. Created by Icek Ajzen and Martin Fishbein, it purports three constructs:

>   behavioral intention, attitude, and subjective norm.

Attitude and *subjective norms* combined determine *behavioral intention*.

Behavioral intention is the strength of the intention to perform a behavior. A person's behavior is determined by their attitude and how others perceive them for that behavior. Research has found that the most relevant application of this theory is in consumer behavior. The theory (and associated mathematical formula) predicts consumer behavior very well.

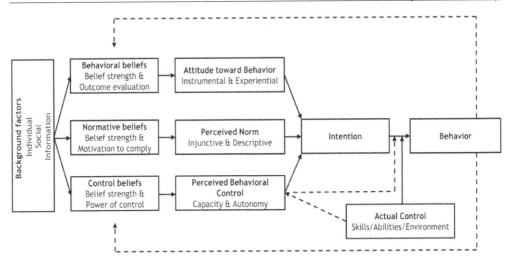

Reasoned action approach is a psychological model to explain and predict behavior

Not all attitudes are equal. The stronger the attitude is, the more likely it predicts behavior. Research has shown that individuals with a strong attitude have spent more time learning about the object of the attitude. This learning process serves to solidify the attitude and makes it not only difficult to change but a better predictor of behavior.

Individuals with firm attitudes are more likely to have experience with the object of the attitude. Again, these *experiences strengthen the attitude* and serve as a *stronger predictor* of behavior.

Cognitive dissonance theory

Cognitive dissonance theory is when attitudes, beliefs, and behaviors do not correspond. One can have two competing thoughts or beliefs, creating tension within that individual. Because this tension is uncomfortable, the individual will try to reduce it.

For example, a high school senior may want to attend Harvard. He may believe that Harvard is the only school worth attending if one is going to go to college and, therefore, spends his time studying and trying to get good grades. However, when he applied, he was rejected. Thus, there is tension between his goals and the reality of the situation. As a result, the high school senior may downplay how much he wanted to attend Harvard and proclaim that "there are better schools out there anyway." In this way, the high school senior *reduces the tension.*

Cognitive dissonance is when two thoughts compete (i.e., cognition) or are inconsistent (i.e., dissonance). Dissonance is uncomfortable, so the person attempts to lessen it.

Cognitive dissonance is essential to studying attitudes and behavior because changes in attitudes due to cognitive dissonance impact behavior.

For example, a child might want to purchase a gift for his mother. When he goes into the store to purchase the gift, he discovers he does not have enough money. However, he steals the gift, knowing this is what his mother wants.

The child thinks: "I stole the gift" and "stealing is wrong," conflicting, so dissonance occurs.

Resolving dissonance:

> 1) return the gift to the store and admit his wrongdoing or

> 2) think, "Stealing may be a bad thing sometimes, but when it is done to help someone, it is not that bad."

A change in cognition (2) reduces dissonance while allowing the behavior (i.e., stealing a gift).

Theories of Attitude and Behavior Change

Changing attitudes

How attitudes form and change is not entirely understood.

However, research has led to the Elaboration Likelihood Model and Social Cognitive Theory.

Further, several factors that affect attitude change have been identified.

Elaboration likelihood model

Elaboration Likelihood Model is a theory of persuasion for attitude change.

It states that there are two persuasion routes: *central* and *peripheral*.

Central route (or *direct route*) involves individuals gathering information and using logic to form attitudes over time. If an attitude change occurs, it tends to resist change over time and predict later behavior.

Most people would like to believe that their attitudes derive from utilizing the central route; however, research has shown that the *peripheral route* forms many attitudes.

Peripheral route involves quick judgments based on positive or negative cues. Often, there is limited evidence and little time to research and logically think about the object of the attitude.

The peripheral route involves some vague impressions, emotions, and the characteristics of the message (as discussed below) when forming the attitude. One example of the peripheral route is the foot-in-the-door phenomenon.

Motivation and *ability* determine which route is taken.

Motivation is the desire to process messages, affected by relevance and existing attitudes.

Ability is the capability for critical evaluation and is influenced by distractions and familiarity.

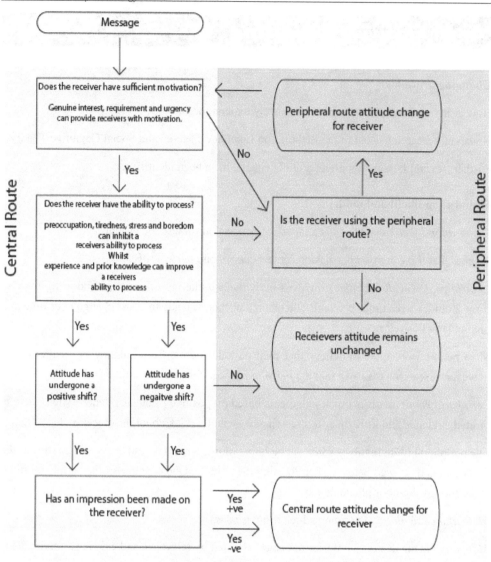

Elaboration Likelihood Model

Social cognitive theory

Albert Bandura developed *Social Cognitive Theory* and posits that an individual learns through observing others. Research shows that individuals learn behaviors and attitudes by observing others in the media, during social interactions, and experiences with external actors. In this way, humans do not have to evaluate the results of behaviors independently; they learn the consequences through observing others.

If an individual sees a desired consequence because of another having a particular attitude (or behavior), there is a likelihood that the individual will emulate that attitude (or behavior).

For example, suppose a celebrity goes on television and states that he or she lost much weight by eating food at a specific fast-food chain. In that case, someone watching this commercial may change their attitude toward that chain and now decide it is healthy eating.

Albert Bandura, psychologist

Factors that affect attitude change

Many factors affect attitude change and the ease at which people change their attitudes. One factor is the message source. Our willingness to change our attitude based on what someone says depends partially on the characteristics of that person (i.e., the communicator).

People are more likely to change their attitude with communicators who are more attractive and perceived as trustworthy or experts in a given topic.

Not only is the communicator influential, but so is the message content. Two-sided messages are when the communicator's message and the opposing viewpoint are presented. These are more effective than one-sided messages, where only the communicator's message is presented, assuming that the opposing side's viewpoint can be easily refuted. The characteristics of the target of the message also influence whether an attitude change will occur.

Even after the communicator has delivered the message, the characteristics of the target will determine if the message changes attitudes. Previous research has shown that less intelligent people are easier to persuade than more intelligent people.

Gender differences also seem to exist, but they are small. Women are more easily persuaded than men when these differences are found, especially with little background. However, men and women are equally likely to change their private attitudes.

Changing behavior changes attitude. In the *Stanford Prison Study*, the guards' attitudes began to shift, and they engaged in the brutal treatment of the prisoners. Likewise, after a few hours of "acting" like prisoners, the prisoners' attitudes began to shift, and they started to see the guards as powerful oppressors and themselves as inferior, bringing about a change in their behaviors (i.e., they became more submissive).

Individuals with similar attitudes often form groups; sometimes, these groups are formalized, and other times, they may be friends who share similar attitudes. Regardless, when members of the group discuss their attitudes with members of opposing groups, the original attitudes tend to become stronger and more solidified.

Group polarization is when discussion makes the attitudes of group members more pronounced.

Relationship matrix

Notes for active learning

CHAPTER 3

Social Psychology

How people relate to social situations is of great interest to psychologists. To explore social interactions, researchers analyze social attitudes, influences, and phenomena that illustrate how group and individual behavior is influenced.

Social psychology studies personality and interpersonal relationships, including such concepts as social thinking, attribution theory, and social cognition. This research offers perspectives on the formation of attitudes and how they might be transformed.

Breadth of social influence must be considered, particularly conformity, compliance, obedience, and altruism.

Human Social Behavior

Social behavior

Social behavior refers to behavior between members of the same species.

Social behaviors include communication and social actions to induce a response in another.

Specific social behaviors include attraction, aggression, attachment, and altruism.

Attraction

Attraction is related to how much someone likes (or dislikes) someone, often leading to friendships and romantic relationships.

Well-studied factors of interpersonal attraction between people include proximity, familiarity, similarity, physical attractiveness, and reinforcement.

Attraction is influenced by *proximity*; long-distance relationships are challenging to form.

Similarly, people familiar with each other are more likely to experience interpersonal attraction, a concept known as the *propinquity effect* (or *exposure effect*).

Attraction is related to how much individuals like or dislike another person.

Similarity is another factor influencing attraction. The more similar two people are regarding attitudes, interests, personality, and communication skills, the more likely they will be attracted.

Matching hypothesis is that similar individuals, regarding physical attractiveness, tend to form relationships. Studies have found that people rate those who are physically attractive as having more desirable internal qualities, such as kindness and sociability.

Reinforcement-affect model of attraction is a well-known reinforcement model that focuses on positive effect as a reinforcer for engaging in social behavior with others. Studies have found that couples stay together longer if they continuously exchange resources and rewards.

Social psychology theories use *reinforcement* to explain attraction. Accordingly, individuals form and stay in relationships due to receiving reinforcement from being with the other person.

Aggression

Aggression refers to social behaviors intended to hurt or damage another.

Two types of human aggression are controlled-instrumental and reactive-impulsive aggression.

Controlled-instrumental aggression refers to aggression used as a means to a goal.

Reactive-impulsive aggression (or *hostile aggression*) stems from anger and is intended to cause pain to another.

Physiologically, aggression is linked to higher levels of testosterone. One study found that testosterone levels are higher among prisoners convicted of violent crimes than those convicted of nonviolent crimes. There appears to be a bidirectional relationship between aggression and testosterone. While injecting animals with testosterone increases aggressive behaviors, behaving aggressively increases the levels of testosterone in an animal's blood.

Social learning is influential in whether people engage in aggressive behaviors.

For example, in Bandura's *Bobo doll* experiment, children were likelier to play aggressively with a Bobo doll if they had seen an adult do the same earlier.

Some theorists argue that violence in the media contributes to the perpetuation of aggressive behaviors through the mechanism of social learning.

Reactive-impulsive aggression is a social behavior intended to hurt another individual.

Though aggression is typically considered physical, researchers have identified another form.

Relational aggression causes harm to another by damaging their relationships or social status.

Physical aggression occurs more in males, while *relational aggression* is greater in females.

Relational aggression has typically been studied in adolescents and is associated with *bullying*.

Relational aggression includes excluding the individual, spreading malicious rumors, and humiliating them in front of others.

Relationally aggressive behaviors are more common for females

Alcohol is associated with increased aggressive behaviors by lowering inhibition. Violence may contribute to alcohol consumption; violent individuals may be more likely to seek out social situations that encourage heavy drinking.

Attachment

Attachment is a deep emotional bond connecting two individuals. John Bowlby and Mary Ainsworth first researched attachment and attachment theory. Bowlby theorized that individuals develop an attachment style based on past interactions with their caregivers.

Attachment styles develop based on an infant's ability to trust their caregivers. The primary purpose of attachment is to develop and sustain a sense of security. These attachment styles persist into adulthood and shape the romantic relationships that an individual will have.

Elements leading to attachment in infancy and adulthood include holding, touching, smiling, desire to be comforted when distressed, anxiety after separation, and happiness upon return.

This theory proposes three attachment styles: *secure*, *anxious*, and *avoidant*.

Anxious and *avoidant styles* are often grouped and considered *insecure attachments*.

According to attachment theory, having a sensitive, caring, and responsible caregiver would lead to a *secure attachment*, where children show some distress when their caregiver leaves but can eventually comfort themselves knowing that their caregiver will return. Upon the return of the caregiver, a child exhibits joy.

Secure attachment is considered the best form of attachment when infants feel comfortable with their caregivers, and later in life, it is easier for them to become emotionally close to others as adults. Similarly, securely attached adults are more likely to view their relationships positively.

Anxious attachment style results in children with caregivers who are unpredictably responsive. Infants with unpredictable caregivers cannot predict whether their needs will be met at any given time. Anxiously attached adults tend to look for and find signs that their relationships are ending, often without basis. They tend to have low self-esteem and seek constant reassurance from their partners; they are often characterized as being needy or clingy.

Children with caregivers who are unresponsive to their needs and attempts at communication are believed to form an *avoidant attachment*. Children with an avoidant attachment tend to ignore their caregivers. Avoidant attachment style adults have trouble forming meaningful relationships and are uncomfortable with close emotional bonds.

Research has found that adults who have an anxious or avoidant attachment style are more likely to identify their romantic partners as safe havens or secure bases.

Insecure attachment styles are associated with low self-esteem.

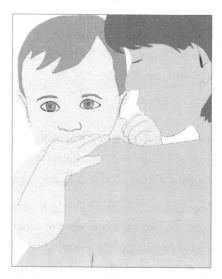

Secure attachment is when infants feel comfortable with their caregivers, and later in life, it is easier for them to become emotionally close to others as adults.

Avoidant attachment style is divided into *dismissive-avoidant* and *fearful-avoidant*.

Dismissive-avoidant attachment style fosters comfort without close emotional bonds and highly values independence. Individuals with this attachment style tend to suppress their feelings.

Fearful-avoidant (or *anxious-avoidant*) attachment styles differ from dismissive-avoidant individuals because people want emotionally close relationships but find it difficult to trust others enough to form them. It is characterized by a fervent desire to be in a relationship while wanting to protect oneself from getting hurt by another.

Anxious-avoidant attachment style individuals can mistrust their partners and be uncomfortable expressing affection.

Altruism

Altruism (or *selflessness*) is behavior with concern for the well-being of others.

Altruism is characterized by costing the individual engaging in it while benefiting another.

Social exchange theory posits that altruism occurs when the benefits of an altruistic act outweigh the costs, suggesting that true altruism does not exist.

Empathy-altruism hypothesis proposes that altruistic behaviors are evoked by the desire to help someone suffering, suggesting that altruism exists. It proposes that altruistic behaviors stem from empathy.

Reciprocity norm theory suggests that people are most likely to engage in altruistic behaviors when others are likely to reciprocate. Research has found that individuals who have received help from someone tend to become more helpful toward others.

Social support

Social support is the perception that one is cared for by others. It refers to the social resources an individual has available.

Resources are categorized into:

emotional, instrumental, informational, and appraisal support.

Emotional social support includes expressions of empathy and love.

Instrumental social support refers to tangible aid; loaning money to a friend, for example, is instrumental social support.

Informational social support refers to advice-giving.

Appraisal social support helps others reframe their thoughts about a situation.

Social support is strongly linked with mental and physical health. People with strong social support networks are at lower risks of depression and anxiety and experience less overall psychological distress than individuals with poor social support.

Individuals with poor social support show higher rates of post-traumatic stress disorder, panic disorder, social anxiety disorder, and suicidal ideation.

People with strong social support networks have been found to have lower mortality rates following a heart attack and have fewer cardiovascular diseases and better immune system functioning than their low-social-support counterparts.

Social support is strongly linked with mental and physical health. Individuals with strong social support networks are at lower risks of depression and anxiety and experience less overall psychological distress.

Buffering hypothesis and direct effects hypothesis theories explain the role of social support in health and stress management.

Buffering hypothesis proposes that individuals need social support only during stressful times since this type of social support protects the individual from the detrimental effects of stress.

Direct effects (or main effects) hypothesis states that individuals with high levels of social support have a better quality of life, regardless of stress levels.

Individual Behavior in the Presence of Others

Social facilitation

Social facilitation is the tendency of people to perform better when in the presence of others. This phenomenon was identified in 1898 by Norman Triplett, who noticed that cyclists went faster when racing against one another than when racing alone against the clock.

Many believe that social facilitation is caused by an arousal response based on apprehension about receiving negative evaluations from others.

Two social facilitations have been identified: *co-action effects* and *audience effects*.

Co-action effects refer to social facilitation when individuals are engaged in the same activity. It has been observed in humans and animals. For example, animals eating together tend to eat more than animals eating alone. Ants that work in view of one another have been found to work more than ants working independently.

Audience effects are social facilitation when an individual engages in a task and is observed by others who are not participating. In experiments involving word output, the presence of an audience increased individuals' output and the number of errors made.

Social facilitation via audience effects is when individuals engage in tasks they experience.

Social inhibition occurs when they engage in a novel task under the same conditions.

Deindividuation

Deindividuation refers to losing one's sense of self-awareness and self-restraint within a group. This occurs when people engage in group behaviors that they would not perform independently.

Diffusion of responsibility is linked with deindividuation. It refers to individuals being less likely to take responsibility for their actions when others are present.

Deindividuation can lead to a "mob mentality," resulting in riots and deviant behavior.

Philip Zimbardo studied deindividuation in his 1971 prison experiment at Stanford University. In this experiment, twenty-four men were randomly assigned either the role of a "guard" or a "prisoner." The guards were not instructed on how to treat the prisoners. The experiment had to be aborted due to the guards' cruel treatment of the prisoners. Zimbardo believed that this behavior resulted from the deindividuation of the guards.

Bystander effect

Bystander effect is when individuals do not help victims when in the presence of others. It was popularized following the murder of Kitty Genovese in 1964. Many people saw Genovese being stabbed, but no one stepped in or called the police.

Social psychologists who studied this murder determined that the onlookers saw others not helping and concluded that their help was not needed.

Like deindividuation, the bystander effect is tied to the *diffusion of responsibility*. People tend to believe that if others are around, their help is unnecessary.

Bystander effect is the tendency of people not to help victims when in the presence of others. It is closely tied to the diffusion of responsibility.

Further research into the bystander effect found that the more bystanders present, the less likely people are to help a victim. This may stem from individuals assuming that more qualified bystanders are available to help or that if help is needed, someone else will step in.

Social loafing

Social loafing describes the loss of motivation when people exert less effort while performing a task in a group than when they work alone.

Social loafing stems from individuals believing their efforts will not matter to the group.

Ringelmann effect is that loafing is more likely in larger groups than smaller ones.

An early experiment on social loafing was conducted in 1913 by Maximilien Ringelmann when he was studying the relationship between performance effectiveness and group productivity.

Experiments show that people pulling on a rope in a group did not pull as hard as when alone.

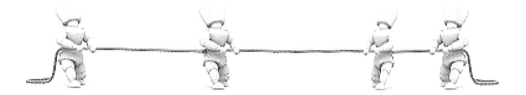

Social loafing refers to losing motivation when people perform a task in a group compared to working alone.

Ringelmann discovered that the *bigger the group*, the *more inefficient* it becomes, which went against a common notion that group effort and teamwork result in an increased effort by the group members and increased overall productivity.

Ringelmann concluded that groups fail to reach their full potential due to various interpersonal processes, one of the main ones being a *loss of motivation* (i.e., social loafing).

Peer pressure

Peer pressure is the influence exerted on an individual to change their behavior.

Peer pressure is not necessarily negative, but it is associated with misconduct in adolescence. It contributes to the likelihood of *substance abuse, unsafe sexual practices,* and *deviance.*

Research suggests that women, people from a collectivist culture, and people with low self-esteem are *more susceptible* to peer pressure.

Responses to peer pressure are:

    compliance, conversion, congruence, and non-conformity.

Compliance is when an individual privately or publicly disagree with the group but goes along anyway.

Conversion is when an individual changes their opinion to match the group's.

Congruence is when an individual's opinion already matches the group's.

Non-conformity is when individuals refuse to go along with the group.

Peer pressure is the influence exerted by peers to change behavior

Conformity

Conformity (or *majority influence*) refers to changing one's beliefs and behaviors to fit into a social group. It is often adaptive; it allows individuals to benefit from the ideas and knowledge of others without exerting much energy.

Conformity refers to changing one's beliefs and behaviors to fit into a social group.

In one of the first experiments examining conformity, Arthur Jenness asked individual participants to guess the number of beans in a bottle. The participants were then brought together into a group, and they changed their answers to be closer to what others had guessed.

There are six types of conformity:

Normative conformity is when individuals yield to group pressure out of fear of rejection.

Informational conformity is when individuals yield to group pressure due to their lack of knowledge and accept the views and behaviors of the group as their own.

Compliance is when individuals change their behavior to match the group's behavior while disagreeing privately.

Internalization is when individuals publicly change their behavior and privately adopt the group's views.

Ingratiational conformity is when individuals conform to gain acceptance from others.

Identification is when individuals conform to expectations stemming from a social role.

Obedience

Obedience is a form of social influence involving compliance with someone else's authority.

Obedience involves an order or demand from someone of a higher status, thus involving a hierarchy of power and prestige.

Stanley Milgram's *shock experiment* is a famous experiment about obedience. Participants were instructed to shock someone in another room in response to each wrong answer. The person in the other room was a Confederate and was not shocked.

To Milgram's surprise, participants persisted in following instructions and continued to "shock" the person in the other room even when the person being "shocked" said they wanted it to stop.

Results highlighted the powerful influence that *authority figures* exert.

Experimental results have been used to explain why ordinary people took part in the Holocaust, a concept that Milgram studied because much of his extended family was killed in the atrocities.

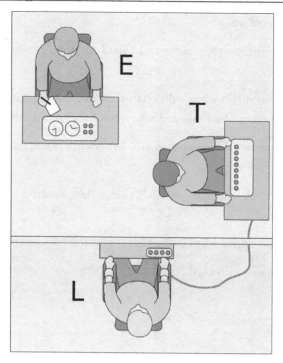

Stanley Milgram's shock experiment illustrates obedience

Group Decision-Making Processes

Group polarization

Group polarization is when groups form more extreme opinions than individuals within the group when alone.

Individuals in a group also advocate for *riskier actions* than when they are alone.

Two theories explain this: *social comparison* and inf*ormational influence theories.*

Social comparison theory is when individuals attempt to gain the approval of peers within a group by taking on the opinion most pervasive in the group but making it slightly more extreme.

Social comparison theorists assert that this allows them to assert themselves as *group leaders*.

Informational influence theory is when individuals in a group become more convinced of their original position after hearing arguments supporting their position by others.

Groupthink

Yale University psychologist Irving Lester Janis coined *groupthink*.

Groupthink is *decision-making errors* by *homogenous groups* making *collective decisions*.

Janis identified eight symptoms of groupthink:

      1) an illusion of invulnerability,

      2) collective rationalization,

      3) belief in inherent morality,

      4) stereotyped views of outgroups,

      5) pressure on dissenters,

      6) self-censorship,

      7) an illusion of unanimity, and

      8) self-appointed "*mind guards*."

Groupthink occurs when groups are:

      1) highly cohesive,

      2) isolated, and

      3) under pressure to decide,

These factors result in the group's *failure to consider alternative decisions.*

For example, some propose that groupthink was involved prior to the bombing of Pearl Harbor. American officers did not act on warnings about the potential for a Japanese invasion due to groupthink that the Japanese would not attack the United States.

Groupthink is decision-making errors by homogenous groups making collective decisions

Attributing Behavior to Persons or Situations

Attributional processes

Attribution is the process by which individuals explain events.

Specifically, attribution refers to the explanation of events through internal or external factors. People typically view events, often inaccurately, in terms of cause-and-effect relationships.

Fundamental attribution error is people's tendency to view and explain the behavior of others through internal attributions while explaining their behavior through external attributions.

For example, an individual might believe that others are obese due to poor self-control while believing that their obesity is a result of being poor. The first is an example of a *dispositional attribution*; obesity results from the person's disposition. The second attribution is an example of *situational attribution*; obesity results from uncontrollable circumstances.

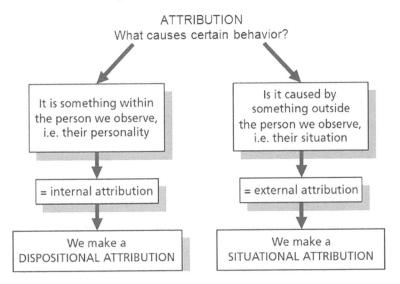

Attribution is used to explain behaviors

Culture is vital in how people form attributions. The differences in attribution between people from *individualist* and *collectivist cultures* are extensively studied.

Individualistic cultures are more likely to engage in *self-serving biases*, meaning that they will attribute their *successes to internal factors* and their *failures to external factors*.

Collectivist cultures are more likely to engage in *self-effacing* biases, meaning they are more likely to attribute their *successes to external factors* and their *failures to internal factors*.

Self-perceptions shape perceptions of others

How individuals perceive *themselves* shapes how they perceive *others*.

For example, people tend to assume that others share their beliefs. However, differences emerge and become apparent through interactions rather than being assumed.

People tend to view others concerning their *goals*.

For example, someone looking for a dating relationship views people through this perspective and identifies characteristics differently than they would if they were looking for a babysitter.

Perceptions of the environment shape perceptions of others

How individuals perceive their *environment influences* how they *perceive others*.

This idea is closely related to *social norms*.

For example, someone who swears when walking down the street will be perceived differently than someone who swears in an office setting due to *the social norms* surrounding each setting.

The importance of the environment on the perception of others was established experimentally when eight healthy researchers claimed to hear voices and admitted into mental health hospitals. Once admitted, the researchers acted normally and reported that the "voices" had stopped. Nevertheless, the mental health hospital staff persisted in classifying the researchers with ongoing schizophrenia.

Relationship matrix

Topic

Notes for active learning

CHAPTER 4

Social Culture & Behavior

Social culture and behavior are not biologically inherited phenomena but acquired through social observations and interactions. Socialization is the process by which individuals learn social behaviors.

Culture determines social behavior, which is how individuals interact. Social behavior is influenced by cultural values and traditions of society and is characterized by various social interactions and relations.

Individuals and groups may change their behavioral patterns depending on situations and circumstances. When exploring culture and social behavior, it is important to recognize the power of stereotypes, prejudice, and bias to affect attribution.

Society and Social Culture

Cultural sociology

Culture is the variety of codes used by society.

Sociology of culture examines culture and the codes that comprise it as manifested in society.

Cultural sociology focuses on aspects of a society's culture, such as ways of thinking and acting and the material objects that collectively build a society's life.

Cultural sociology was explored in Weimar, Germany, in the 1920s and reemerged in the English-speaking world during the cultural upheaval of the 1960s when the development of *structuralist* and *postmodern approaches* to social science incorporated aspects of *cultural analysis* and *critical theory*.

Cultural sociology relies more on words, artifacts, and symbols than scientific methods.

Ascent of cultural sociology to a mainstream discipline has infused the concept of culture into strains of *"empirical"* sciences and increased *quantitative* cultural research.

Ethnographic strategies analyze and describe global cultures with intersections of *sociology* and *anthropology* to form *cultural sociology*.

Theoretical perspectives in cultural sociology:

> *functionalism*
>
> *conflict theory*
>
> *symbolic interactionism*

Social constructionism, social exchange theory, and *feminist theory* are main theoretical perspectives of cultural sociology.

The essence of the early development of the field is evident in the:

> *methods* (tendency toward qualitative research)
>
> *theories* (critical approaches to sociology central to research communities)
>
> *substantive focus* (societal manifestation)

For instance, relationships between popular culture, political control, and social class were early and lasting concerns in the field.

Elements of culture

Culture, an integral component of being human, is a set of general codes followed by a group of people developed throughout history.

"A culture" is a community's customs, traditions, and values (e.g., ethnic group or society).

Multiculturalism is the mutually respectful coexistence between cultures within the same area.

Specific customs of a society's subgroup, subculture, or counterculture may be called *culture*.

Cultural relativism is a vital ideology and analysis of culture. It asserts that cultures cannot be held to any objective evaluation system because any evaluation is necessarily situated within the value system of the evaluating culture and is, therefore, inherently subjective.

Culture comprises numerous elements, including material, expression, human behavior, beliefs, and values. The material encompasses food preparation, shelter, architecture, and technologies. Expression can be a culture's art, writing, dance, or music.

Human behavior accounts for specific practices of a culture, such as language, kinship, gender norms, and marriage.

Beliefs and values stem from principles of social organization (including political organization and social institutions), written and oral history, literature, mythology, and philosophy.

A hierarchical perspective of culture, focusing on the degree to which sophistication in the arts, sciences, education, or manners has been achieved, has been employed on larger scales, distinguishing civilizations from less complex societies. It has been applied to class-based distinctions between the high, elite culture of the upper class and the low or popular culture of the lower or middle class.

Hierarchical culture is associated with mass culture, or mass-produced and mediated consumer culture, which has become extremely prevalent in the twentieth century.

Material *vs.* symbolic culture

Material culture is a culture's physical evidence (e.g., objects and architecture). It is the interdisciplinary study of relationships between people and their things. This field focuses on the making, history, preservation, and interpretation of objects.

Material culture encompasses anything from buildings to toothbrushes to jewelry.

Symbolic culture is the culmination of learned and transmitted behavioral traditions that emerge, and habituate generationally based on beliefs and values situated entirely in the symbolic realm.

Symbolic culture can include concepts such as good and evil, religion and mythology, and constructs of a purely social nature—like promises or sporting events.

The ability of symbolic culture to exist is based on collective belief in its existence.

As a domain of objective facts, symbolic culture only exists if those subscribing to the culture maintain belief in those facts.

Symbolic culture frequently interacts with *semiotics* or the mediation of human culture through signs and concepts.

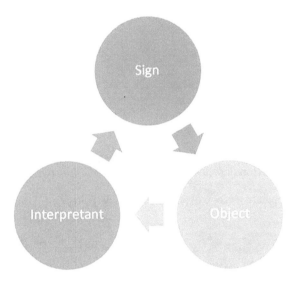

Semiotics chart

Culture lag

Culture lag is the phenomenon of a society's culture taking time to catch up with society's technological advances and other social changes. It addresses the social problems and conflicts that arise when *progress* and *social practices* move at different speeds through theory and explanations of these occurrences.

American sociologist William Ogburn (1886–1959) coined *"culture lag."* He focused his reasoning on material and non-material aspects of culture. He concluded that this conflict occurs in a society when the *non-material* culture struggles to adapt to *material changes*.

Technological determinism resonates with culture lag because both assume technology affects the broader society. Culture lag does *not* necessarily label technology as the central causative element of societal conflict but examines a society's adjustment to innovative technologies.

Ogburn designated the differences between material and non-material. He believed that while material culture tends to evolve and change rapidly, voluminously, and exponentially, non-material culture usually resists changes and likes to remain *relatively fixed*.

Culture lag manifests itself in many ways and is prevalent in most modern societies.

Culture shock

Culture shock is an individual's disorientation when exposed to an unfamiliar location, a way of living, or a social situation. This frequently happens to people visiting foreign countries and can occur upon immigration.

Distinct phases of culture shock are:

> *honeymoon*
>
> *frustration*
>
> *adjustment*
>
> *mastery*

Culture shock includes *information overload, language barrier, generation gap, technology gap, skill interdependence, formulation dependency, homesickness* (cultural), *infinite regress* (homesickness), *boredom* (job dependency), and *response-ability* (cultural skill set).

Culture shock may happen to anyone experiencing a new culture.

Assimilation

Cultural assimilation is when a group's culture transforms to resemble the culture of another. For example, a person can go through the process of assimilation individually or in a group, such as immigrants or a native population dominated by a different population.

Assimilation may occur quickly or happen gradually.

Complete assimilation is when there is no distinction between a new and an original member of the society. There is controversy over whether it is positive or negative for a minority culture to assimilate into a dominant culture.

Multiculturalism

Multiculturalism is the view that cultural differences within society should be accepted, promoted, and encouraged. It involves coexistence in which multiple cultures live peacefully in a single society without assimilating.

Multiculturalism is a "melting pot," "salad bowl," or "cultural mosaic," and the idea of it has several interpretations. It encourages cultures to retain native aspects because losing a diverse culture is detrimental and undesirable. It promotes equal rights and representation of cultures in society and promotes policies that maintain cultural diversity.

Multiculturalism, interested in retaining the distinctiveness of multiple cultures, is often at odds with proponents of social integration and cultural assimilation.

Two incompatible government strategies for multiculturalism policy-making have developed.

Interculturalism has an objective intent on the interaction and communication between cultures.

Intercultural competition has an objective intent on diversity and cultural uniqueness.

Cultural isolation can maintain the individuality of a culture and add to global cultural diversity. A commonality of many policies following *intercultural competition* is that they do not present specific ethnic, religious, or cultural community values as central.

Subcultures and countercultures

Subculture is a group of people with beliefs, norms, and values who exist within mainstream society and maintain some foundational principles of mainstream culture.

Subculture shares much with mainstream culture but stands out because of specific differences.

*Counterculture*s have norms and values that differ significantly from mainstream societies. They are actively separate and opposed to the mainstream culture, often politically active and motivated to change their society.

"Trekkies," a subculture of Star Trek fans

Mass media and popular culture

Mass media is mass communication intended to reach a large audience simultaneously. It can occur through various mediums, sometimes more than one at a time.

Mass communication is achieved through broadcast media (e.g., film, radio, music, television), digital media (e.g., e-mail, social media, websites, streamed radio and television), print media (e.g., books, magazines, newspapers, pamphlets, comics), outdoor media (e.g., billboards, blimps, storefronts, subway cars), event organizing and public speaking.

Mass communication can be achieved through digital media comprised of Internet services, such as e-mail, social media sites, online communities, Internet-based radio, and television.

Mass media became prevalent and indispensable in society between 1860 and 1920. In 1956, C. Wright Mills defined two critical characteristics of mass media as the fact that a limited number of people can use it and, therefore, communicate with many people at one time and that there is no effective way of answering back.

Mass media is an ever-growing and ever-changing entity. The Internet has made disseminating mass media even faster, easier, and more ingrained in the fabric of society.

Popular culture encompasses the ideas, attitudes, images, and other phenomena mainstream culture embraces. This includes music, film, art, fashion, literature, television, and radio, generally consumed by the middle or lower class.

Popular culture is heavily influenced by and primarily distributed through the mass media.

Popular culture includes music, film, art, fashion, literature, television, and radio. It is heavily influenced by and primarily distributed through the mass media.

Evolution and human culture

Evolution is a successive change of biological populations' heritable traits.

Processes of evolution have created a diversity of species, individual organisms, and molecules.

The early twentieth century saw the integration of classical genetics with Darwin's theory of *evolution by natural selection.*

Sociocultural evolutionism addresses formal social theorizing and scientific research. It assumes that if organisms develop over time according to discernible, deterministic laws, then it seems reasonable that societies could evolve as well.

Human society was compared to a biological organism, and concepts like variation, natural selection, and inheritance were introduced, from a sociological perspective, as factors resulting in the progress of societies.

Sages through which human societies progress:

> *savagery*

> *barbarism*

> *civilization*

However, many more stages have been proposed for the progression of societies.

Most social scientists have adopted a general systems approach, examining cultures as *emergent systems* and *constituent parts* of a whole social environment, including *political* and *economic relations* among cultures.

Humanistic approaches focus on:

> *historical contingencies,*

> *contacts between cultures* and

> *operation of cultural symbol systems.*

Humanistic notions of progressive evolution shun modern, complex cultural evolution theories in discourse and research.

Transmission, learning and diffusion

Cultural transmission (or *cultural learning*) is how a society learns and relays information.

How cultures socialize young people dramatically affects their learning style. Unlike a child's physical traits, a person does not attain all their experiences and knowledge from their parents.

Enculturation is the process of a child understanding their culture, and the skills and knowledge children learn from this process are more than they would learn alone.

Humans, as opposed to other species, depend on caretakers for a relatively long time once they are born before they are independent, allowing time to observe and understand culture. The basis of cultural learning allows people to create, remember, understand, and deal with ideas and understand and apply systems of symbolic meaning.

Cultural learning relies on the ability to communicate or imitate the behavior of others and create new responses to the environment based on processed knowledge.

Intercultural competence is the successful communication between people of other cultures.

Diffusion is the spreading of something from the point of high concentration to the point of low concentration. From a sociological perspective, culture is being diffused (or elements of which culture is composed are being spread) to places where those elements did not exist.

Diffusion includes spreading ideas, religions, technologies, languages, and fashions between individuals within a single culture or in diverse cultures.

Diffusion is considered positive. For example, novel ideas of agriculture and technologies have spread among nations, increasing productivity and efficiency.

Normative and Non-Normative Behavior

Social norms

Social norms are behaviors, values, and beliefs deemed appropriate for a specific social group.

These norms, though unwritten, establish expectations for the behavior of others.

Social norms vary by social group and situation. Social norms can range from the religion of a group to how individuals in a group wear their hair.

Individuals who do not follow group norms typically suffer social consequences, such as rejection. Social norms influence individual behavior within a social group through conformity.

Individuals' behavior changes accordingly when they move to a different social group.

Social control and sanctions

Social control is how society influences human behavior. Social control is maintaining order and social norms. It is exerted by sanctions conducted by members of society.

Sanctions can be positive rewards or negative punishments for behavior.

Negative sanctions follow when an individual has violated the group's social norms and can be informal (e.g., displays of shame, criticism, disapproval) or formal (e.g., fines, imprisonment).

Positive sanctions are rewards for following the social norms of a group.

Informal sanctions can cause the group's social values to become internalized in the individual, resulting in lasting behavioral change.

Folkways, mores, and taboos

Folkways, or customs, are social norms followed for tradition's sake. Dressing in a culturally appropriate way is one example of a folkway. Violation of a folkway does not typically have lasting or severe consequences.

Mores are norms based on morality and ethics. People typically feel stronger about mores (i.e., characteristic customs and conventions of a community) than folkways.

For example, the belief that individuals should be clothed in public areas is commonly held. Religious doctrines are also forms of mores.

Violation of a more is severe and results in informal (or formal) sanctions.

Taboos are firmly held social norms; their violation results in rejection and disgust. For example, in most countries, cannibalism is taboo. Some taboos have formal sanctions.

Anomie

Anomie breaks social norms and ethical standards within a social group. This state does not understand common values, and new values have not yet developed.

Emile Durkheim popularized the term in his book on the social influences of suicide. Due to rapid change, Durkheim viewed anomie as a *mismatch* of societal values and ideals.

Major economic depressions are often the cause of anomie in societies.

Anomie theory proposes that a lack of social norms and standards results in people feeling purposeless and worthless.

Common reactions to anomie include *delinquency*, *crime*, and *suicide*.

Emile Durkheim, French psychologist

Socialization

Socialization is the process by which individuals acquire social norms and ideologies, enabling them to function within a society. It is a lifelong process, but many sociologists agree that important socialization occurs in childhood.

Primary socialization refers to the socialization beginning at birth by caregivers. During primary socialization, children learn the values and attitudes their caregivers hold.

Agents of socialization

People become socialized through interaction with a variety of people and environments.

Main agents of socialization are the *family*, *mass media*, *peers*, and the *workplace*.

Family is typically the earliest unit of socialization for an individual. Parents, siblings, and extended family members provide basic needs and guidance to children. The family heavily influences an individual's language, religion, and social class.

Mass media includes television, movies, the press, and the internet. Mass media influences individuals' political views, as well as how they view women and people of color. Some theorists believe that the depiction of violence in the mass media affects violent behavior.

Peer groups influence a person's personality the most. Peer groups are social groups in which members of similar ages influence each other. Exposure to peers allows individuals to decide what norms to keep and reject.

Workplace acts as an agent of socialization. The workplace environment and employers have their culture and sets of norms.

The workplace is typically seen as an agent of mild *resocialization*, learning new norms when entering a new social group.

Deviance

Deviance is engagement in behaviors that violate social norms. These behaviors can be criminal or non-criminal. Alcoholism, for example, is a form of non-criminal deviance.

Deviance is culturally bound because social norms vary by social group and culture.

Several theories, typically from criminology and sociology, explain why individuals engage in deviant behaviors.

Deviance focuses on the process by which some people are labeled deviant by others (and thus take on deviant identities) rather than the nature of the behavior. Identity and behavior are influenced by how individuals are labeled or specific terms describing or categorizing them. Deviance and conformity result not so much from what people do but from how others respond to those actions; it highlights social responses to crime and deviance. Deviance is that which is so labeled.

Perspectives on deviance

Differential association theory proposes that deviant behaviors are learned from an individual's environment, specifically intimate personal groups. According to this theory, deviant individuals have witnessed others acting in a deviant manner and, through exposure to their motives and attitudes, come to adopt those motives, attitudes, and behaviors themselves.

Labeling theory proposes that the attitudes and reactions of others to deviant acts, not the acts themselves, influence further engagement in deviant behaviors. According to this theory, behaviors are only deviant when society labels them as such.

For example, labeling individuals as "deviant" may create a self-fulfilling prophecy.

Strain theory proposes that the gaps between individuals' goals and the means they have to achieve them lead individuals to engage in deviant behaviors. This social strain was initially viewed as resulting from the social structures within a society but has been expanded to include the individual difficulties experienced in a person's life.

Collective behaviors

Collective behavior is a form of social behavior that typically opposes existing social norms. Collective behavior differs from group behavior because it is spontaneous and temporary.

Two collective behaviors have been identified: *localized* and *dispersed*.

Localized collective behavior is when members are in a crowd or proximity.

Dispersed collective behavior is when members are not nearby but still impact one another. For example, social media use has increased the potential for dispersed collective behavior.

Three main collective behaviors are:

> *fads*
>
> *mass hysteria*
>
> *riots*

Fads are behaviors that gain and lose popularity very quickly among many people.

Mass hysteria refers to fear reactions spread through rumors or incorrect information. In mass hysteria, people typically act irrationally due to their unwarranted fear. For example, major storms, health scares, and terrorist acts often result in mass hysteria.

Riots are large groups of people unified, for the moment, by their excited engagement in deviant behaviors. Riots are costly and damaging to society.

Elements of Social Interaction

Status

Social status refers to one's position in the social hierarchy and standing within the community. It reflects factors, including occupation, income, moral values, and perceived influence.

Social mobility is an individual's movement up or down the social hierarchy. Social status is, therefore, malleable. Social status can be a synonym for prestige, which refers to an individual's reputation as perceived by their peers.

Theories of social mobility define social status by social "tastes" that divide classes.

Others determine social status, grouping individuals into a social class by social stratification, which occurs within all societies.

Status types

Ascribed social status is inherited when born into a particular social class.

Individuals acquire an ascribed status by *marrying* into a particular social class.

People raised in different social classes are treated differently and given different opportunities.

Race, gender, religion, and age affect an individual's ascribed status.

For example, the caste system in India is social stratification based on ascribed status. Each level of social status is a *caste*. Individuals are born into their caste and unable to move up or down within the system.

Achieved social status is earned through individual achievement. Individuals achieve higher social status from a prestigious job or earning substantial money.

People move into a lower social status with a less prestigious job or suffer financial losses.

Overall, *social status* is the combination of *ascribed status* and *achieved status*.

Role

Role theory proposes that individual and community members' expectations influence behavior.

Roles function as social categories with a set of norms that guide the behavior of individuals. Roles emphasize predictable behavior because predictability preserves stasis and reduces risk.

Role theory emphasizes the social context in which behaviors occur. Typical roles include gender, occupational, situation-specific, and familial roles.

Roles are "defined" by society through predictable expectations for behavior; a person's actions should be consistent with their social role.

Therefore, people have a variety of roles that change depending on social context.

For example, a political joke told by a cashier to a customer may be viewed as offensive and inappropriate because it violates the established social norms for this role and type of social interaction. If the cashier tells the same political joke to a friend, it might not be offensive or inappropriate.

People have a variety of roles that change depending on social contexts, such as gender, occupational, situation-specific, and familial roles.

Role conflict and role strain

Role conflict is when an individual performs roles with different norms and expectations.

For example, the CEO of a large company might find that her expectations as a mother conflict with the expectations of her as the head of the company.

Role conflict is distressing, as one role must be compromised for another.

Role strain is when an individual cannot meet the demands and expectations of a single role.

For example, a mother may feel she cannot get her kids ready in the morning, help them with their homework, and make breakfast, all within an hour. Role strain results from the inability to meet expectations set by her role as a mother.

Like role conflict, role strain is usually distressing for the individual experiencing it.

Role exit

Role exit refers to disengaging from a particular role to establish a new role.

Individuals usually exit a role if role conflict or role strain becomes too distressing for them.

Individuals can undergo role exit due to changing circumstances (e.g., moving, divorce, or childbirth). Role exit is often discussed in terms of leaving a place of employment.

Role exits can have an enormous impact on an individual's self-identity, particularly if the role they are leaving was one they highly identified with.

Role exiting may not be planned and can be distressing.

Helen Ebaugh identified four stages of the *role exit process*.

First stage, the individual doubts and becomes frustrated with their current role.

Second stage, the individual searches for alternatives to their current role.

Third stage, the individual exits their current role.

Fourth stage involves the individual assuming a new role and identity.

Groups

Social groups interact, share a sense of unity, and consider themselves part of the group.

People can, and often do, belong to many social groups.

Social groups are a significant source of identity for many individuals but can have a role in discrimination and prejudice against these individuals.

Primary and secondary groups

Sociologist Charles Cooley proposed the concepts of *primary* and *secondary groups*.

Primary group is a close-knit social group and is a primary source of socialization. They are long-lasting, and members typically have intimate relationships.

Primary groups are essential influencers of an individual's identity; the members within the group typically feel a strong connection between their identity and the group.

Nuclear families, close friend groups, and sports teams are examples of primary social groups.

Primary groups are essential influencers of an individual's identity; members typically feel a strong connection between their identity and the group.

Secondary groups are larger, temporary groups. The relationships within secondary groups are weaker than those in primary groups.

Relationships in secondary groups are goal-oriented and less meaningful to members.

Secondary groups are often found at work and school but can refer to groups exchanging commodities (e.g., doctor-patient).

The relationships within secondary groups are weaker than in primary groups; they are goal-oriented and less meaningful to the individuals within them.

Ingroup *vs.* outgroup

Ingroups are social groups in which an individual feels they belong.

Outgroups are social groups that an individual does not identify with.

Ingroup bias is when individuals have positive beliefs about ingroup members.

Outgroup derogation is when individuals have contempt for outgroups.

Ingroup favoritism causes ingroup bias when members help each other with resources and exclude those in the outgroup.

Intergroup aggression is behavior intended to harm another solely because they are an outgroup member. It is more likely for a perception of intergroup conflicts of interest.

Ingroups and outgroups are divided by *race*, *ethnicity*, *age*, *gender*, and *political affiliation*.

Outgroup homogeneity effect is when people perceive outgroup members as more similar than ingroup members.

Cross-race effect (or *ingroup advantage*) recognizes others of their racial group.

Group size

Size categorizes social groups and influences the group's strength, organization, and attitudes.

Dyads are social groups with two people. Dyad members must cooperate for the relationship between them to continue. Thus, social interaction in a dyad is typically more intense than triads or larger groups.

Dyads can be formed through romantic, family, school, and work relationships.

Dyad members must cooperate for the relationship to continue.

Triads are social groups of three people. Triads can be intense but are usually less so than dyads; triad members do not have to be as *engaged* as dyad members because more people are responsible for keeping the group integrated.

Triads are more *stable* than dyads because one member can mediate between the other.

As group size increases beyond triads, *intimacy* between members decreases.

Large groups require *leadership* to ensure that the group functions properly.

As a group size increases, individual members can become *isolated*; when this happens, the creation of smaller subgroups within the main group occurs.

Networks

Social networks are social structures made up of social relationships. They are self-organizing, meaning they are spontaneous and not directed by an agent.

Social actors are the individuals within a social network. Social actors are the smallest units of analysis in a social setting.

Social network theory studies social networks using nodes and ties.

Nodes are the individual social actors.

Ties are the relationships between actors. According to social network theory, an individual's ties with other actors are more important than their attributes.

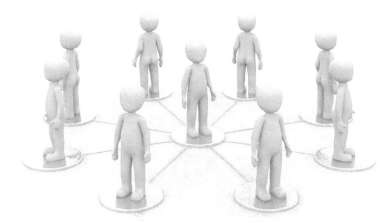

Social networks are people connected with others (directly or indirectly)

Social network theory uses six degrees of separation and the rule of 150.

Six degrees of separation theory proposes six or fewer contacts among anyone. Research on social networking sites (e.g., Facebook and Twitter) supports this idea.

Rule of 150 was proposed by anthropologist Robin Dunbar (in the 1990s), which states that humans can comfortably maintain no more than 150 stable relationships.

Organizations

Organizations are institutions that exist for a *specific purpose* or *collective goal*.

Organizations are divided into three types:

> *utilitarian*
>
> *normative*
>
> *coercive*

Utilitarian organizations are when people are paid for their membership in the organization. Payment is not necessarily monetary; students at a university, for example, are paid with a diploma. Thus, the members' goal within a utilitarian organization is to receive remuneration.

Normative organizations (or *voluntary organizations*) have a shared commitment to a moral goal. Membership in normative organizations is voluntary and without compensation.

Individuals join normative organizations to promote a social cause. Typically, members have equal opportunity to make decisions regarding the organization's direction. Examples include Mothers Against Drunk Driving (MADD) and religious institutions.

Coercive organizations are characterized by involuntary membership. They use force to keep members within the organization, and members are usually not allowed to leave. Rules and regulations are fundamental within these organizations. Members are expected to conform and relinquish their identity. Prison and the military are two examples of coercive organizations.

Organizations often do not fit into one of these three categories but may be a combination.

For example, while the US military is typically considered a coercive organization, members are compensated for their time and have joined voluntarily to fulfill a moral or other goal.

Military combines utilitarian, normative, and coercive features

Formal organizations

Formal organizations are a type of secondary group (e.g., large corporations) deliberately constructed for a shared goal. In corporations, this shared goal is usually to increase profits.

Three things characterize formal organizations.

1) *division of labor and power*. For example, doctors, nurses, and staff have specific roles at hospitals. The goals and responsibilities of the members align with the organization's goals.

2) *written set of rules, policies, and procedures*. For example, most places of employment have an employee handbook that serves this function.

3) *system for replacing members*. For example, large organizations often have a human resources department dedicated to this function.

Bureaucracy

Bureaucracy organizes enormous amounts of people in the public and private sectors.

Used in everyday speech, bureaucracies typically have a negative connotation.

Traditionally, bureaucracies refer to a body of non-elected government officials.

Three well-known models of bureaucracy are:

> *Weberian model*
>
> *acquisitive model*
>
> *monopolistic model*

Weberian model is a bureaucracy with:

> 1) a clear hierarchy
>
> 2) an area of *specialization*
>
> 3) *divide work* into smaller tasks
>
> 4) *standard rules* for operating

Acquisitive model is a bureaucracy characterized by expansion and turf wars.

Turf wars refer to disagreements over the duties and responsibilities of a particular agency.

Monopolistic model proposes that bureaucracies use monopoly and inefficiency.

Ideal bureaucracy

Max Weber proposed a model for an ideal bureaucracy, dividing the defining characteristics of this ideal bureaucracy into six principles.

First principle of an ideal bureaucracy is that *subordinates follow superiors' orders*. Each level of workers controls the level below and is controlled by the level above it.

Second principle is the existence of *rules* consistent across all levels of the bureaucracy.

Third principle is *fixed areas of activity*; people are organized by their work type.

Fourth principle in an ideal bureaucracy is that positions require *specialized skills and training*.

Fifth principle is *task-oriented activities*; a worker in an ideal bureaucracy must complete an assigned task rather than work for an allotted time.

Sixth characteristic of an ideal bureaucracy is that individuals in management positions have exhaustively written rules that can be learned.

Max Weber, sociologist and political economist

Iron law of oligarchy and McDonaldization

Iron law of oligarchy is a political theory that rule by elites is inevitable. This theory was developed by Robert Michels, who believed that it is impossible to eliminate elite rule through a representative democracy.

The common saying associated with this theory is, "*Who says organization, says oligarchy.*"

Michels believed that large organizations must create a bureaucracy. For this bureaucracy to be effective, centralization of power must occur, resulting in a small elite who hold power.

McDonaldization was proposed by George Ritzer in 1993 as the process by which a culture adopts the characteristics of a fast-food restaurant.

McDonaldization has four components: efficiency, calculability, predictability, and control.

Robert Michels, sociologist

Social institutions

As structures of social order, *institutions* govern the behavior of individuals in a community.

Institutions are defined based on their social purpose and transcend individual intentions by controlling the rules or laws that govern behavior.

The term "institution" is commonly applied to customs and behavior patterns important to society (such as the institution of marriage).

Institutions may function as formal mechanisms of societies' essential structures, such as the law and legislature (governmental political rule-making and enforcement) and education.

Individuals tend to view institutions as *natural* and as an *unchanging and inherent factor*.

However, studying institutions has revealed the nature of institutions as social constructs. They are relics of a specific moment in society, culture, and time and produced by *collective human choice*—not necessarily by the intent of individuals.

Social institutions are usually studied by examining the roles and expected behaviors that comprise them. The proper fulfillment of roles carries out an institution's social function.

The institutions of marriage and family have proven necessary for procreation, childrearing, and other basic human requirements. These institutions are upheld by adhering to an elaboration on behaviors expected of husband/father, wife/mother, and child/parent.

Sociology looks at the fundamental relationship between institutions and human nature.

However, institutions are seen as organically forming from and conforming to human nature—a fundamentally conservative view—or institutions are viewed as artificial, almost accidental. From this fundamentally progressive perspective, institutions require much structural revision (inspired by expert social analysis) to serve human needs better.

Education

Formal education

Education facilitates learning. Knowledge, skills, values, beliefs, and habits are transferred to younger members during education. This transfer can be conducted through storytelling, discussion, teaching, training, or research.

Education frequently takes place under the guidance of educators in the form of a student-teacher dynamic. Those who self-educate are *autodidacts*. Experiences that have a profound or lasting effect on an individual's thinking, feelings, or acts may be considered educational.

Formal education commonly divides the education system into stages: preschool, primary school, secondary school, college, university, or apprenticeship.

Pedagogy is the methodology of teaching.

At the global level, the United Nations' 1966 International Covenant on Economic, Social, and Cultural Rights recognizes every person's right to an education. Some governments have recognized a right to education, although education is often mandatory until a certain age.

Formal education commonly divides the education system into stages. The United Nations recognizes every person's right to an education.

Attendance at a traditional school building is flexible, and some parents homeschool their children. Parents home-schooling children use electronic educational technology (e-learning).

Hidden curriculum

Hidden curricula are unintentional lessons learned as a side effect of education. These curricula are learned but not blatantly meant to be taught, such as transferring or enforcing norms, values, and beliefs in a classroom and the social environment.

Hidden curriculum refers to formative knowledge gained by young primary and secondary school students. These lessons usually inform and reinforce social inequalities, including designations of class, race, disability, or gender.

Formal educational institutions claim to strive for equal intellectual development of students. Thus, the term "*hidden curriculum*" usually has a negative connotation.

Hidden curriculum is formative knowledge gained by primary and secondary school students.

Unequal distribution of cultural capital in a society (non-financial assets that promote social mobility beyond economic means, such as education) mirrors a corresponding distribution of knowledge among its students.

Factors within the learning process add to disseminating a hidden curriculum, including practices, procedures, rules, relationships, and structures.

Specific sources that may contribute to the success of a hidden curriculum are specific to the school environment and include the social structures of the classroom, the teacher's exercise of authority, rules governing the relationship between teachers and students, standard learning activities, the teacher's use of language, textbooks, audio-visual aids, furnishings, architecture, disciplinary measures, timetables, tracking systems, and curricular priorities.

Disparities are common in analyzing the hidden curricula across societies.

Sources of hidden curricula deserve as much scrutiny as didactic school lessons.

It may be unintentional, but the moral characteristics and ideologies of teachers and authority figures become inherently translated into their lessons, often adversely affecting their students. This is particularly apparent concerning *social* and *moral lessons*.

Like interactions with teachers and authority figures, *peer interactions* promote certain moral and social ideals.

In the case of hidden curriculum transferred by peers, there can be beneficial outcomes, such as basic socialization and fostering exchanges of information, ideas, culture, and experience.

Peer interactions promote certain moral and social ideals

Teacher expectancy

Canadian Professor Victor H. Vroom (1964) created the *expectancy model* based on motivation.

Motivation results from an expectation that a behavior will lead to an intended performance. The instrumentality of this behavior to achieving a specific result, and the desirability of this result for the individual, is *valence*.

Expectancy theory proposes that an individual's behavior is motivated, consciously, or subconsciously, based on that behavior's expected result or reaction. Naturally, desirous outcomes are the primary source of motivation for an individual's behavior choice.

However, expectancy theory examines an individual's cognitive decisional process because the outcome is not the only determining factor in making a behavioral decision.

Based on Vroom's original expectancy model, psychologist Jere Brophy and Professor Thomas Good created a comprehensive model of the relationship between teacher expectations and student achievement.

Brophy and Good's model details how teacher expectations and student achievement are linked: based on many factors, teachers form expectations of students; however subtle or blatant, teachers adjust their behavior toward students based on these expectations.

Teachers behave differently toward students based on expectations; students notice and internalize how a teacher behaves toward them, often compared to others. From these internalized observations, students understand *what the teacher expects from them*.

When a student accepts expectations and behavior of a teacher toward them, the student often acts to confirm the teacher's expectations.

Expectancy theory has been criticized for o*versimplification*.

Educational segregation and stratification

Segregation (i.e., enforced separation) in education has occurred throughout public education.

Segregation occurs with *gender*, *class*, and *racial segregation*.

In the U.S., there was a concerted effort at racial desegregation of public schools during the 1960s Civil Rights Movement. Though this effort succeeded within the legislature, economic status still creates racial segregation within education today.

Segregation includes *racial isolation* (exposure) and *racial unevenness* (imbalance).

Racial isolation looks at a student of a certain race and the percentage of students of the same race who surround her/him in the educational environment. If a student attends a school with an overwhelming number of students of the same race, the student is *racially isolated*.

Analytical approach of racial isolation receives criticism because it inherently depends on demographic composition changes. Suppose a certain minority percentage in the area increases. In that case, students will necessarily attend a school with different racial populations. However, there will be no insight into the increase in individual percentages of different races.

As a result, analysts prefer to define segregation according to measures of racial imbalance or the extent to which racial and ethnic groups are distributed unevenly across schools.

Racial stratification is a systematic social classification based on race. It is directly related to economic segregation because students of a lower economic status tend to live in the same areas and attend the same schools.

Racial segregation in schools effectively shows the results of racial stratification in the quality of the education that students receive. Students of low socioeconomic standing, a majority of whom are of a racial or ethnic minority, receive lower-standard education.

Nationwide, minority students are concentrated in high-poverty, low-achieving schools, while white students are more likely to attend high-achieving, more affluent schools.

Resources, such as funds and high-quality teachers, attach unequally to schools according to their student body's racial and socioeconomic composition.

Protest march against segregation in U.S. schools.

Notes for active learning

Family

Immediate and extended family

A *family*, as recognized by human society, is an affiliated group. This term has far-reaching meanings, which are continually expanding.

Affiliations commonly include birth, marriage, co-residence, or another shared characteristic.

Immediate family includes spouses, parents, siblings, and children.

An immediate family widens to the *extended family*, consisting of grandparents, aunts, uncles, cousins, nephews, or nieces.

Extended families are widespread in the U.S. In societies where divorce and remarrying are common, stepparents, stepsiblings, and step-extended families are widely accepted.

Adoption is when *non-blood-related* individuals are legally family members.

An immediate family of spouses, parents, brothers, sisters, and children widens to the extended family, which may consist of grandparents, aunts, uncles, cousins, nephews, and nieces.

Families are constantly redefining whom they include in their immediate and extended circles. In many cases, close family friends, religious or educational figures, or others who may have stood in for an absent family member are considered family. However, they are not of one bloodline.

"Family" is an inclusive metaphor for specific designations (e.g., community, nationhood, global village, and humanism).

Experts trace extending lineage and ancestry of families using the field of *genealogy*.

Evolutionarily, the family is a *system of reproduction and raising offspring*. In most societies, the family is the initial and most fundamental institution for the socialization of children.

In modern society, the vital act of rearing children generally takes place in a few different typical family structures:

> *matrifocal* (a mother and her children)
>
> *conjugal* (a husband, wife, and children; a nuclear family)
>
> *avuncular* (for example, a grandparent, a brother, his sister, and her children)
>
> *extended* (parents and children co-reside with members of one parent's family)

Forms of kinship

Anthropologist Lewis Henry Morgan (1818–1881) was the first to observe *kinship* worldwide.

Though his work is outdated, he was the first to deconstruct kinship worldwide.

Lewis Henry Morgan, anthropologist

Kinship can be designated into two groups:

> affiliated based on *consanguinity* (consanguineous kinship) or
>
> affiliated based on *marriage* (affinal kinship); primary, secondary, or tertiary.

Nuclear family has eight primary kinship relationships:

> husband-wife, mother-daughter, mother-son, father-daughter, father-son, younger sister-older sister, younger brother-older brother, and brother-sister.

Thirty-three secondary kin relationships are outside the nuclear family. For example, mother's brother, brother's wife, sister's husband, and father's sister.

Tertiary kin is the secondary kin of primary kin. There are 151 recognized tertiary kin relationships. For example, the wife's brother's son and sister's husband's brother.

Kinship terms distinguish kin. These terms can function in either the *classificatory system* or the *descriptive system.*

Morgan determined that kinship terminologies reflect *different categorizations*. For example, most kinship terminologies distinguish between the *sexes* (a brother and sister) and between *generations* (a child and parent).

Classificatory system includes kin under one category and with the same term. For example, a child calls his mother and sisters of her "mother." Similarly, that child calls any child of his mother's sister "brother" or "sister."

Descriptive system uses terminology given to kin describing the relationship between kin. A child would call his mother "*mother*" and her sister "*aunt.*"

Kinship usage is the behavioral pattern of kinship.

Distinct societies normalize certain behaviors between specific kin or family members. For example, most societies have a taboo and illegalization of *incest*.

Morgan's classification differentiates *classificatory kinship systems* (i.e., not distinguish lineal and collateral relationships) and *descriptive kinship systems* that do.

He identified six basic patterns of kinship:

Hawaiian: only distinguishes relatives based on sex and generation;

Sudanese: no two relatives share the same term;

Eskimo: distinguishes relatives based on sex and generation but distinguishes between lineal relatives and collateral relatives;

Iroquois: in addition to sex and generation, distinguishes siblings of opposite sexes in the parental generation;

Crow: a matrilineal system with some features of the Iroquois system but with a "skewing" feature whereby the generation is "frozen" for some relatives;

Omaha: same as the Crow system, but patrilineal.

Family forms

Family as an institution, as opposed to a biological fact, is accepted based on diverse and wide-ranging data from ethnography, history, law, and social statistics. What is considered "family" is no longer strictly adherent to a basis of *consanguinity*.

Diverse families exist in many settings, each with functions and meanings in conjunction with their relationship to other social institutions.

Nuclear family (or *conjugal families*) are a wife, a husband, and unmarried, underage children.

Sociologists distinguish between conjugal and nuclear families by the closeness of ties with kin (conjugal families are independent, while nuclear families remain close with kin).

While conjugal or extended families are normative family structures found societies, family forms vary in the composition and conception of families.

A nuclear family consists of a wife, a husband, and unmarried, underage children.

Matrifocal family consists of a mother and her children. This kind of family is common, where women have resources to rear children by themselves or must do so out of necessity and when men are absent.

Family (or *domestic group*) is matrifocal when centered on a woman and her children. These children's fathers may be intermittently present in the group's life and occupy a secondary or inconsistent place. The matriarch is not necessarily married; if she is, her husband is not necessarily any of the children's father.

Blended family or *stepfamily* can refer to a family with parents who have divorced, remarried, or have children from other partners. Societies are moving toward tolerance of same-gender relationships, and family structures consisting of two mothers, or two fathers are becoming more common and accepted within society.

Monogamous family is based on legal and social monogamy between parents. From a legal perspective, an individual can be married to only one person.

Polygamy is a relationship with more than two partners and exists in three forms:

polygyny, where a man is married to more than one woman at a time;

polyandry, where a woman is married to more than one man at a time, and

polyamory (or group and conjoint marriage) is when more than two people are married.

Many polygamous practices exist, varying within diverse cultures. In some cases, the whole family co-inhabits a single household. In other instances, each family's wife has her household where she lives, possibly with her children.

The laws of polygamy vary worldwide, and group marriage is illegal and not widely practiced in most places today, including the U.S.

In places where polygamy is illegal, the act of marrying more than one person is *bigamy*.

In places where marriage to more than one person is allowed, it tends to refer to *polygyny*.

Marriage and divorce

Marriage is the legal recognition of two people as partners in a relationship. The age of legal consent to marry varies, and in some places, there is no age requirement for marriage with approval by parents or courts.

Marriage can be a declaration of love and devotion to another person, a step in building a family, significant in the unification of two families, or, in some cases, a business agreement or arrangement between individuals or the families of individuals.

Divorce is the dissolution of a marriage by a court or another competent authority. Reasons for divorce vary but include sexual incompatibility, infidelity, spousal abuse, or personality clash.

Though divorce laws differ worldwide, some legal sanction from a court or another authority is required to finalize a divorce. Divorce includes alimony (spousal support), child custody, child visitation, child support, division of debt, and distribution of property and assets.

Where monogamy is the only marriage structure allowed by law, divorce allows each former partner to marry another. Where polygamy (which can be understood here as polygyny) is legal, divorce allows a woman to marry a new husband.

Annulment is the declaration of marriage null and void, which differs from divorce. After an annulment, it is as though the marriage never happened, with no lasting legal effects. An annulment may be preferable to avoid divorce's stigma or legal entanglements.

Situations such as *de facto separation* (spouses stop cohabiting) and *legal separation* (a married couple formalizes a *de facto* separation while married) should not be confused with divorce.

Domestic abuse and violence

Violence within a family is *domestic violence*. Worldwide and within cultures, what is legally and socially considered domestic violence can vary drastically.

Domestic abuse has different implications in diverse contexts (e.g., medical, legal, political);

> *physical, sexual, emotional* (e.g., stalking), *psychological, cyber,* and *economic abuse.*

Domestic abuse *victims* are spouses, children, cohabitants (roommates, romantic partners), and sexual or dating partners.

Family violence and domestic violence overlap.

Family violence is explicitly used for *child abuse, elder abuse,* and *spousal abuse.*

As dependent, impressionable, and physically smaller individuals, children can easily be subject to abuse.

Child abuse is the physical, sexual, or emotional maltreatment or neglect of a child or children. This definition informs the major designations of child abuse, which are neglect, psychological or emotional abuse, physical abuse, and sexual abuse.

As people age, becoming physically and perhaps more mentally frail, they are more dependent and vulnerable to abuse.

Elder abuse includes physical, sexual, psychological, or emotional abuse, caregiver neglect or self-neglect, financial exploitation or abuse, and health care fraud or abuse.

Laws protecting the elderly from abuse are like laws protecting dependent adults. These express that the fundamental element of elder abuse is the *expectation of trust* that the older person holds toward their abuser.

Religion

Sociology and psychology of religion

Religion consists of cultural structures and practices, worldviews, and beliefs that assist its members' understanding of the order of existence (the tripartite order consisting of the natural, social, and divine orders).

Over many years, most religions have constructed sacred narratives and symbolism that attempt to deconstruct and explain existential queries, such as the meaning of life and the origin of life and the Universe. These narratives and sacred histories may explain the formation of the religion and usually contain some divine framework or set of laws about how members of the religion should conduct their lives.

Religion has many forms and using different symbolism to express their faith

Beyond prescribed rules and laws, people may choose certain portions of a religion's teachings to follow, such as aspects of morality or ethics or a preferred lifestyle. A religion's teachings can be disseminated through organized gatherings, sermons, scripture, missionaries, or clergy.

Many religions incorporate holy places, rituals, prayers, commemoration, and public service.

Sociology of religion studies religion's beliefs, practices, and organization using sociological methods. Objective investigation of religion includes quantitative and qualitative methods.

While quantitative methods (e.g., surveys, polls, demographic and census analysis) are frequently employed, qualitative approaches, including participant observation, interviews, and analysis of archival, historical, and documentary materials, can be applied too.

Sociology was applied to the study of religion when Émile Durkheim (1858–1917), a French sociologist known as the father of sociology, conducted an 1897 study of suicide rates among Catholics and Protestants. This was a foundational work because it brought the study of religion and sociology together and distinguished the sociological approach from other disciplines, such as psychology or philosophy.

Psychology of religion focuses on the *uses of religious beliefs and behaviors*.

Philosophy of religion attempts to assess the *validity of religious beliefs*.

In contrast, the *sociology of religion* operates with an *assumed indifference* to the supernatural and usually focuses on the *socio-cultural reification* of religious practices.

After Durkheim's initial work, sociologists began bringing the sociological study of religion in different directions. Karl Marx and Max Weber emphasized the relationship between religion and society's *economic or social structure*.

In contemporary discourse, there have been debates centered on trends of secularization, such as secular humanism and atheism. Discussions have encompassed civil religion and the cohesiveness of religion in the context of globalization and multiculturalism.

Religiosity

Religiosity (or *religiousness*) is a comprehensive sociological term applied to many aspects of religion, such as religious activity, dedication, faith, and religious doctrine.

On a small scale, religiosity refers to a person's degree of religiousness. It is less concerned with *how* a person is religious (i.e., practicing certain rituals, retelling specific stories, revering certain symbols, or accepting certain doctrines about deities and the afterlife).

Religiosity is studied from many perspectives, and sociologists propose that religiousness has multiple dimensions. Sociologists propose four to twelve dimensions, though measures of religiosity acknowledge differences in religious doctrine, religious practice, and spirituality.

Most widely referred to are the *six dimensions of religiosity*.

Cognition, affect, and behavior have two cross-classifications, resulting in six dimensions.

> *cognition* (i.e., knowing) is traditional and particularistic orthodoxy;

> *effect* (i.e., feeling) is a palpable and tangible effect, and

> *behavior* (i.e., doing) is religious actions and participation.

These six dimensions comprise a measure of the spectrum of religiosity. Individuals measured on these dimensions may score high in one category and low in another, though there is usually a correlation between specific dimensions.

Religiosity distinguishes *religious doctrine*, *religious practice*, and *spirituality*.

Religious organizations

All religions have members who make up *religious communities*. These communities, which include institutions, practitioners, and structures, can be organized in different forms, including religious movements, churches, sects, and cults.

Religious movements are when people join to spread a new religion or reinterpret an old one. Movements are typically open and accepting to new members to build a following.

A movement may not continue after a leader has lost influence, been replaced, or passed away.

If a movement gains support and followers, it may grow and establish a church or denomination; a movement develops adherence to symbols, rules, discipline systems, rituals, and methods of governance.

Non-denominational church does not have an affiliated denomination.

Denomination is a broader structure exercising some authority over a group of churches and is integrated into society but not the state.

Sects and cults

Sects are typically relatively newer offshoots of a larger denomination. They are formed when some members disagree with the larger denomination and desire to preserve what they believe to be the true views of the denomination.

Sects usually retain characteristics and beliefs like the denomination, with specific exceptions. They may have practices *conflicting* with *societal norms* and *values*. Sects may fail as independent entities, dissolving or becoming absorbed into the larger denomination.

On rare occasions, sects may attract or recruit enough people who feel similarly and eventually become a religious institution, growing over time into a denomination.

Cults, sometimes confused with sects, are transient and informal religious institutions. Unlike sects, they do not necessarily stem from a larger denomination but typically form around the teachings of a single, charismatic leader.

Unlike sects, cults tend to rely more on secrecy and privacy and do little proselytizing. Cults are criticized for secrecy, power over members' lives, and domination by a singular leader.

Cults' values and beliefs vary, sometimes drastically, from societal norms and values. Although many significant religions began as cults, the term *"cult"* holds a pejorative connotation today.

Because of complicated definitions and implications, many prefer not to use *"sect"* or *"cult"* and instead refer to an emerging religious group as a *"new religious movement"* or *"NRM."*

Religion and social change

Religion and society are inextricably linked, influencing one another as they evolve and develop.

Religion is affected by shifts in a worldview, which may result in more or less interest in religion or interest and needs of a different kind. Society can be shaped and influenced by believers of a religion performing their beliefs in societies worldwide.

Three significant shifts in a worldview that incorporate and affect religion and society are:

> *modernization, secularization*, and *fundamentalism*.

Modernization within societies is the progression from pre-modern to traditional to modern societies. Proponents of modernization operate under the assumption that citizens of more modern societies have more freedom to enjoy a higher standard of living based on the resultant increase in wealth and power of the society.

As a result of modernization, traditional (in many cases, synonymous with religious) values, beliefs, and practices tend to hold less importance to societies.

Modernization can be linked to increases in urbanization, industrialism, globalization, and education and rationalization. Aspects of modernization include the progression of technology, increase in infrastructure, and development of governance based on abstract principles.

Critics of modernization say it has been conflated with Westernization to the detriment of traditional, in many cases religious, and Indigenous populations worldwide.

Secularization is the process by which society no longer attaches significance, meaning, or fulfillment to religious ideologies, practices, or institutions. During this process, religion loses social life and governance authority and holds little power.

Societal shifts to *modernization* and *rationalization* align with shifts toward *secularization*.

From a sociological perspective, secularization uses *differentiation* (i.e., the process by which society and individuals' lives become categorized as society moves toward modernization).

For example, during the Age of Western Enlightenment, secular bodies overtook education and welfare systems, decentralizing the role of religion. Due to secularization and corresponding modernization, science progressed exponentially.

Fundamentalism

Fundamentalism, often viewed as a response to modernization or secularization, is the belief in the strict adherence to an *irreducible set of beliefs*.

Religious fundamentalists typically react to a perceived marginalization of their religion; often, occurrences perceived as marginalization are the result of modernization and secularization, and fundamentalists are willing to fight to reverse this marginalization.

Fundamentalism can be characterized by selectivity regarding promoting specific religious traditions and accepting (or condemning) aspects of modernity.

Characteristics include *moral dualism* and an *inflexible, literal interpretation* of the holy text.

Organizational features among fundamentalist organizations include:

>   elected or divinely chosen membership,

>   moral and even physical boundaries between themselves and sinful others,

>   charismatic leaders, and

>   strict behavioral guidelines (e.g., clothing, sexuality, and child-rearing).

Fundamentalist groups may spread their message to others in several ways.

Conqueror is when, like religious terrorist groups, a fundamentalist organization attempts to dominate society to impose religious rule. This can be attained through militarized coercion, force, or elimination of those deemed enemies and gives rise to fundamentalist political groups.

Transformer is when fundamentalists attempt to convert others, possibly by political means.

Creator is when fundamentalist organizations create alternative social structures and education systems to give believers a domain separate from the mainstream, non-believing society.

Notes for active learning

Government and Economy

Government

Government is the system by which a nation, state, or town is managed and controlled.

Government typically consists of legislators, administrators, and arbiters, who are the means for creating and enforcing laws and policies.

When studied through the lens of sociology, government is *political sociology*, which focuses on *relationships between* the state, society, and citizens.

Political sociology studies how social trends, dynamics, and institutionalized structures affect the political process.

Economy

Economy (or *economic system*) is a country or region's *wealth* (i.e., valued resources), especially concerning the production and consumption of limited goods and services by different agents. Economic agents can be individuals, businesses, organizations, or governments.

Economy involves culture, values, education, technological developments, history, social organization, political structure, legal systems, and geography.

Market-based economy has uninterrupted production of goods and services, which are exchanged based on supply and demand. This economy uses an exchange system calibrated to free-market pricing.

Command-based economy is controlled by a central political agent and usually results in frequent instances of goods shortages.

Green economy is socially inclusive and driven to preserve the natural environment and resources by enhancing resource and energy efficiency and sustainable development.

Economic sociology

Economic sociology is the social cause and effect of economic phenomena, divided into *classical economic sociology* and *contemporary sociology*.

Classical economic sociology approaches economic phenomena with a focus on the role that economic structures and institutions have in society and the influence that an economy holds over these economic structures and institutions.

Contemporary economic sociology focuses on the *social consequence* (or outcome of economic exchanges) and the *social meanings* they incorporate, encourage, or obstruct.

Socioeconomics (or used synonymously with *economic sociology*) focuses on the intersection of economics and society from broad interdisciplinary perspectives.

Power and authority

The relationship between *power and authority* is close and often confusing.

Power is the ability to influence or direct events or others' behavior.

Authority is permission (i.e., right) to give orders, make decisions, and enforce obedience.

> An individual with power does not necessarily have authority.

> An individual with authority is given the right to exert power.

Social sciences have initiated approaches to *authority vs. power* and their differences. They can be analyzed for families, schools, churches, armies, industries, bureaucracies, and societies.

Comparative economic and political systems

Comparative economics is a subfield by economist Calvin, who critically examined economic systems such as feudalism, communism, socialism, capitalism, and mixed economies.

Comparative economics focuses on comparisons, such as societies' transitions to different economic systems, the merits and detriments of a system as applied to a society, and the emergence of mixed economies in countries worldwide.

Comparative economics remains relevant even without substantial system differences between countries. The analysis illuminates essential information about specifics, such as resource allocation within markets and households, customs, and centralized allocation.

Comparative politics involves elements of political science and political sociology.

Comparative politics is the study and comparison of political systems and the social basis of politics. It focuses on the relationships between *society*, the *political sphere*, and *social and political institutions*.

Division of labor

Division of labor is dividing a single task into multiple, more specific tasks or roles performed by separate, specialized workers. It relates to gender (childrearing historically being performed by women laborers) and class.

Historically, it is closely linked to the rise of capitalism, the expansion and complexity of industrialization processes, and increased economic growth and output.

Influential thinkers have had differing opinions and theories on whether the division of labor is *beneficial and essential* or *detrimental to production* and a prospering economy.

Proponents of the division of labor point to efficiency. Division of labor offers enormous reductions in time spent training workers (because of the simplicity of the assigned tasks) and having them move between different tasks; division of labor increases productivity and profits.

Workers are believed to become more skilled at working within a division of labor system because they perform tasks repeatedly.

There are criticisms of the division of labor between laborers and businesses. Laborers may suffer alienation from their task and the larger product they have a part in making.

This could lead to decreased productivity and a lack of interest in their position. Workers are only trained in a single task and do not get diverse experience. This may be detrimental for businesses with a strict dependence on the system, which could fail if even a single section does not work correctly or at the correct speed.

Division of labor systems often has high start-up costs because they tend to require expensive machinery involved in the labor process.

Notes for active learning

Medical Sociology

Health and medicine

Medical sociology studies medical organizations and institutions from a sociological perspective. This includes examining healthcare professionals and their interactions or actions, experiences of patients, and disparities of health issues among different races and classes.

On a broader scale, this analysis can include the effects of medical practices on cultures and societies and the interrelation of globalization and the medical and healthcare fields.

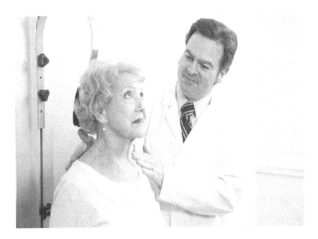

Population health is monitored and treated by a society's healthcare system

A healthcare system uses resources, institutions, and people working in tandem to administer healthcare services to society.

Healthcare systems exist worldwide, as diverse in history and organization as their nations. They attempt to match available resources with the health needs of their people.

Most healthcare systems employ primary healthcare and public health programs.

Medicalization

Medicalization is how human conditions, problems, or experiences become culturally and medically defined as *pathological* and *treated as medical conditions*. This results in pathology or condition becoming the subject of medical study, diagnosis, prevention, or treatment.

Medicalization can occur from current information, evidence, or hypotheses about a condition. It depends on shifting societal thinking, economic conditions, or the development of technology, medications, or treatments.

Medicalization in sociology is analyzed regarding professionals, patients, corporations, and public health organizations and the power structures that lie therein.

Sociology examines the implications for citizens who rely on certain evolutions or setbacks in medicine for their sense of self-identity and, in some cases, their lives and life decisions.

After a pathology becomes classified as medical, a *"medical model of disability,"* instead of a social model, is associated with the condition.

Pathologization (or pejorative *disease mongering)* may be used instead of medicalization.

Sick role

Sick role was conceptualized by American sociologist Talcott Parsons in 1951. He viewed sickness from a sociological and socio-cultural perspective (his ideas emanate from *role theory)* instead of a physiological phenomenon.

He emphasized the rights and responsibilities of the ill. Parsons, a functionalist, argued that a sick person is not a productive member of society and, upon becoming ill, enters *sanctioned deviance.* A sick person, who should not be held accountable for their illness, must *receive competent medical help* and *get well.*

Sick role ties into a concept of legitimization; a society allows the sick to deviate from everyday responsibilities because the sick have proven their illness *legitimate* and that they are *unable* to perform their typical responsibilities.

A sick person's rights and responsibilities vary based on the severity and illness and can last while the individual is ill.

Criticisms of the sick role theory exist. In many societies, the medical profession is expanding its reach, and the sick role theory does not account for illnesses based on lifestyle choices.

Though there has been progress toward acceptance of certain illnesses, some sufferers are still stigmatized or blamed for their illnesses. Sick role theory does not account for discrepancies between the social status of ill people, their access to competent health care, or their treatment by the healthcare industry. Sick role theory assumes the power and authority of the medical profession and functions on ideal patient-doctor relationships.

Society is becoming more open to ideas of chronic illness; chronic illness patients often cannot be helped by the medical profession and are encouraged to live independent lives. It is widely accepted that, in many cases, those with chronic illnesses can live whole and productive lives.

Sick role theory assumes that an ill individual *accepts the sick role* and *acts appropriately.*

Illness experience is a personal account of a patient's illness not limited to clinical symptoms. It is a concept used in patient interviewing and may refer to the individual's illness process.

Illness experience has five steps:

1) experiencing a symptom,

2) assuming a sick role,

3) acquiring health care,

4) being dependent (accepting the role of the patient), and

5) recovery and rehabilitation.

Healthcare delivery

Trained interdisciplinary medical professionals deliver modern healthcare. This includes medical practitioners of every medical discipline, allied health, public health practitioners, community health workers, and assistive personnel. These clinicians provide populations with personal and population-based preventative, curative, and rehabilitative services.

In most societies, the healthcare process begins with primary care and continues to secondary and tertiary levels of care if necessary.

Home and community care are healthcare and include programs of public health interest and health and social work programs, such as residential and community programs for the elderly and rehabilitation services.

Healthcare can be private or public.

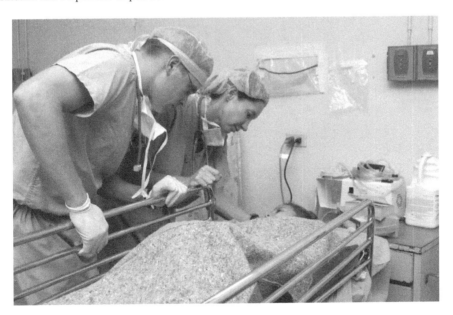

Social epidemiology

Social epidemiology is the socio-cultural study of epidemiology, focusing on the stratification of advantages and disadvantages regarding the distribution or acquisition of health and disease.

Social epidemiology is applied on multiple levels, from focusing on individuals to broader, emergent social trends that do not necessarily correlate at the individual level.

Analysis from both a narrower and broader social epidemiology perspective is valuable.

Models of multilevel analysis, known as hierarchical and mixed effects models, have increased, but this approach has theoretical and practical concerns like observational epidemiology.

Social epidemiology may overlap with medical anthropology, sociology, and geography; it uses social concepts to explain a population's health patterns instead of using health and sickness to demystify social phenomena.

Processes Related to Stereotypes

Stereotypes

Stereotypes are widely held, oversimplified ideas about a group of people. They allow people to simplify the world and make rapid judgments.

Stereotypes can be positive but are often negative. They lead to social categorization, or the formation of ingroups and outgroups, and can form the basis of prejudice.

Stereotypes neglect to acknowledge individual variations existing within groups of people. They are often *exaggerated generalizations*.

Racial stereotypes typically favor the race of the stereotype holder and can be harmful to individuals stereotyped (through stereotyping threats and self-fulfilling prophecy).

Self-fulfilling prophecy

Self-fulfilling prophecy is a prediction that becomes true due to the prediction being made.

For example, an employer who believes his employees will be lazy and incompetent behaves in a way that will likely result in the employees acting in a lazy and incompetent manner.

Self-fulfilling prophecies occur because *beliefs* and *expectations influence behavior*.

Self-fulfilling prophecies have typically been studied in classroom settings and have been found to have more of an effect on students who are *ethnic minorities*.

Negative stereotypes of ethnic and racial groups create self-fulfilling prophecies for individuals.

Stereotype threat

Stereotype threat is when an individual feels at risk of confirming a negative stereotype about their social group.

Stereotype threat causes anxiety and decreases individual performance within a stereotyped group across many domains.

Individuals do not need to believe the stereotypes about their social group for stereotypes to affect them.

Studies have shown that stereotype threat can result in decreased performance on the SAT by students from low-income families due to the stereotype that low-income students are less intelligent than other groups.

Stereotype boost and lift

Stereotype boost is when people perform a task better after exposure to *positive stereotypes* about their social group.

Stereotype lift is when individuals perform better at a task after exposure to *negative stereotypes* about a *different* social group.

Stereotype boost and *stereotype lift* are hypothesized to result from decreased anxiety.

Stereotype threat is hypothesized to result from increased anxiety.

Prejudice and Bias

Factors contributing to prejudice

Prejudice is adverse judgments made about individuals not based on reason or experience.

Prejudice often leads to *discrimination*, treating a person *differently* based on groups.

Prejudice typically stems from differences in physical or cultural characteristics, which become socially significant.

When examining prejudice, *power* typically refers to economic and political power. Groups that hold power can keep laws in place to benefit and maintain their power, often putting those without economic or political power at a disadvantage.

The existence of social classes contributes to prejudice by creating a hierarchy in which some individuals are better off than others.

Just world phenomenon contributes to prejudice. This phenomenon refers to the belief that when dreadful things happen to others, they usually do something to deserve it.

Prestige is the respect and admiration of an individual and is typically based on occupation. People in prestigious positions may look down on those who are not and prevent them from achieving a higher status.

Emotion and prejudice

Emotions are integral in prejudice and prejudicial behavior through their associated behaviors.

Fear, disgust, anger, contempt, and *jealousy* contribute to prejudicial behavior. These emotions do not cause prejudicial behavior *per se* but increase the likelihood of occurrence.

For example, *fear* and *disgust* function as social emotions contributing to prejudice, making people more likely to avoid group members.

Anger and *contempt* can contribute to an individual acting out against outgroup members.

Jealousy can alert individuals to the benefits others are receiving and cause them to demand similar benefits, sometimes acting resentfully.

Cognition in prejudice

Cognitive appraisals can lead to emotions of *fear, disgust, anger, contempt,* and *jealousy.*

For example, individuals from one group may think that individuals in another group will take their power, resulting in fear and discrimination against that group.

Individuals can learn to *reappraise cognitions* to reduce the effects of prejudicial behavior.

For example, those who believe that individuals from a minority group receive special treatment by having special admission criteria and more scholarship opportunities might consider the ways those individuals have received advantaged treatment based on minority status.

Stereotypical beliefs about outgroup members can contribute to *prejudice* and *discrimination.*

For example, a teacher who holds the stereotype that Asians are good at math might overlook an Asian student who needs additional help with the subject.

Stigma

Stigma is the disapproval of a group based on perceived characteristics that distinguish them from other members of society.

Perception of these characteristics matters, not actual existence.

Erving Goffman, an American sociologist, interprets stigma as "spoiling" identity.

Goffman proposed three types of stigma: character, physical, and group association.

Character stigma is when characteristics become apparent through interaction with another.

Physical stigma results from visible deformities or an atypical appearance.

Group association stigma results from negative stereotypes about an individual's social group.

Ethnocentrism and cultural relativism

Ethnocentrism is judging another culture based on the standards and values of one's culture.

Ethnocentrism typically implies the belief that one's culture is superior to others. It often occurs outside of one's conscious awareness.

Cultural relativism asserts that cultures are equal; therefore, there is no "superior culture." It assumes something is "good" or "bad" relative to its cultural context.

Cultural relativists accept that people's perspectives are significantly influenced by cultural background, acknowledging that studying cultures from a neutral position is nearly impossible.

Discrimination

Individual *vs.* institutional discrimination

Discrimination is the *prejudicial (or unfavorable) treatment* of others based on a perceived membership in a specific group.

Discrimination is an *action based on distinctive factors* such as age, gender, weight, and race.

Discrimination can be divided into *institutional* and *individual discrimination*.

Institutional discrimination occurs on a macro scale and is the mistreatment of individuals by organizations, including government organizations, public institutions, and corporations. Law enforcement, housing, employment, and educational institutions are often cited as contributing to discrimination.

Studies have found that African Americans are more likely to have their mortgage applications declined than white people, even when income and credit history are controlled for.

Institutionalized discrimination stems from widely held and stereotypical systemic beliefs that may be conscious or unconscious. Institutional discrimination is believed to contribute heavily to the racial wealth gap.

Individual discrimination occurs at the micro (or individual) level. It can stem from conscious or subconscious prejudice and bias.

Individual discrimination can include derogatory remarks, excluding an individual from a group, or limiting the opportunities of another solely based on their group membership.

Prejudice and discrimination

Prejudice is unjustified attitudes towards others based on social group membership.

Prejudice does not mean action but *holding certain beliefs*, prejudice without action.

Prejudice typically *precedes discrimination*.

Prevailing social norms within a society influence prejudice; if a peer group is prejudiced against a specific group, the person shares the prejudicial beliefs of the group.

Social factors identified as contributing to prejudice and discrimination include *conflict theory*, *group closure*, and an *authoritarian personality*.

Conflict theory is when privileged individuals and groups who wish to keep their power may act in specific ways to prevent members of minority groups from gaining power.

Group closure explains prejudicial beliefs; according to this theory, group members maintain clear boundaries between themselves and others.

Authoritarian personalities think rigidly and reject those considered inferior.

Group closure excludes others who are different

Power, prestige and class facilitate discrimination

Power typically refers to economic power or political power. Individuals with economic and political power can put individuals like themselves into political office. Similarly, these individuals will more likely protect the interests of people who put them in office and the interests of those who are most like them.

Minority groups are often underrepresented in political positions. People who hold economic power may be more likely to share this power with individuals like them through the hiring process. This inhibits individuals from minority groups from gaining economic power.

People may discriminate against others based on social class. Social classes form hierarchical structures, enabling individuals in higher social classes to discriminate against those who are beneath them in the social class hierarchy.

Prestige is how an individual is viewed within society, often based on occupation and income. Jobs associated with high prestige often go to members of the majority group, while jobs associated with low prestige tend to go to individuals belonging to a minority group.

Intersectionality

Intersectionality studies the interrelationships between forms (or systems) of oppression, domination, or discrimination by analyzing complex facets of an individual's identity (e.g., race, gender, class, sex, and age). Recognizing that people rarely experience oppression of a single factor, intersectionality adds additional layers of complexity to the understanding of social inequality.

Intersectionality holds that traditional conceptualizations of oppression within society, such as racism, sexism, biphobia, homophobia, and belief-based bigotry, do not act independently. Oppressions interrelate, creating systems of structural inequalities that reflect the intersection of multiple forms of discrimination.

Intersectionality is an essential paradigm in cultural studies. However, difficulties arise from the complexities encountered in making *multidimensional conceptualizations* to explain how *socially constructed categories* of differentiation interact to create a *social hierarchy*.

Notes for active learning

Social Movements

Types of social movements

Social movements are group actions to enact *societal change* or *retain the status quo*.

Formal or *informal* social movements unite people over *social* or *political issues*.

American Civil Rights Movement (1954–1968) was a notable social movement during which African Americans used nonviolence and civil disobedience to increase social awareness and enact legislation abolishing legalized racial segregation.

There have been many social movements, some of which caused *human loss* during war and civil unrest. Others increased *emigration* during political instability.

Social movements can be *proactive* or *reactive*.

Proactive social movements lobby for a cause. In the U.S., initiative-taking movements include the *Women's Rights Movement* and the *Green Movement* (or Environmentalism).

Reactive social movements involve people protesting an aspect of society, including anti-immigration and anti-globalization movements.

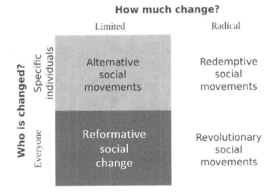

Limited vs. radial social movements with alternative and reformative social change

Relative deprivation

American sociologist Robert Merton (1910-2003) studied social deviance and developed *relative deprivation*.

Relative deprivation is the experience of being *deprived of something one feels entitled to*.

Relative deprivation is applied to a group compared with society or people compared to others. It may emanate from a person seeing another obtain (or possess) something they believe they should have (e.g., diet, amenities, activities, or lifestyle).

Relative deprivation may be applied to an *entire population*, noting fewer resources or rights than another society.

Relative deprivation describes *relative rather than absolute feelings* (or measures of economic, political, or social deprivation).

Relative deprivation is consequential for behaviors and stress. It can be impactful on a large scale in social movements and social deviance and potentially contributes to rioting, civil wars, and terrorism. On a smaller scale, individuals who suffer from relative deprivation may resort to social deviance or crime.

Deprivation theory suggests that people deprived of money, resources, justice, privilege, dignity, or rights will use political activism to redress their grievances. It is a starting point for analyzing why people join social movements. It also points to criticism of relative deprivation, which explains people who feel discontented but refuse to act.

Counter-criticism explains that not all discontent takes action because people avoid conflict, have only short-term goals, or feel life difficulties may increase because there is no guarantee of social action making a change.

Social movements involve people protesting an issue

Social movement stages

Social movement is a group bonded by the goal of stopping (or creating) *social change*.

Social movement organizations (SMO) are groups comprising the broader social movement.

The organization of a social movement is related to its goals, including what the movement is trying to change and the amount of change it is attempting to enact.

Movements may set their aims for change on individuals, groups, or society. It can advocate for minor changes (e.g., a policy of local governments) or radical changes (e.g., Prohibition).

Social movements have four stages:

> *Emergence, coalescence, bureaucratization*, and *decline*.

Emergence can be considered the unhappiness of people with certain conditions. It is the vague time before any real organization or collaboration forms, when individuals may express their discontent and look for people who feel similarly.

Coalescence is the second stage when a group with specific grievances forms and organizes its mission, demands, and strategies. Leaders emerge, and demonstrations may begin to take place.

Bureaucratization is the creation of a high-level organization that formalizes a movement. At this stage, a coordinated mission has developed across subsections of the larger movement, a trained staff administers daily operations, and the movement may begin to hold political power.

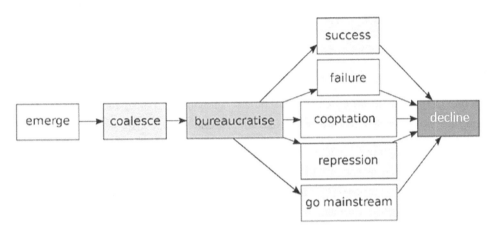

Stages of social movements evolution and final stages of decline

Social movement decline

Decline is the final stage but does not mean failure of a movement; there are four ways a movement can pass through a stage of decline (repression, co-option, success, and failure).

Movements may decline from *repression*, control by authorities or agents of authority, sometimes by violent or illegal means, or by enacting biased policies.

Co-optation is when a movement relies heavily on a *charismatic leader* or *centralized authority*, and that leader becomes integrated into the opposition.

Movements may decline because they have *succeeded*, more common among smaller, localized movements with specific goals, although the women's suffrage movement is an example of a successful national movement.

Movements reaching their goal may shift focus to another component of the issue.

Social movement's decline may be due to *failure,* which occurs from organizational mistakes, often caused by factionalism or encapsulation.

Movement strategies and tactics

Movements rely on strategies and tactics to gain support for their cause by attracting bystanders, media, or authorities. Strategies are various, and a movement may use more than one strategy.

Strategies include protest marches, parades, vigils, sit-ins, demonstrations, rallies, pickets, or boycotts. Tactics include singing, chanting, signs, public speakers, musical performances, book readings, and physical formations such as human chains or walls.

Other social movement strategies can be employed using forms of media, such as news coverage, television appearances, radio interviews, news and editorial articles, flyers, pamphlets, handouts, books, and the internet and social media.

Canvassing is a strategy with members speaking to people on the street to gain support.

Strategies and tactics must be well-planned to execute the mission of a movement correctly.

Specific factors are location, content, resources, individuals, police or authority, legality, timing, public outreach, advertisement, execution, repetition, follow-through, and follow-up.

A movement attempting to enact social change in legislation often uses civil disobedience or nonviolent resistance to achieve its goals. For example, during the American Civil Rights Movement, activists purposefully put themselves in situations where they would be arrested while breaking laws they deemed to be unjust to African Americans.

When they were subsequently tried for these crimes, they would appeal the decision in the hope of making it to the Supreme Court. This way, they could have their issues examined on a federal level and enact legislative change regarding segregation laws.

Dr. Martin Luther King, Jr.

African Americans engaged in non-violent resistance by sitting in stores that served only white people and marching in protests until they were physically removed. Though they were treated violently, they would not respond with violence. This strategy raised awareness of their cause through media coverage and awareness in the communities where these actions occurred.

Relationship matrix

Notes for active learning

CHAPTER 5

Demography

Demography is the statistical and mathematical study of human populations to analyze their size, movement, and structure over space and time. It utilizes methods from history, economics, anthropology, sociology, and other disciplines. Demographers also analyze how economic, social, institutional, cultural, and biological processes influence populations.

Demography provides sociologists with a framework for understanding the social and economic factors that influence populations. For instance, sociologists use demographic data to study the relationship between population growth (or decline) and urbanization, social inequality, environmental sustainability, among other factors.

Demographic Structure of Society

Demography

Demography is the statistical study of indicators to capture evolving population composition.

Demographers gather and report statistics (e.g., number of deaths and births) to describe how the structures of societies change over time and space.

Demographers sample entire societies (populations) or smaller sections (samples).

For example, if the question focuses on a specific indicator (e.g., level of education), a demographer may sample a population subsection (i.e., adults) or the entire population.

Every ten years, the U.S. Census Bureau gathers demographics about every person living in the United States. This data offers demographers the complete picture of the contemporary composition of U.S. society, including indicators such as race, age, education level, and gender.

Demographics reveal the composition of a population

Demographers use two main methods to collect data: *direct* and *indirect methods*.

Direct data collection methods include birth and death certificates, marriage and divorce registries, censuses, and official depositories.

Indirect data collection methods collect data when direct methods are not possible, such as in developing countries where registries are lacking or when polling an entire population is not feasible (e.g., too expensive, lack of access to the entire population).

One indirect method used in Africa, where it is hard to poll every person due to the heavily rural areas and the lack of regularly updated registries, asks participants how many of their sisters are alive or dead. This data estimates population birth and death ratios for that society.

It is imperative to gather statistics on the people who comprise a society and how a society's composition may change over time to form an understanding of social interactions and other important aspects of society.

Demographics study age, gender, race and ethnicity, immigration status, and sexual orientation in society or its subgroups.

Demographics includes categorizes society members

Age

Age is an important indicator within society. It can be divided into qualitative categories, such as young and old, or it can be categorized by the number of years since a person was born.

Regardless of how the data is categorized, the age spread of a population is essential in making policy-level decisions, such as which age groups need the most resources.

For example, the high number of *"baby boomers"* in the United States represents a substantial portion of America's aging population beginning to retire. They are placing strain on medical and government resources compared to previous generations.

"Baby boomers" were the highest-earning generation, and their decisions impacted economics. For example, the Baby Boomers generation controls more than fifty percent of consumer spending in the United States, and they purchase over three-quarters of prescription drugs sold in the United States.

Aging and the life course

Aging is much more than simply becoming older and combines *biological* and *sociological processes* through which a person *develops and matures*.

Populations are increasing worldwide, which means more people are aging than ever before. People live longer, which poses challenges and benefits to society. Because more people are living to old age, healthcare systems, social security systems, and pension plans are experiencing increased strains.

For example, more elderly patients are being diagnosed with dementia and Alzheimer's disease. This has led to an increased demand for long-term care facilities able to manage the unique challenges that people with these diseases face. Pension plans and social security systems were never designed to last as long as people are now living.

While there are certainly some economic and healthcare challenges associated with an aging population, society benefits from the growing population of older adults. The elderly contribute *wisdom and life experience* to benefit their families and communities.

Statistics suggest that more older adults are helping raise their grandchildren, are actively involved in families, and are helping with domestic responsibilities.

Many retirees contribute socially and economically to society by obtaining part-time jobs.

Social gerontology (a subfield of gerontology) examines the social aspect of aging and asserts that aging is more than just a physical and biological process.

Age cohorts

Demographers look at aging through *generations* or *age cohorts*.

Age cohorts are people who have lived through similar experiences in the same period.

Age cohorts are determined by year of birth and constructed based on *defining historical events* or *changes in social structure* that occurred during their lives.

Age cohort implies that cohort members have aged similarly and distinctly from others. Typically, *cross-sectional research* studies examine *behavior* and *attitude* among age cohorts.

Research draws from qualitative and quantitative studies, including field interviews, survey data, oral histories, and other methods.

Familiar age cohorts within the United States include:

> *Greatest Generation* (born between 1901 and 1924)
>
> *Silent Generation* (born between 1925 and 1942)
>
> *Baby Boomers* (born between the mid–1940s and the early 1960s)
>
> *Generation X* (born in the early 1960s to early 1980s)
>
> *Millennials* or *Generation Y* (born from the early 1980s to early 2000s)
>
> *Generation Z* (born mid-2000s to present)

For example, the Greatest Generation adults lived through the Great Depression and WWII. Baby boomer cohort shared critical historical milestones, such as the Cuban Missile Crisis, the Vietnam War, and the first person to walk on the moon, which are culturally significant events.

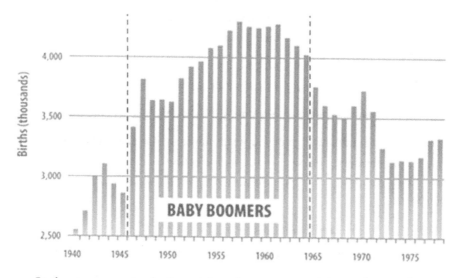

Birth rate vs. year tracks the number of persons comprising each age cohort

Countries develop cohorts based on significant political or human rights changes (e.g., Armenia's Independence Generation). However, cohorts may form by other criteria or events, such as survivors of the *terrorist attack on the World Trade Center* or *tsunami survivors*.

Social significance of aging

Aging is not simply the biological process through which humans mature. Humans are social creatures, and it is essential to consider how humans understand and maneuver aging and what age means for social significance. For example, some cultures value youth more than age.

These cultures tend to put older family members in nursing or assisted living homes and often consider the elderly a burden, both socially and economically. In other cultures, aging is valued and respected; the elderly are often the heads of their families and revered for their knowledge. They are taken into a family's home and cared for as they become more dependent with age.

Labels of "young" and "old" are socially constructed with various meanings in societies. For example, countries like Japan and United States have long life expectancies, and it is common for Japanese and American people to live into their eighties, which necessitates a different view of the roles of "the young" and "the old" compared societies with a low life expectancy.

Ageism is discrimination or stereotyping of a person based on age. While examples of ageism directed toward the elderly are abundant, it is essential to remember that ageism can happen to anyone throughout their lifespan.

Ageism is when children's ideas are considered worthless or the treatment of recent graduates struggling as they enter the workforce.

Gender

Gender is a socially constructed identity based on a person's biological sex traits. It is the ideas society holds about the *appropriate behavior*, *actions*, and *roles* of a sex.

Cultural norms and *values* shape *gender roles* and *gender differences.*

Societal ideas of gender are imposed upon every individual, regardless of the personal gender identity of the individual.

Most people are *cisgender* and have a gender identity based on the sex assignment at birth. For example, a baby pronounced a girl at birth and grew to identify as female is cisgender.

Most societies adhere to a strict gender binary (classification of sex and gender into two distinct, disconnected, and opposite forms, feminine and masculine); some people born with a specific biological makeup (female or male) identify between female and male for gender.

Gender roles impact the expression of emotions and societal gender norms cause people to express emotions differently depending on expectations.

The concept of *emotional expectations* is illustrated by a common belief that men should not cry because it is not "masculine behavior," and women should not act loud and aggressive because it is not "feminine behavior."

The language of gender identity constantly develops and changes and means different things. Beyond the established genders of male and female, an individual can identify as *genderqueer*.

Genderqueer is a broad term for people who do not identify with binary gender categories but who identify as bi-gender (identifying with two genders), genderless (not identifying with any gender), or genderfluid (identity varies with time, fluctuating between genders).

Genderqueer people may undergo physical alterations to fit their gender expression.

Gender benders purposefully *"bend"* expected (or normalized) gender roles, undertaken as personal expression, awareness raising, or political activism.

Transgender is when individuals feel there is a discrepancy between their sexual assignment and their gender identity.

Transgender is an umbrella term and can refer to people in any stage of transition from one sex to another and genderqueer individuals.

The precise way to know how a person gender-identifies and what that means is to ask them.

Gender and sexuality are not necessarily linked; a person of any gender identity may have any sexual orientation.

Sex vs. gender

There is often confusion between sex and gender, but it is essential to know that sex and gender are not the same.

Gender is a *socially constructed identity*, while *sex is a biological assignment.*

Sex refers to chromosomes.

> XY genotype is *male.*

> XX genotype is *female.*

Gender encompasses *psychological, behavioral,* and *cultural traits* rather than biological traits.

Transgender individuals have a mismatch between their biological sex and gender identity. Some undergo sexual reassignment surgery as one part of an individual's transition, which may include physical, social, psychological, and therapies.

Hermaphroditism (or *intersex*) is uncommon; people born with both male and female anatomy.

Gender and sexuality are not necessarily linked

Social construction of gender

The culture of a society largely influences the prescribed roles, attitudes, and beliefs of gender. Society influences how individuals speak, dress, think, and act for males or females.

Gender schemas are cognitive frameworks deeply rooted within society and individuals, influencing what differentiates males and females.

Gender schemas are reinforced by socializing agents (e.g., teachers, peers, caregivers, media, and religion).

Society exerts pressure on children to conform to gender roles, and research indicates that parents have different expectations and treatment for boys and girls.

Gender stereotypes are when generalizations are made about a specific gender or their roles. These can have a positive or negative connotation.

For example, a female stereotype is that a woman should marry, conceive children, and raise a family. Furthermore, a woman should feel compelled to put others' needs before her own while attending to her husband. This contradicts the experience of many working mothers who must balance a career, a family, and self-care.

For example, a stereotypical male role is to protect and provide financial stability for his family. In addition, he should control emotions and be dominant in career and personal relationships.

Sexual orientation

Sexual orientation is an individual's sexual attraction to the same gender or sex, the opposite gender or sex, or to either sex or more than one gender.

Variations are usually discussed using:

>*heterosexuality* (attraction to people of the opposite sex or gender),

>*homosexuality* (attraction to people of the same sex or gender), or

>*bisexuality* (attraction to people of the same sex and the opposite sex or gender).

Pansexuality (defined as attraction to any sex or gender identity) and *polysexuality* (attraction to multiple – but not all – sex and gender identities) are more specific designations of bisexuality but sometimes are used interchangeably with it.

Bisexuality symbol

Asexuality, the lack of sexual attraction to others, is sometimes viewed as a fourth designation of sexual orientation.

Sexual orientation is a spectrum ranging from exclusive attraction to the same sex or gender to exclusive attraction to the opposite sex or gender and preferences in between.

Most humans identify as heterosexual. Throughout history, there has been evidence of non-heterosexuality in individuals and within societal and cultural norms.

Non-heterosexual individuals have been considered deviant and suffered discrimination and violence, and often not afforded equal rights.

Race and ethnicity

Race is the shared genetic or physical characteristics that differentiate members of racial groups. It refers to observable differences in phenotypes between groups of individuals.

These may be biological differences based on skin color or other visible characteristics. It is important to note that race is socially constructed, and some researchers feel that race is an invalid classification type given the high genetic variations that exist within racial groups.

Ethnicity is a classification based on shared religious, cultural, ancestral, or linguistic features.

While race and ethnicity may be highly related, one significant difference exists. People can choose whether to reveal their ethnic identity, but racial identity is visible and cannot be masked. A person may look Caucasian based on observable physical characteristics, but their ethnic identity may be African or Latino.

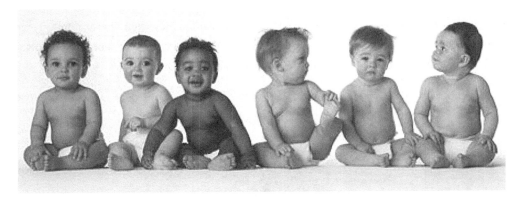

Observable differences among children based on race and ethnicity

Social construction of race

Social constructions of race have changed over time. Presently, designated categories of race in the United States include African Americans, Native Americans, Hispanic Americans (or Latinos), Asian Americans, and European Americans.

Racial minorities in the U.S. are people of any race who do not hold the majority of power.

Historical, geographical, socioeconomic, and political factors contribute to and determine the racial makeup of society and the interaction between racial majorities and minorities.

Social constructions have led to various levels of discrimination and prejudice against certain racial groups throughout history.

A person's race has implications for several reasons. Racial minorities receive fewer resources than members of racial majorities, leading to disparity in intelligence, education, employment, and living standards.

Minorities tend to have decreased access to health care, preventative care, and health insurance.

Racialization

The concept of racialization was vital to the idea of race being a process and social construction.

Racialization refers to giving a new ethnic or racial identity to a social practice, a group of people, or a relationship that did not identify as such.

Racialization is the process by which certain people are identified for unique (often negative or detrimental) treatment because of actual or imagined characteristics.

Historically, "race" referred to people who shared similar aspects of culture, such as language or religion (e.g., Catholic or Jewish). However, racialization morphed the meaning of race.

Racialization is the process of converting a *biological characteristic* into a *status determination*.

Racialized objects and subjects display the somatic (i.e., morphology and phenotype) and cultural characteristics that others attribute to the idea of race.

Since race is socially constructed, these characteristics may not be actual. For example, Tiger Woods is Chinese, Thai, White, Native American, and African American, but because he looks black, his treatment is based on society's racial connotations of *"Blackness."*

Tiger Woods is Chinese, Thai, White, Native American, and African American.

Racialization often targets the common physical characteristics of a group, resulting in a racialized group continuing itself biologically. Racialization is typically initiated by a group exerting dominance over others.

Ascribed racial or ethnic identity by the dominant group is used for continued dominance.

For example, early European colonists failed to recognize African culture, instead ascribing to Africans a culture based on their ignorant prejudices and agenda of exploitation.

Racialization is associated with colonialism, imperialism, and foreign occupation.

Racialization produces a racialized population that slowly accepts and then embodies and embraces the ascribed attributes and identities.

Racialized populations become a *self-proclaimed* and *self-ascribed* race or ethnicity.

Racial formation

Racial formation theory deconstructs and examines race as a *construct of social identity*.

Social identity groupings differ compared with political, economic, and social trends.

Instead of accepting categories assigned by society, researchers suggest that racial categories are changing based on ongoing micro-level and macro-level relationships.

Context: the dominant consensus on race

National values   Contemporary culture

Current manifestations: social and institutional dynamics

| Process that maintains racial hierarchies | Racialized public policies and institutional practices |

Outcomes: racial disparities

| Racial inequalities in current levels of well-being | Capacity for individual and community improvement is undermined |

Ongoing racial inequalities

Social constructs of race with context, manifestations, outcome, and racial inequalities

Notes for active learning

Immigration

Immigration status

Immigration status refers to whether a person was born in a country. If a person born in a foreign country moves to a new society, they are immigrants.

Recently, major shifts have changed the composition of the immigrant sector of the United States demographic makeup. In the 1960s, one in twenty people (5%) in the United States was an immigrant. However, there are now many more immigrants in the United States, and in 2022, one in seven people (14%) of the U.S. population were immigrants.

Immigrants to America are likely from Latin America and Asia and live in the West or South. Before shifting, immigrants were more likely from Europe and lived in Northeast or Midwest.

The U.S. Census Bureau suggests that the immigrant population will continue to increase.

Immigrants may be "legal" (i.e., those who followed the country's immigration procedures and maintained lawful status) or "illegal" (i.e., those who unlawfully entered the country or failed to maintain their lawful status).

Regardless of immigration status, immigrants face barriers and difficulties when entering or living in the United States. To enter the United States, legal immigrants must contend with acquiring, filling out, and submitting proper documentation and the potential separation from their family members. Illegal immigrants often endure economic exploitation and violence at border crossings, as well as emotional and physical strain or exhaustion.

In the United States, barriers and obstacles immigrants face include educational barriers (e.g., enrolling a child in school or enrolling in continuing education), language barriers, and the inability to adequately access the host culture, community resources, and social services.

Some immigrants experience discrimination in employment. Immigrants with low education levels or poor knowledge of the language frequently take jobs for which they are underpaid and overworked, such as agricultural, domestic, or tourism-related jobs.

Patterns of immigration

In the United States, immigration patterns occur along three main streams. One stream is in the *Northeast*, the second in the *Midwest*, and the third is the *Western* state's stream.

Regardless of the pattern of immigration, immigrants face some degree of cultural assimilation. This means that they go through a process of adapting to aspects of the host culture. This can include language, customs, foods, and even religion.

Enculturation is related to assimilation, which refers to the process during which people adopt only the requisite aspects of their host culture to fit in with its mainstream values and behaviors.

The United States has a long and varied immigrant history. While immigrants continuously arrived, they did so at drastically different numbers according to the era. In the 17th-century colonial period, England sent 400,000 colonists to the Thirteen Original Colonies.

Between 1836 and 1914, European immigration accounted for more than 30 million new arrivals. In 1933, in the depths of the Great Depression, a meager twenty-three thousand arrived. In the ten years between 2000 and 2010, marked by the acceleration of globalization, an estimated 14 million immigrants from other countries arrived in the United States.

Government policies before 1965 generally limited opportunities for immigrants from outside Western Europe to gain entrance or obtain naturalization.

Racial quotas dictated the influx rather than per-country limits now in place. Discriminated groups deemed undesirable included the Chinese, Jews, Italians, and Slavs, to name a few.

Reforms made in the 1960s and inspired by the civil rights movement quadrupled the number of first-generation immigrants, profoundly changing the ethnic composition of America.

As of 2014, the top countries of immigrant origin were Mexico (27.6%), India (5.2%), China (4.6%), the Philippines (4.5%), El Salvador (3.1%), Vietnam (3%), Cuba (2.8%), South Korea (2.5%), the Dominican Republic (2.4%) and Guatemala (2.2%).

In 2021, Department of Homeland Security estimated that the top six countries of origin for illegal immigrants were Mexico, El Salvador, Guatemala, India, Honduras and China.

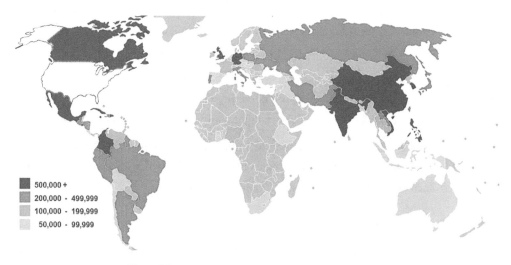

United States immigrant country of origin in 2000

The decision to admit immigrants is based on three categories. By 2009, the reason for family ties in the U.S. accounted for 66% of accepted immigrants, while employment skills were 13% and humanitarian reasons were 17%.

Among the immigrants that have arrived in recent history, a 2009 survey indicated that seven out of ten questioned stated that they wished for the U.S. to be their permanent home.

Intersections with race and ethnicity

Numerous factors, including geographical proximity, the prevalence of economic opportunity, and the motive for migration, influence rates of specific ethnicities and races immigrating.

According to the Migration Policy Institute, 45.3 million immigrants lived in the U.S. in 2021. Immigrants are primarily of minority racial and ethnic backgrounds.

American Community Survey reports that 28%, or 12 million, of immigrants are Mexican.

Immigration and Nationality Act (1965) increased the number of immigrants from Asian countries. In 2019, 14.1 million Asian immigrants reside in the United States, representing a 29-fold increase from 1960.

Historically and worldwide, attitudes of host societies towards immigrants have shifted based on events such as terrorist attacks or civil wars, scarcity of resources (such as housing, food, water, and jobs), and clashes based on cultural or religious differences. Often, these attitudes have been directed at a specific demographic based on *racial or ethnic characteristics*.

One million Irish people immigrated to America throughout the Irish Potato Famine (1845–1852). The Irish had to fight for jobs and places to live and were hated by Americans and other immigrant groups.

The host society was unfriendly towards these immigrants because of differences in cultural characteristics and fear of the Irish taking jobs and resources from Americans. The Irish were only able to work at low-paying jobs and were relegated to living in slum neighborhoods, which bred crime and disease. This perpetuated a cycle of the society's dislike and discrimination toward the Irish, preventing them from experiencing economic prosperity or progress.

Irish immigrants in America

Notes for active learning

Demographic Shifts and Social Change

Demographic transition theory

Demographic transition theory aligns changes in society with technological advances. Before industrialization, populations remained relatively stable because the birth and death rates remained reasonably comparable.

Agricultural societies of the time required *high birth rates* to increase the number of laborers in the workforce. *High mortality rates* counteracted these high birth rates in preindustrial societies due to poor living conditions, ravaging diseases, and lack of advanced medical care.

Industrialization increased access to food and decreased the number of people working in the agricultural sector. *Medical care* and *technological improvements* helped people *live longer*. Birth rates remained high, but death rates decreased, which led to rapid population growth.

Another shift occurred with the continuation of industrialization; *birth rates* decreased as child mortality rates plummeted. Large families became less desirable because of the longer lifespans and the economic considerations of raising children. As the *death rates* continued to decline with improved medical technology, the population continued to grow at a *steady pace*.

After the industrialization of society, living standards were higher, which led to a decrease in births and constant death rates, thus *slowing population growth*.

Population growth and decline

Distinct factors and approaches are relevant when examining a region's population growth or decline. The ways and the reasons that population growth or decline occurs in a city, as opposed to the globe, differ. Population growth varies in countries based on status.

Underdeveloped countries tend to increase in size due to unreliable birth control options.

Developed countries tend to grow due to internal factors, such as lower infant mortality rates, longer life expectancies, and immigration. Countries that experience dramatic increases in development may also experience population growth as a result.

Population decline can be due to long-term demographic trends or sudden reductions. These decreases can be triggered by lower fertility rates, "white flight" or rural flight, urban decay, or large, sudden declines due to disease, war, or famine.

Population projections are estimates of a particular region, country, or the world's population at a point in the future. They are usually determined by consistency, using data from the recent decennial census. The cohort-component method is commonly used to calculate projections.

Projected populations for each birth cohort (people born in any given year) are calculated for components of population change, including fertility, mortality, and net migration. Projections forecast population change based on assumptions about future births, deaths, net international migration, and domestic migration.

Population pyramids

Population pyramids are graphs used to help determine the distribution of various population age groups. They can be applied to the population of a city, country, region, or the world. They take the shape of a pyramid when the population they represent increases.

Population pyramids show an age-sex distribution, with age on the *y*-axis, the percentage of the population on the *x*-axis, and male/female shown as a side panel. A population pyramid does not show the exact number of people in a population but displays percentages that measure how many people fall into each age bracket or cohort.

Population pyramids comparing previous populations with projected increases or decreases.

Four population pyramids:

Stable – an unchanging pattern of fertility and mortality;

Stationary – a somewhat equal proportion of the population in each age group;

Expansive – a vast base, a large population of young people, high birth and death rates, lower life expectancy;

Constrictive – showing constriction on the bottom, a low percentage of young people, declining birth rates, and a lower population in successive age groups.

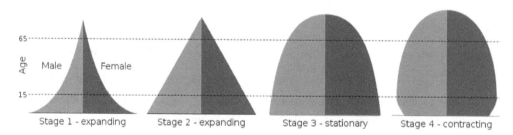

Population pyramids depict and examine the age-sex distribution of a population.

Fertility, migration, and mortality

Fertility, migration, and mortality impact a society's population composition.

Economic, political, cultural, and technological factors influence societal makeup.

Fertility is the number of births in the population of interest (measured using crude birth rate).

Migration is how demographers measure the immigration and emigration of a population.

Immigration refers to people entering a society, while *emigration* refers to people leaving. Demographers use both to determine changes in the composition and size of populations.

Mortality is the number of deaths in a population, measured using *crude* or *infant mortality*.

Fertility and mortality rates

Fertility and mortality rates largely determine the size of any population. Fluctuations in these rates can be influenced by some factors, including the economic status of a state (how many children a family or government can afford), political sanctions on reproduction (limits on the number of children), medical resources, natural disasters, disease, and war or unrest.

Crude birth rate is the number of live births for every one thousand people each year.

Mortality rates indicate the number of deaths in a given number of people per unit of time, typically deaths per one thousand individuals per year.

Crude death rate is the number of deaths each year per one thousand people.

Infant mortality rate compares the number of infant deaths yearly per one thousand live births.

Fertility rate is the average number of children a woman bears, often higher in underdeveloped countries, where children are less likely to survive into adulthood than in industrialized countries.

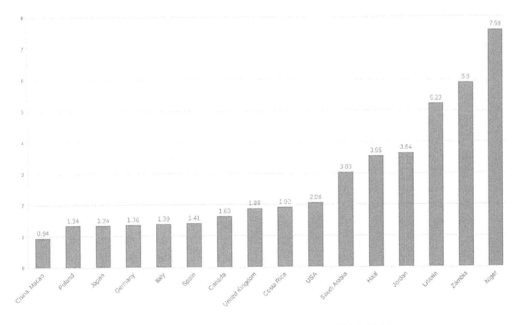

Total fertility rates for select countries, 2005-2010

Patterns in fertility and mortality

Patterns in *fertility* and *mortality* are essential factors in determining and projecting patterns within given subsets and the entire population.

Fertility rates exhibit a variety of patterns, usually based on scale. Averages of rates in areas can mask a wide variation across countries. Similarly, country averages can disguise worldwide differences.

Fertility rates can be studied with other factors (e.g., race). For example, in the United States, fertility rates of minorities are higher than those of the majority white population, which could have a significant sociopolitical impact.

Mortality is the counterbalance to fertility. Like fertility, mortality varies significantly. Mortality is most affected by *poor health conditions*.

A natural disaster puts a population in dire living conditions and influences mortality rates.

Infant mortality is an essential factor in measuring the overall quality of life, making mortality patterns focusing on infant mortality especially helpful to examine.

Push and pull factors in migration

Factors contributing to migration are numerous. Often, it is a combination of factors that may lead to migration and the decision of migrants to move to one place as opposed to another.

   Push factors drive migrants to leave their homes.

   Pull factors compel migrants to move to a region or country.

Push and pull factors can be economic, cultural, or environmental.

Push Factors	Pull Factors
Unemployment	More employment opportunity
Lack of services and amenities	Better services and access to them
Poor safety and security, high crime rates	Safer environment, low crime rates
Crop failure, droughts, floods	Fertile land, good climate for agriculture
Poverty	Greater wealth and affluence in population
War	Political security
Harsh climate conditions	More desirable climate and weather
Low quality of life	More attractive quality of life

Primary economic push factor is a lack of adequate job opportunities.

Primary economic pull factor is plentiful job opportunities.

Cultural push factors include forced migration into slavery, trafficking or prostitution, political instability, war or civil unrest, or fear of persecution.

Cultural pull factors include political and religious freedom, political stability, and peace.

Environmental push factors are natural disasters (e.g., drought or flood).

Environmental pull factors are a non-harmful or non-hazardous climate.

Theories of demographic change

The composition of the population of any given society is constantly evolving. It is likely that as the group composed of a society changes, societal attitudes and values shift. Therefore, it is essential to understand the main factors that cause a change in the composition of a population.

Malthusian theory suggests that population growth quickly overwhelms resources, such as food, which will, in turn, lead to social problems and conflict. The ideas of the English scholar Reverend Thomas Robert Malthus (1766–1834) pointed to the need to control the size of the population to avoid *mass casualties*, which would occur through *war* or *resource scarcity*.

Malthus suggested that people who are unable to refrain from having more children than they can support should face criminal punishments. He advocated abstinence and sterilization.

Overpopulation still threatens modern-day society; technological advances have increased food availability. Malthus's ideas can be seen in modern-day China, where, until recently, Chinese parents were limited to one child. Chinese families faced government sanctions, such as lower income and decreased support if they had additional children. Atrocities such as forced abortion, sterilization, and infanticide were common.

Today China faces a gender imbalance, with too few people entering the workforce to support the economy and a disproportionate population of elderly. The Chinese government repealed the one-child policy effective January 2016, allowing families to have two children. In July 2023, the government repealed limits on family size to address the looming demographic crisis. Despite the loosening of the one-child policy, China's fertility rate has decreased precipitously in recent years.

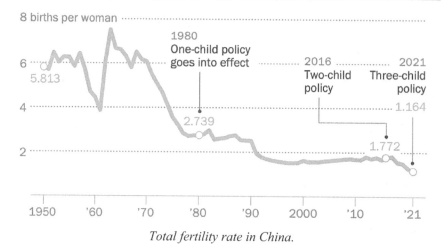

Total fertility rate in China.

Total fertility rate is the expected number of children a woman who lives to the end of her childbearing age and has children will have based on the given age-specific rates.

Source: UN Population Division's World Population Prospects (2022 revision)

Globalization

Process of globalization

Globalization is when organizations develop international influence or operate internationally.

Globalization purports that societies will be global and less confined geographically. For example, essential aspects of society, such as law, culture, religion, and economics, have become highly internationally integrated.

Globalization is due to the increasing exchange of ideas, goods, and attitudes, which is possible because of increased contact between cultures. This increased contact can be attributed to the decreased cost of traveling internationally, technological advances such as electronic communication, and increased prosperity, all metaphorically shrinking the world and bringing cultures closer. The current pace of globalization will likely continue for years.

Factors contributing to globalization

Globalization did not begin in modern times; people have been buying and selling with others and setting up enterprises in foreign lands for thousands of years. These trade routes led to an exchange of goods, services, culture, and traditions.

In modern history, globalization is driven by economic interdependence and technology.

Since the mid-20th century, there has been a substantial increase in governments adopting a free-market system of economics. In the free-market system, nations gain access to cross-border trade opportunities and a consequential increase in production potential.

In addition, governments have negotiated to remove international trade obstacles and sanctions instead of creating agreements encouraging the international exchange of goods, services, and investment. With the expansion of foreign markets, corporations have grown internationally, building industries in foreign lands and marketing to foreign populations.

Global financial system is a development within the banking and economic sector. Institutions are economic actors, and legal agreements have contributed to the financial integration of the world market. They regulate and maximize the effectiveness of international markets, resulting in economic interconnectedness and interdependency between nations.

Technology contributed to the expansion of global economics and sociocultural globalization. Emerging technologies, such as advancements in information technology, allowed economic actors to expand to a global level more readily. For example, technologies provide information on foreign market trends, easy ability to transfer funds, and opportunities for collaboration and instant communication with international partners.

Sociocultural exchange is enabled by technology, with foreign cultures readily available, and communications worldwide are maintained effortlessly and instantaneously.

Perspectives on globalization

Globalization includes:

> *Hyperglobalist perspective*
>
> *Skeptical perspective*
>
> *Transformationalist perspective*

Hyperglobalist perspective is that globalization unites nations politically and economically. It denationalizes economies with less dependency on traditional nation-states.

Hyperglobalist purports that the *current marketplace*, not governments, controls the world.

Globalized economics have diminished the government's ability to influence economic policy. The importance of transnational governance organizations has increased, resulting in a decrease in the influence of national governments due to the need to adhere to a set of laws not created by the state but by a supra-national or transnational organization.

Some scholars believe this model is unsustainable, while others posit that the decline of nation-states will promote universal economic and political organization principles.

Hyperglobalist scholars agree on the causes of globalization but disagree on whether the outcomes of globalization are positive or negative. Some think that all nations benefit from a global economy, though some may be worse off. Others disagree, believing that global capitalism reinforces existing inequalities between nations and promotes new ones.

Skeptical perspective of globalization is the opposite of the hyperglobalist perspective, which asserts that this international shift is occurring fragmentarily and by region instead of globally. It maintains that the height of globalization was at the end of the nineteenth century. Skeptics argue that developing nations are increasingly exploited and marginalized; the nation-state is not irrelevant because multinational corporations are tied to their national governments and primarily benefit home nations, and a few powerful economies control foreign investments.

Skeptical perspective scholars reject ideas of universal economic and political principles leading to a global governance structure. A global governance structure masks neo-liberal economic strategies beneficial only to Western interests.

Transformationalist perspective has two fundamental assertions:

> 1) *no single factor* caused globalization and
>
> 2) the result of globalization *cannot yet be determined*.

Transformationalist perspective is broader and less certain.

Transformationalist scholars acknowledge that the role of government is shifting but are unsure whether the government is gaining or losing power and believe distinctions are too simplistic.

The emergence of a different stratification pattern is examined, but the transformationalist perspective does not conclude whether this leads to the marginalization of developing countries.

Hyperglobalist and *skeptical perspectives* are criticized as unsound teleologically (i.e., design or purpose). They assume globalization is automatically moving to an "ideal" state.

Another critique is that they rely heavily on empirical data. Data cannot stand alone but needs to be interpreted and applied in many contexts.

Social changes in globalization

There is no definite answer to how globalization promotes terrorism and civil unrest. Since the emergence of globalization, there has been an increase in terrorism, and it may be connected.

Motivation for terrorist behavior can be a backlash against encroachment by another culture. It is widely accepted that globalization has promoted the pervasion of Western culture worldwide.

Terrorist networks have recruited members, spread messages, and enacted violence using technologies of globalization.

A global economy has created opportunities for businesses to expand internationally. In many cases, large corporations offshore labor to developing nations to manufacture products cheaply.

Corporations have wreaked havoc on developing nations through environmental and agricultural catastrophes, unfair and unlivable wages, oppressive working conditions, and economic collapse when corporations no longer operate in a particular area.

For example, a corporation may abruptly leave an area that has become reliant on the employment and economic opportunities it provides. Civil unrest in protest by a takeover or in the wake of their destruction or departure can be related to globalization.

Globalization weakens nation-states, according to some.

With weakened and less relevant national governments, there is the threat of civil unrest as political groups compete for power positions and people make unattainable demands from an increasingly irrelevant or powerless government.

Notes for active learning

Urbanization

Urban growth

Urbanization is when people leave rural areas and move to urban centers. While people have tended to congregate and cohabitate in large groups since ancient times, this tendency has increased in recent years.

Urbanization is common in first-world societies but growing in underdeveloped countries.

Urbanization impacts the economy and the environment of a society.

Urban areas tend to have a larger labor force than is necessary, and urbanization decreases rural agricultural labor.

Increased population size means more infrastructure and negative externalities, such as paved roads and transportation systems, more buildings for offices and housing, overcrowding, and increased pollution from car emissions and industrial factories.

As urban areas grow, there is less land for agriculture and food production.

Industrialization

Industrialization is a society's shift from a primarily agricultural society into an industrial or manufacturing economy.

Industrialization and *urban growth* are *linked*.

After the American Industrial Revolution of the late eighteenth and early nineteenth centuries, the establishment of industrial units generated demand for industrial workers. This led to a large population movement from the rural agricultural sector to industry hubs in urban cores.

As industry expands in urban environments and cities grow larger, rural inhabitants move to cities for economic opportunities.

Foreign migrants add to the influx by immigrating to cities for economic opportunity.

Urban sprawl (i.e., uncontrolled expansion of urban development) is related to urbanization.

Suburbanization and urban decline

Suburbanization is city inhabitants moving out of urban areas and into suburbs or residential communities surrounding cities.

Suburbanization is often examined in conjunction with *urban decline,* which is the deterioration of the inner city based on a lack of investment and maintenance.

During suburbanization trends throughout history, higher-income residents have been more likely to move out of the city and into the suburbs. These higher-income residents can afford homes and vehicles instead of renting an apartment and commuting on public transportation. They tend to have families who require more space than a crowded and congested city offers and children who need safe neighborhoods and good school systems.

With a sizable portion of the higher-income inhabitants leaving a city, low-income ones remain. Lower socioeconomic communities experience higher crime and drug use rates and worse living conditions and underperforming school systems. They have less expendable income, which causes the local economy to suffer. These and other factors contribute to urban decline.

Suburbanization is connected to the concept of "white flight." *White flight* is the migration, of white people, to suburban or rural areas to escape the influx of minorities into urban areas.

Gentrification and urban renewal

Uurban renewal and *gentrification* are often confused and used interchangeably, though they have significant distinctions.

Urban renewal is the governmental restoration and revitalization of deteriorating urban areas. It was popular in cities across America in the 1950s and 1960s after the federal 1949 *American Housing Act,* which funded the demolition of *decaying* neighborhoods (i.e., *slums*) and the construction of *low-income public housing.*

Gentrification is when higher-income individuals renew and rebuild a deteriorating area, displacing the existing lower-income property or business owners and families. In the past, the phenomena have been connected with urban renewal plans leading to an area's gentrification.

Gentrification tends to target and exploit minorities living in urban communities, which are priced out of the areas after development heightens property values or are bought out or forcibly removed from their communities to make way for development.

Gentrification revitalizes decaying urban cores

Urban renewal demolished historic communities to make way for expanded infrastructure, housing developments, and office buildings. More recently, urban renewal has been focused less on destruction and displacement and more on renovation and investment.

Relationship matrix

Notes for active learning

CHAPTER 6

Social Inequality

Social inequality analyzes the context of spatial inequality, social class structure and patterns, and health disparities about class, race, ethnicity, and gender. Inequalities are typically interconnected.

Disparity (linked to social inequality) is differences in unequally distributed resources. Communities may suffer from economic, education, health, and healthcare disparities. Effects of disparity, specifically economic disparity, are among the most significant issues the United States experiences today.

Social disparity is examined from many perspectives, including race and ethnicity, sexual orientation and assignment, age, disability, socioeconomic status, and geographic location.

Gender Inequality

Feminist theory

Feminist theory brings the concept of feminism into the theoretical and philosophical discourse. It illuminates the *reality of gender inequality* while understanding its nature and consequences.

Feminist theory uses analysis of women's social roles and experiences through the lenses of many disciplines, such as sociology.

Feminist theory gives representation and recognition to women and incorporates a non-discriminatory study of their experiences into an inclusive sociological perspective.

Feminist theories explain men's and women's societal roles:

> *gender difference,*
>
> *gender inequality,*
>
> *oppression,* and
>
> *structural oppression theories.*

Gender difference perspective specifies and analyzes how women's traditional place in, and experience of, social situations is dissimilar from men's.

Cultural feminists consider values commonly attached to womanhood and femininity parallel to, but separate from, those attached to manhood and masculinity as an explanation of why social spheres are experienced differently by men and women.

Gender differences in women's and men's traditional place in society

Some feminist theorists believe that different institutional roles provide men and women with an explanation for gender differences, emphasizing the gender-based division of labor that takes place in the domestic sphere.

Feminist analysis from an existential or phenomenological perspective may point to women's marginalization. Since women have been historically defined as "other" in societies that uphold patriarchy as the status quo, they are frequently seen as objects. Women are denied agency and the opportunity for self-realization.

Gender-inequality and oppression feminist theory

Gender-inequality feminist theory emphasizes that women's traditional place in, and experience of, social situations are dissimilar and unequal to men's. Proponents of women's equality advocate that women have an equal capacity to men for moral reasoning and agency.

They point to an oppressive patriarchal system, which has historically denied women the opportunity to express and practice this moral reasoning and agency in spheres such as academia and the workplace. Women have been confined to the private, domestic sphere and left without representation in the public sphere. Even if women enter the public sphere, they are expected to manage the private sphere and take care of household duties and child-rearing.

Gender inequality feminist theorists emphasize that marriage provides gender inequality and that the gender-based division of labor must be altered for women to achieve equality.

Gender oppression feminist theory differs from *gender difference* and *gender inequality* theories by arguing that women and men have differences. However, women are sometimes oppressed, subordinated, and abused by men. Some commenters propose that women are victims of systematic oppression, which deprives them of their rights to agency and independence, the opportunity to realize their potential, or the opportunity to progress to equal status to men in male-dominated spheres.

Structural oppression feminist theory

Power is the critical variable in the two leading theories of gender oppression: psychoanalytic feminism and radical feminism.

Psychoanalytic feminists theory examines subconscious and unconscious human emotions and childhood development to understand the continued patriarchal power structure.

Radical feminists theory proposes that being a woman is a positive thing in and of itself, but that this is not acknowledged, and the opposite view exists in patriarchal societies where women are oppressed.

Identification of physical violence as the foundation of patriarchy and belief in action toward neutralization of the patriarchy are tenets of radical feminism.

Radical feminists believe that if women recognize, accept, and utilize their intelligence, strength, and value, build foundational female bonds of trust, retaliate against oppression, and form female-operated networks in social spheres, then patriarchy can be eradicated.

Structural oppression feminist theory asserts that women's oppression and inequality result from overarching structures, such as capitalism, patriarchy, and racism.

Socialist feminists, in agreement with Karl Marx and Friedrich Engels, believe that the working class is exploited due to capitalist production. However, they seek to extend this exploitation not just to *class* but also to *gender*.

Structural oppression theorists overlap with intersectionality theories, which attempt to explain and examine oppression and inequality across variables (e.g., class, gender, race, ethnicity, and age). The conclusions of structural oppression theory indicate that women do not experience oppression in the same way, but all women experience oppression.

Friedrich Engels, German philosopher

Intersectional feminist theory

Intersectionality came to the forefront of sociology in the late 1960s and early 1970s in conjunction with the multiracial feminist movement. It appeared as part of a critique of radical feminism developed in the late 1960s, known as *revisionist feminist theory*. This theory questioned the notion that gender was the primary factor determining a woman's fate.

Intersectional feminist theory was named by Kimberlé Crenshaw in 1989, although the concept can be traced to the 19th century. It asserts that biological, social, and cultural categories, such as gender, race, class, sexual orientation, religion, caste, age, and other identities, interact on multiple and often simultaneous levels, contributing to *social inequality* and *systemic injustice*.

Intersectional feminist theory suggests that others shape discrete expressions of oppression. Understanding the racialization of oppressed groups and how racializing structures, processes, and representations are shaped by gender, class, sexual identity, and others is required.

For example, black feminists argue that the experience of being a black woman cannot be understood by considering being black and being a woman separately. Interactions between the two identities must be considered, frequently *interacting with,* and *reinforcing each other*.

Intersectional feminism explores the oppression of women within society. Today, sociologists strive to apply it to all people and explore the intersections of group membership.

For example, intersectionality holds that knowing a woman lives in a sexist society is insufficient to describe her experience; instead, it is necessary to know her race/ethnicity, sexual orientation, class, etc., as well as the society's attitudes toward each of these to understand her position within the society entirely.

The movement led by women of color disputed the idea that women were a homogeneous category, sharing essentially the same life experiences. This argument coalesced from the realization that the experiences of white middle-class women could not accurately represent the problems faced by the feminist movement.

Recognizing that the forms of oppression understood by white middle-class women were different from those understood by non-white, poor, or disabled women, feminists sought to understand how gender, race, and class combined to determine the female experience.

Spatial Inequality

Factors of spatial inequality

Spatial inequality is unequal resources or services in different areas or locations.

Communities may have a disparate range of resources and services, and those who can diminish or eradicate these disparities do not live near the less advantaged communities and will not move to these areas, producing a cycle that is difficult to change. These distinct areas of disparate resources and services are usually designated by the groups of people living there with similar socioeconomic statuses.

Spatial inequality is influenced by factors such as religion, culture, or race. Impoverished areas will remain as such until the acquisition of complex resources (e.g., access to fresh drinking water) and services (e.g., educational institutions, hospitals, police services, markets).

Spatial inequality in regional development refers to disparate levels of socioeconomic development in different areas, districts, provinces, or states.

Residential segregation

Residential segregation is a form of physical separation of two or more groups into different neighborhoods. Traditionally, it has been associated with racial segregation but can refer to any sorting based on criteria populations (e.g., race, ethnicity, income, religion).

Direct segregation is illegal, at least in Europe and the United States, but housing patterns show significant segregation for certain races and income groups.

Residential segregation is influenced by:

suburbanization, *discrimination*, and *personal preferences*.

Residential segregation produces adverse socioeconomic outcomes for minorities, but public policies attempt to mitigate these negative effects.

U.S. Census data indicates that racial separation has diminished significantly since the 1960s and that the dissimilarity index has declined in eighty-five of the largest cities, continuing to drop in the last decade.

Despite current trends, Black people remain the most segregated racial group. They are hyper-segregated in most large metropolitan areas across the U.S., including Atlanta, Baltimore, Chicago, Cleveland, Detroit, Houston, Los Angeles, New Orleans, New York, Philadelphia, and Washington, D.C.

Hispanics are the second most segregated racial group, mostly in northern metropolitan areas.

Patterns of income segregation are analyzed using data from the *National Survey of America's Families*, Census, and the *Home Mortgage Disclosure Act*. The dissimilarity and neighborhood sorting indices show that income segregation grew between 1970 and 1990 when the dissimilarity index between affluent and low-income people increased, meaning low-income families became more isolated.

Pew Research Center, in 1970, reported that 14% of low-income families lived in impoverished areas; however, by 1990, the number increased to 28%.

Most low-income people live in the suburbs or central cities, with more than half of low-income working families being racial minorities.

Black and Hispanic low-income families, the two most racially segregated groups, rarely live in majority-white neighborhoods. Some low-income white families live in high-poverty areas.

Low-income families experience poor housing conditions

Neighborhood safety and violence

Neighborhood safety is community members' ability to control others for a safe environment.

Collective efficacy is the effort of residents to monitor children playing in public areas, attempt to prevent street corner loitering by teenagers, and confront individuals who exploit or disturb public spaces. These measures increase community control over individuals, thus creating an environment where violent crime is less likely.

Communities with elevated levels of active neighborhood watch have lower rates of violence and homicide, implying that *community participation* prevents violence and reduces crime.

Safety depends on the *values shared* by community members; if members *trust each other* and *cooperate to prevent violence and crime*, they will be able to create a safe community environment.

The neighborhood safety concept is used to explain why urban neighborhoods differ in the amount of crime occurring in them.

Collective efficacy develops more readily in specific communities than in others.

Economic downturns affect some areas more than others, leading many individuals in affected areas to move to neighborhoods offering better economic opportunities. Developing mutual trust and cooperation with neighbors requires time; those communities where individuals are more likely to move have lower neighborhood safety levels. In communities seriously affected by residential instability, social bonds between residents are weaker, and they are less likely to cooperate in monitoring the behavior of others.

Neighborhood Watch is an organized group of civilians that discourages crime and vandalism. It is a crime prevention plan in which civilians agree to monitor one another's property, patrol the streets, and report suspicious incidents to law enforcement members. Such organizations aim to achieve a safe neighborhood and educate residents.

Neighborhood watch sign

Lower-income racial or ethnic minorities tend to live close and lack the resources to live in areas with affluent individuals. They are, therefore, more likely to be excluded from contact with more advantaged people. This isolation creates feelings of helplessness and lack of control among residents of lower-income neighborhoods.

Lack of trust and cohesion between individuals reduces the probability that they will be willing to monitor the behavior of others or intervene to prevent crime.

Environmental justice

Environmental justice appeared in the United States in the early 1980s with two distinct uses. The term's first use describes a social movement focusing on equitable environmental benefits and burden distributions. The second use is an interdisciplinary social science literature that includes theories of environment, justice, environmental law and governance, environmental policy and planning, development, sustainability, and political ecology.

Environmental justice implies the fair treatment of people under laws, regardless of race, color, national origin, or income. It supposes everyone will receive the same degree of protection from environmental hazards and access a healthy environment to live, learn, and work.

Environmental justice includes *equitable distribution of environmental risks and benefits*, meaningful participation in *environmental decision-making*, recognition of *community ways of life, local knowledge, and cultural differences*.

Environmental justice addresses racism and discrimination against minorities by a socially dominant group, often resulting in privileges for the dominant group and mistreatment of non-dominant minorities. The distribution of these privileges and prejudices is one reason waste management and high-polluting sites tend to be in minority-dominated areas.

Environmental discrimination is evident from the location of hazardous sites, such as waste disposal, manufacturing, and energy production facilities. For example, transportation infrastructure, including highways, ports, and airports located in poor and racially oppressed neighborhoods, are considered environmental injustices.

A study of *toxic waste site distribution* in the U.S. documented environmental racism. From the study results, waste dumps and incinerators have been the target of environmental justice lawsuits and protests.

Environmental injustice harms people in high-poverty areas and racial minority groups.

Poor people account for more than 20% of the human health impacts from industrial toxic air releases, compared to 13% nationwide.

A typical example of environmental injustice among Latinos is the exposure to pesticides faced by farmworkers. After several pesticides were banned in the United States in 1972, farmers began using more acutely toxic organophosphate pesticides such as *parathion*.

A sizable portion of farmworkers in the U.S. are working illegally and are not able to protest regular exposure to pesticides.

African Americans are affected by a variety of environmental justice issues.

Indigenous groups arc the victims of environmental injustices.

For example, some severe illnesses that Native Americans suffered were due to the side effects of uranium mining and atomic bomb testing in the American West, beginning in the 1940s.

Uranium mill in Shiprock, New Mexico, near the Navajo community

Internationally, exposure to chemical pesticides in the cotton industry affects farmers in India and Uzbekistan.

For example, endosulfan is a highly toxic chemical banned in much of the world because of the threat to human health and the natural environment. It persists in the environment long after it has killed the target pests, leaving a deadly legacy for humans and wildlife. Safe use cannot be guaranteed in the many developing countries it is used in.

Toxic industries concentrate in minority neighborhoods or poor neighborhoods because these populations lack political power. In the case of Latinos in the United States, there is often an inability to participate politically because of their status as non-citizens. Many workers are illegal immigrants, so they are not represented in the political system, making them vulnerable to economic injustice.

Notes for active learning

Social Class

Construct of class

In the social sciences and political theory, *social class* refers to concepts centered on models of social stratification. People are grouped into *hierarchical social categories*, the most common being the upper, middle, and lower classes.

The word class's etymology is the Latin *classis*, which census takers used to categorize citizens by wealth to determine military service obligations.

Class is an essential metric for sociologists, political scientists, anthropologists, and social historians. Nevertheless, there is no consensus for definition of "class;" consequently, it has different contextual meanings.

In everyday language, "*social class*" is synonymous with *socio-economic class*, a group of people with the same social, economic, or educational status (e.g., the working class).

Researchers debate and evaluate social classes in detail, including how they are formed, what motivates them, and what inequalities result.

Academics distinguish social class from socioeconomic status:

> *class* refers to a stable *sociocultural background* and

> *socioeconomic status* is the current social and economic situation, which can change.

Social standing, social class, and social life can all be impacted by social inequality, which is connected to an imbalance in the distribution of wealth and resources.

Modern capitalist society

According to Karl Marx, class is determined by the relationship to the means of production.

In a modern capitalist society, classes are the:

> *proletariat* (i.e., those who work but do not own the means of production),

> *bourgeoisie* (i.e., those who invest and live off surplus generated by the former),

> *aristocracy* (i.e., those with land which is used as a means of production).

The roles in the analogous context of big business relate to a factory worker, an overseer or manager, and the company CEO.

In the late 18th century, "class" was used instead of classifications such as estates, rank, and orders to organize society into hierarchical divisions. This corresponded to a general decrease in the significance ascribed to heredity and an increase in wealth and income as indicators of one's position in the social hierarchy.

Social stratification

Social stratification is a society categorizing people into socioeconomic strata based on *income and occupation, wealth, and social status*, or *derived social and political power*.

Stratification is the social position of persons within a social group, category, geographic region, or social unit.

In modern Western societies, social stratification is distributed among the upper, middle, and lower social classes.

Each class can be subdivided into upper, middle, and lower strata.

Social stratum can be formed based on kinship, caste, or both.

Classification of people according to social strata occurs in all societies. The determination of structures of social stratification appears based on status inequalities among persons.

Therefore, the degree of social inequality determines a person's social stratum.

The greater the social complexity of a society, the more social strata there will be as a modality of social differentiation.

Four principles govern *social stratification*:

socially defined by society rather than by individuals within that society;

reproduced from generation to generation;

encountered in every society but differs according to time and place;

involves quantitative inequality and qualitative convictions.

Social stratification exists in all complex societies.

In complex societies, goods are distributed unequally, with the most privileged individuals and families enjoying a disproportionate share of income, power, and other valued resources.

Stratification produces inequalities

Stratification system is the complex social relationships and structure generating inequalities.

Critical components are *socio-institutional processes* to define goods as valuable and desirable.

rules of allocation that distribute goods and resources across positions in the division of labor;

social mobility processes that install individuals in desirable positions and thereby generate unequal control over valued resources.

Social mobility concept classifies systems of social stratification.

Open stratification systems are when people are ranked by achieved status and have mobility between strata, typically by putting a value on the achieved status characteristics of individuals.

Societies with the highest levels of intragenerational mobility are considered the most open and flexible systems of stratification.

Systems without mobility, even intergenerational systems, are *closed stratification systems*.

For example, in the system of castes, all aspects of social status are ascribed, so one's social position at birth will be the position one holds for a lifetime.

Inequality of conditions is the imbalanced and unequal distribution of wealth and income. For example, in the United States, the wealthiest 10% of people held 69.8% of the nation's net worth, with the top 1% controlling 32.1 percent in 2021.

Inequality of opportunities is the unequal availability of opportunities (e.g., education, criminal justice, jobs, and health care). For example, the Centers for Disease Control and Prevention (CDC) states that non-Hispanic black women have more than double the rate of stillbirths compared to non-Hispanic white women. To reach conclusions and promote change, a sociologist would investigate contributing factors and social inequalities that disproportionately affect black mothers.

Socioeconomic status

Socioeconomic status is the economic and sociological sum of a person's work experience and an individual or family's economic and social position, compared to others, based on their income, education, and occupation.

In analyzing a family's socioeconomic status, the household income and the earners' education and occupation are considered.

In analyzing an individual's socioeconomic status, only their attributes are assessed.

Socioeconomic status is typically divided into three categories to describe the areas in which a family or an individual may be included. Income, education, and occupation can be assessed when situating a family or an individual into one category.

Income is wages, salaries, profits, rents, or earnings, including unemployment, social security, workers' compensation, pensions, interests or dividends, royalties, trusts, alimony, or other governmental, public, or family financial assistance.

Income can be considered *relative* and *absolute*.

Absolute income is when, as income increases, so will consumption, but not at the same rate.

Relative income determines a person or family's savings and consumption based on the family's income in relation to others.

Income is a criterion for assigning a social stratification status

Income is a frequently used measure of socioeconomic status because it is easy.

Low-income families and individuals focus on meeting their immediate needs and do not accumulate wealth that can be passed on to future generations, thus increasing inequality.

Higher-income families (and a greater share of expendable income) can accumulate wealth while dedicating a generous portion of capital to luxury goods and developing an ability to weather economic crises.

Education, occupation and wealth influence socioeconomic status

Education plays a vital role in income. Education systems serving lower socioeconomic populations tend to have fewer and worse resources than affluent school systems.

Higher levels of education are associated with better economic and psychological outcomes, and education plays a significant role in teaching skill sets for acquiring jobs.

The rate of earnings increases with each level of education. Those with the highest degrees, professional and doctoral degrees, earn the highest weekly earnings, while those without a high school diploma earn less.

Studies have demonstrated that parents from lower socioeconomic status households are more likely to discipline their children more severely and more likely to give orders in their interactions; conversely, parents with higher socioeconomic status are more likely to interact and play with their children.

Education attainment relates to differences in parenting styles. Children born in lower socioeconomic status households have weaker language skills than those raised in higher socioeconomic status households.

Language skills eventually affect their learning ability and increase the educational disparity between low and high-socioeconomic-status neighborhoods.

Occupational prestige is a socioeconomic status component, including income and education. It reflects the education level required to obtain the job and income levels that differ with different jobs and within ranks of occupations. Moreover, it shows achievement in skills required for the job.

Occupational status measures social position by describing job characteristics, decision-making ability and control, and psychological job demands. Occupation is challenging to measure, especially on a competing scale, because of the number of occupations of various types and complexities.

Scales rank occupations based on the level of skill required (e.g., unskilled manual labor, skilled manual labor, or professional).

Occupational scales use a combined measure incorporating the education needed and income.

Wealth (i.e., economic reserves or assets) represents a source of security, measuring a household's ability to meet emergencies, absorb economic shocks, and provide the means to live comfortably. This reflects intergenerational transitions and the accumulation of income and savings.

Income, age, marital status, family size, religion, occupation, and education are all predictors of wealth attainment.

Wealth gap (i.e., income inequality) is enormous in the United States and Europe, especially in southeastern and central Europe. A social wealth gap exists due in part to income disparities and differences in achievement resulting from institutional and political discrimination.

Class consciousness and false consciousness

Class consciousness is traditionally used in social sciences and political theory, particularly in Marxism, to define a *person's beliefs* regarding their social *class or economic rank* in society, the structure of their class, and their class interests.

German philosopher Karl Marx rarely used the term class consciousness. Marx distinguished:

> class *in* itself, which he defined as a category of people having a common
> relation to the means of production, and a

> class *for* itself, defined as a stratum organized in active pursuit of interests.

Defining a person's social class can catalyze their awareness.

Marxists define classes by their relation to the means of production— especially on whether they own capital.

Non-Marxist social scientists distinguish various social strata by income, occupation, or status.

193

At the beginning of the 19th century, labels like working class and middle class were already coming into common usage. The old hereditary aristocracy, reinforced by the new gentry who owed their success to commerce, industry, and the professions, formed the upper class. Its consciousness was formed in part by public schools and universities.

False consciousness is a term Marxists use for how material, ideological, and institutional processes in capitalist society *mislead* members of the proletariat and other class actors. These processes hide the relations between classes and the exploitation suffered by proletariats.

Marx renounced ideology, but there is no evidence that he used the term "false consciousness."

Working-class neighborhood in Bishopsgate, England, in the 19th century

False consciousness is linked with the *dominant ideology*, *cultural hegemony*, and, to a lesser extent, *cognitive dissonance*.

Marxist feminists and radical feminists use false consciousness for women's studies.

Marxist academics have argued that members of the proletariat minimize the true nature of class relations because they believe in the probability or possibility of *upward mobility*. Such a belief, or something like it, is required in economies that function on the presumption of the rational agency; otherwise, wage laborers would not be the conscious supporters of social relations antithetical to their class interests, violating that presumption.

Cultural and social capital

Pierre Bourdieu and Jean-Claude Passeron used the terms *cultural capital* and *social capital* in *Cultural Reproduction and Social Reproduction* (1973), an academic work that tried to explain differences in children's socioeconomic outcomes in France during the 1960s.

Bourdieu distinguishes three types of capital:

> *economic capital* (command over economic resources),
>
> *social capital* (resources based on group membership, relationships, networks of influence and support), and
>
> *cultural capital* (knowledge, skills, education, and advantages a person has, allowing them to enter a higher status).

Cultural capital is a non-financial social asset *promoting social mobility* beyond economic means. The term is extended to material and symbolic goods, without distinction, which present themselves as rare and desired in a particular social formation.

Cultural capital is a social relation within an exchange system, including accumulated cultural knowledge that confers power and status. For example, education, intellect, appearance, and speech or dress are cultural capital. Parents offer their children cultural capital by transmitting the attitudes and knowledge needed to succeed educationally.

Symbolic capital (resources based on honor, prestige, or recognition) was added by Bourdieu. It has gained popularity and developed for other capital and higher education.

Social capital is the expected collective (or economic) benefits derived from the preferential treatment and cooperation between individuals and groups.

Although social sciences emphasize distinct aspects of social capital, they share the core idea that *social networks have value.*

Social reproduction

Karl Marx originally proposed the concept of social reproduction in his book *Capital: Critique of Political Economy* (1867), a version of his larger idea of *reproduction*, which emphasizes the structures and activities that *transmit social inequality* from one generation to the next.

Capital is vital in social reproduction: it is passed from generation to generation, keeping people in the same social class as their parents and reproducing inequality through social stratification.

Economic reproduction refers to recurrent (i.e., cyclical) processes in Marxism.

Marx viewed reproduction as how society re-created itself, both materially and socially. Recreating the conditions necessary for economic activity was a vital part.

Capitalists need to reproduce a specific social hierarchy of workers who owned nothing but labor power and a hierarchy of others who controlled the capital necessary.

Reproduction must recreate workers and capitalists.

Economic reproduction is the physical production and distribution of goods and services, trade (circulation through exchanges and transactions) of goods and services, and consumption (both productive and intermediate).

In his second volume of *Capital: Critique of Political Economy* (1865), Marx highlighted the reproduction process for any capitalist society using the circulation of capital.

Marx distinguished *simple reproduction* and *expanded reproduction*.

> *Simple reproduction* has no economic growth.

> *Expanded reproduction* is when more is produced than needed to maintain the economy at the given level, facilitating economic growth.

In the capitalist mode of production, the difference is that in the case of simple reproduction, the new surplus value created by wage labor is spent by the employer on consumption, and in the case of expanded reproduction, part of it will be reinvested in production.

The system of economic reproduction has a direct influence on the evolution and progress of social reproduction.

'Capital: Critique of Political Economy' by Karl Marx

Weber's theory of social stratification

German sociologist Max Weber conceptualized the three-component theory of stratification (or the three-class system).

Weber used a multidimensional approach to social stratification, reflecting the interdependence of wealth, prestige, and power.

Weber argued that power could take a variety of forms.

Person's power is displayed in:

> *social order* through their status
>
> *economic order* through their class
>
> *political order* through their party

Therefore, *class, status*, and *party* are each aspects of power distribution within a community.

Class, status, and party are not self-contained; each aspect influences other areas.

Wealth includes property (e.g., buildings, lands, farms, houses, factories) and other assets (i.e., economic production).

Power, privilege, and prestige

Prestige is the status or respect with which others regard a person or status position.

Power is the ability to achieve goals despite opposition from others.

Weber's theory of status has two dimensions of power:

> *possession of power* and *exercise of power.*

Max Weber speaking with his political fellows

Privilege is the assertion that some groups of people have advantages relative to other groups. The term is traditionally used in the context of *social inequality*, particularly *concerning social class, race, age, sexual orientation, gender*, and *disability*.

Privilege elements include:

> *financial or material* (e.g., access to housing, education, and jobs);

> *emotional or psychological* (i.e., sense of self-confidence and comfort, belonging, or worth in society).

Weber's notion began as an academic concept but became popular outside academia.

Historically, the study of social inequality focused on how minority groups were discriminated against, with little attention to the privileges accorded to dominant social groups.

Social inequality concepts changed in the late 1980s when researchers studied privilege as a function of intersecting variables with differing importance (e.g., race, age, gender, sexual orientation, gender identity, citizenship, religion, physical ability, health, and education).

Sociologists consider race, gender, and social class to be determinative of the level of privilege.

Privilege theory argues that each person is included in a matrix of categories and contexts and will, in some ways, be privileged and, in other ways, disadvantaged.

Privileged attributes lessen disadvantages, and membership in a disadvantaged group lessens the benefits of privilege. For example, a Black student benefits from the advantages that the educational system offers him but is racially disadvantaged from a social standpoint.

Some attributes of privilege, such as race and gender, are usually visible, and others, such as citizenship status and birth order, are not. For example, Southeastern European citizens are disadvantaged compared to Western Europeans.

Some attributes (e.g., social class) are stable, and others (e.g., age, wealth, religion, attractiveness), may change. Attributes of privilege are partly determined by the person, such as education, whereas others, such as race or class background, are assigned.

Privileged people are considered the norm and, as such, gain invisibility and ease in society. Less privileged or disadvantaged individuals are cast as inferior variants.

Privileged people see themselves reflected throughout society in mass media and face-to-face encounters with teachers, workplace managers, and other authorities. Researchers assert that this leads to a sense of entitlement and the assumption that the privileged person will succeed while protecting the privileged from worrying that they may face discrimination from authority.

There is a general reluctance to acknowledge privilege; instead, privileged individuals may look for ways to justify (or minimize) privilege's effects. They may assert that the power of privilege was earned and is, therefore, justified. Sometimes, they acknowledge individual instances of unearned dominance but deny that privilege is institutionalized.

Those who believe privilege is systemic may deny personally benefiting from it and may oppose efforts to dismantle it. Privileged people may refuse to acknowledge their privilege is that by doing so, they would have to acknowledge that whatever success they achieved did not result solely through their efforts but was at least partly due to a system developed to support and empower them.

The concept of privilege brings into question the idea that society is a *meritocracy*. Research notes that false meritocracy is disturbing to Americans, for whom the belief that they live in a democracy is a deeply held cultural value, albeit often characterized as a myth.

Social inequalities and privilege attributes divide people

Economic inequalities

International inequality is inequality between countries.

Economic inequality (or income inequality, wealth inequality, or the gap between the rich and poor) is how economic metrics are distributed among group members, groups in a population, or between countries.

Economists refer to three metrics for economic disparity:

> *wealth* (wealth inequality),
>
> *income* (income inequality), and
>
> *consumption.*

Economic inequality invokes equity, equality of outcome, and equality of opportunity.

Inequality is a destructive social issue because income inequality and wealth concentration affect a nation's general economy and gross domestic product (GDP).

Inequality limits education and long-term economic opportunities for lower-income citizens.

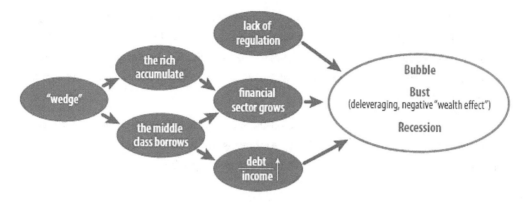

Inequality has many macroeconomic effects

Early statistical studies comparing inequality to economic growth had been inconclusive.

International Monetary Fund (IMF) economists showed that *greater income equality* increased the duration of countries' *economic growth* more than low foreign debt, robust free trade, minimal government corruption, or foreign direct investment.

Economic inequality varies between societies, historical periods, and economic structures. It can refer to the *cross-sectional distribution of income* (or wealth) at a given period or income and *wealth over extended periods*.

Numerical indices measure *economic inequality*.

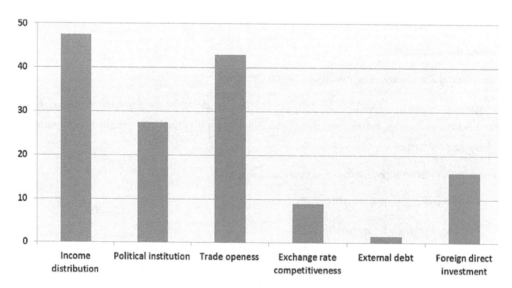

Income equality eclipses trade, political institutions, or foreign investment for economic growth

Evolution of the income gap between poor and rich countries is related to convergence.

Convergence is the tendency for poorer countries to grow faster than richer ones and eventually for income levels among the countries to converge.

Convergence is a matter of current research and debate, but most studies show *no evidence* for *absolute convergence* based on comparisons among countries.

Global income inequality peaked in the 1970s when world income was distributed in a bimodal of "*rich*" and "*poor*" countries with little overlap.

Since then, inequality has rapidly decreased, and has the trend has accelerated.

Global income distribution is *unimodal*, with most people living in *middle-income* countries.

Notes for active learning

Social Mobility

Patterns of social mobility

Social mobility concerns the movement of individuals, families, households, or other categories of people within or between layers or strata in a stratification system. It is a change in social status relative to others' social location within a given society.

Absolute social mobility is the number of people in a stratification different from their parents.

Relative social mobility is the difference in the probability of attaining a specific outcome, regardless of overall structural changes; societies have high absolute and low relative mobility.

Social mobility provides pathways to greater equality in societies with high social inequality.

Mobility is most often quantitatively measured regarding changes in economic status, such as income or wealth. Quantitative and qualitative data analysis uses occupation as another measure of mobility, while other studies concentrate on social class.

Though it is generally accepted that some level of mobility in society is desirable, there is no consensus on how much social mobility is good or bad for society. Indeed, too much social mobility means a constant social flux with no chance to build traditions and social institutions.

Too little mobility leads to *social stagnation* with little opportunity for innovation and, often, to entire classes of people who feel disenfranchised from the benefit of social participation. Thus, there is no international benchmark of social mobility, though one can compare mobility measures across regions or countries or within a given area over time.

Cross-cultural studies comparing economies are possible, but comparing similar economies yield comparable data; comparisons typically study intergenerational mobility, examining the extent to which children born into families have life chances and outcomes.

An academic study comparing social mobility between developed countries found that the four countries with the greatest intergenerational social mobility were Denmark, Norway, Finland, and Canada, with less than 20% having the advantage of having a high-income parent.

Studies show a negative relationship between income inequality and intergenerational mobility.

Countries with low levels of inequality (e.g., Denmark, Norway, Finland) had greater mobility.

Countries with high levels of inequality (e.g., Chile, Brazil) had low mobility.

Intergenerational and intragenerational mobility

Intergenerational mobility refers to movement between generations and typically measures how a person's income compares to that of her/his parents.

Intragenerational mobility, in contrast, refers to movement up or down within a generation — throughout one's life. Research examines how people fare during their working careers compared to when they were eighteen, twenty-five, or thirty.

Intergenerational upward mobility is more common, where children or grandchildren improve in economic terms than their parents or grandparents. In the U.S., this mobility is a fundamental feature of "*the American Dream*," even though the U.S. has less mobility than most OECD (Organization for Economic Co-Operation and Development) countries.

Absolute intragenerational mobility refers to changes in income compared to the income one started with. Suppose a person begins her working career with an income of $25,000. If a decade later, her income is $30,000 (adjusting for inflation), she has experienced upward absolute intragenerational income mobility.

Relative intragenerational mobility is how individuals move up or down compared to cohorts.

For example, if a person's income increases from $38,000 at the start of his career to $51,000 a decade later, most people his age have experienced a larger salary increase; they experienced *absolute upward* but *relative downward mobility*.

For intergenerational mobility, the distinction between absolute and relative is analogous. If a person's inflation-adjusted income is $32,000 and her parents were $26,000 at a comparable point, she has experienced upward absolute intergenerational income mobility.

Economic growth favors upward mobility as the norm. The issue is the degree of absolute upward mobility and how it changes over time.

Relative intergenerational mobility depends on a person's position in the distribution.

If a person's income is at the seventy-fifth percentile of the distribution and his parents were at the fiftieth percentile at a comparable point, he experienced relative upward intergenerational mobility.

Relative mobility is a *zero-sum phenomenon*; if one person moves up in relative terms, another must move down.

Absolute mobility, however, is *not* zero-sum.

Downward and upward mobility

Vertical mobility is when social mobility movement involves a change in social class, upward or downward. For example, an industrial worker who becomes a wealthy businessperson moves upward in the class system; a landed aristocrat losing assets in a revolution moves downward.

Horizontal mobility is when mobility involves a change in position, especially in occupation, but no change in social class.

For example, a person moves from a managerial position in one company to a similar position in another or a factory employee becomes a construction worker.

Revolution alters class structures. Once radically reorganized by social and political unrest, social mobility may be minimal.

Social mobility may come about through slower, more subtle changes, such as the movement of people from a poor, agrarian region to a richer, urban one.

Throughout history, international migration has been an essential factor in upward mobility.

For example, during the 19th century, members of the working and peasant classes migrated from Europe to the United States.

Western European colonial expansion, while benefiting some, served to enslave others.

In modern societies, social mobility is typically measured by career and generational changes in the socioeconomic levels of occupations.

Meritocracy

Meritocracy is a political philosophy asserting that power should be invested in people almost exclusively according to merit. Advancement is based on performance measured through *examination* or *demonstrated achievement*.

Meritocracy conceptualizes merit with competency and ability, measured by IQ or standardized tests. In government and administration systems, meritocracy is a system where responsibilities are assigned to individuals based on merits, namely intelligence, credentials, and education, as determined through *evaluations* or *examinations*.

Proponents of a meritocratic system do not necessarily agree on the nature of merit but agree that merit should be a primary consideration during evaluation. In a more general sense, meritocracy is any organizational form (e.g., government, industry) based on *achievement*.

Like "utilitarian" and "pragmatic," the word "meritocratic" has developed a broader definition and may refer to governments run by a ruling or influential class of able people.

Broadly, meritocracy is any *general act of judgment* upon the basis of demonstrated *merits*; such acts are frequently described in sociology and psychology.

Merit extends intelligence and education to *mental abilities*, *physical talent,* or *work ethic.*

Demonstrating mastery of a subject is an essential task related to the Aristotelian term *ethos.*

Aristotelian concept of meritocracy was based upon *aristocratic* or *oligarchical structures* rather than the modern state.

The term "meritocracy" is recent (1958), but the concept of a government based on standardized examinations originates from the writings and teachings of Confucius, Legalist, and Confucian philosophers. Meritocracy was implemented in China during the second century B.C. by the Han Dynasty, introducing the world's first civil service exams evaluating the merit of those applying for government positions.

Meritocracy spread from China to British India during the 17th century and then into continental Europe and the United States. With the translation of Confucian texts during the Enlightenment, the concept of a meritocracy reached intellectuals in the West, who saw it as an alternative to the traditional *ancient regime* of Europe.

Meritocratic screening today is a college degree. Higher education is an imperfect meritocratic screening system for assorted reasons, such as lack of uniform standards worldwide, scope, and access (some talented people never have an opportunity to attend college because of expense, especially in developing countries).

Nonetheless, academic degrees serve meritocratic screening purposes. Education alone, however, does not constitute a complete system, as meritocracy must confer power and authority, which a degree does not validate independently.

Poverty

Concept of poverty

Poverty represents general scarcity, dearth, or the state of a person who lacks a certain amount of material possessions or money. It is a multifaceted concept that includes social, economic, and political elements.

After the Industrial Revolution (circa 1914), mass production in factories made production goods increasingly less expensive and more accessible. Modernization of agriculture, and introduction of chemical fertilizers, provided enough yield to feed the population.

Responding to basic needs can be restricted by constraints on government's ability to deliver services. These constraints may include corruption, tax avoidance, debt and loan conditions, and the emigration of health care and educational professionals.

Strategies for increasing income to make basic needs more affordable typically include welfare, economic freedoms, and the provision of financial services.

Poverty impacts people

United Nations defines poverty as the inability to make choices, pursue opportunities and violating human dignity.

Poverty is a lack of the basic *capacity to participate effectively* in society.

It means not having enough to feed and clothe a family, not having a school or clinic, not having the land to grow one's food or a job to earn one's living, and not having access to credit.

It means insecurity, powerlessness, and exclusion of individuals, households, and communities, and susceptibility to violence. Poverty often implies living in marginal or fragile environments without clean water or sanitation access.

World Bank defines poverty as a pronounced *deprivation of well-being*, including low incomes and the inability to acquire the basic goods and services necessary for *survival with dignity*.

Poverty includes:

> low levels of *health and education,*
>
> poor access to *clean water and sanitation,*
>
> inadequate *physical security,*
>
> lack of *voice,* and
>
> *insufficient opportunity* for a fulfilling life.

Relative and absolute poverty

Relative poverty is contextual as economic inequality in locations where people live.

Absolute poverty (*destitution*) is the deprivation of basic human needs, including food, water, shelter, sanitation, clothing, and healthcare.

Poverty reduction is a major goal and an issue for international organizations, such as the United Nations and World Bank. 2.8 billion people are living in poverty, and the World Bank estimated that 1.29 billion people were living in absolute poverty in 2008 and 700 million in 2022.

About 400 million people in absolute poverty live in India and 173 million in China.

47% of sub-Saharan Africa has the highest incidence of absolute poverty.

Between 1990 and 2010, about 663 million people moved above the absolute poverty level.

Extreme poverty is a global challenge, and it is observed worldwide, including in developed economies. UNICEF estimates that half the world's children live in poverty.

Absolute poverty is consistent over time and between countries. Introduced in 1990, the dollar-a-day poverty line measured absolute poverty by the standards of the world's poorest countries.

World Bank defined poverty in 2005 as $1.25 a day; in 2015, as $1.90 and in 2022 as $2.15.

Poverty results in poor diets due to scarcity and deficient nutritional value

Copenhagen Declaration on Social Development defines absolute, extreme, or abject poverty as a severe deprivation of basic human needs, including food, drinking water, sanitation, health, shelter, education, and information. It depends on income and *access* to services.

Absolute poverty is synonymous with *extreme poverty*.

Wealth required for survival differs, particularly in advanced countries where few people are below the World Bank's poverty line; so, countries often develop *national poverty measures*.

World Bank's designation of the absolute poverty line at $1 a day was revised in 1993 to $1.08 on a purchasing parity basis after adjusting for inflation.

In 2005, worldwide cost of living studies prompted the World Bank to raise the global poverty line to $1.90 to reflect the observed higher cost of living.

In 2015, the World Bank defined *extreme poverty* as living on less than U.S. $1.90 per day and *moderate poverty* as less than $2 or $5 a day.

In 2022, the World Bank defined *extreme poverty* as living on less than U.S. $2.15 per day.

It is worth noting that a person or family with access to subsistence resources (e.g., subsistence farmers) may have a low cash income without a correspondingly low standard of living because they are not living exclusively on their cash income.

Gross domestic product

In the early 1990s, transition economies of Central and Eastern Europe and Central Asia experienced a sharp income drop. The collapse of the Soviet Union resulted in large declines in the gross domestic product (GDP) per capita, of 30% to 35% between 1990 and when it was at its minimum in 1998. As a result, poverty rates increased, although in subsequent years, as per capita incomes recovered, the poverty rate dropped from 31.4% of the population to 19.6%.

World Bank data shows that the percentage of people living in households with consumption or income per person below the poverty line has decreased in each world region since 1990.

Life expectancy has been increasing and converging worldwide. Sub-Saharan Africa has recently seen a decline, partly related to the AIDS epidemic.

Poverty reduction is not uniform; economically prospering countries such as China, India, and Brazil made more progress in absolute poverty reduction than countries in other regions.

Absolute poverty trends are supported by human development indicators, which improved.

Life expectancy has dramatically increased in developing countries since World War II, and the life expectancy gap between developing and developed countries is shrinking.

Child mortality rates have decreased in every developing region of the world.

The proportion of the world's population living in countries where per-capita food supplies are less than 2,200 calories per day decreased from 56% in the mid-1960s to below 10% in 1990s. Similar trends exist for literacy and access to clean water, electricity, and basic consumer items.

Relative poverty views poverty as socially defined and dependent on context; it is a measure of *income inequality*. Usually, relative poverty is measured as the percentage of the population with an income less than some fixed proportion of the median income.

Relative poverty is the most useful method to ascertain poverty rates in wealthy developed nations. Relative poverty measures are used by the United Nations Development Program, the UN Children's Fund, the Organization for Economic Co-operation and Development, and Canadian poverty researchers.

European Union use the relative poverty measure as the most-quoted social inclusion indicators because *relative poverty* better reflects the cost of *social inclusion* and *equality of opportunity*.

When economic development passes a minimum level, the issue of poverty, from the individual and collective point of view, is not so much the effects of poverty in an absolute form but the effects of the *contrast between* the lives of the poor and the lives of those around them.

Scottish economist Adam Smith (1723–1790) argued, in *The Wealth of Nations* (1776), that poverty is the inability to afford the *indispensable commodities* for the support of life *and* whatever the custom of the country renders it *indecent for creditable people to be without*.

People are poverty-stricken when their income, even if adequate for survival, is markedly below that of their community.

Consequently, the general idea is that no objective definition of poverty exists, as the definition varies over time and across space. When the standard of living rises, so does the notion of what is substandard.

Poverty must be seen in terms of the *standard of living of a given society*.

Adam Smith, Scottish economist and philosopher

The European Union, UNICEF, and the OEDC use relative poverty measures for poverty rates.

Main poverty measures used in the OECD and European Union is based on economic distance, a level of income set at 60% of the *median household income*.

Social exclusion

Social exclusion, or *marginalizati*on, refers to a person or group's social disadvantage and relegation to a fringe society. It is a term used across disciplines, including education, sociology, psychology, politics, and economics.

Social exclusion is the process in which individuals or entire communities are systematically blocked from (or denied full access to) various rights, opportunities, and resources that are generally available to members of a different group and fundamental to social integration within that group (e.g., housing, employment, healthcare, civic engagement, and due process).

Alienation resulting from social exclusion is connected to a person's social class, educational status, childhood relationships, living standards, or choices. For example, exclusionary forms of discrimination apply to people with a disability, minorities, the LGBTQ community, drug users, and the old or young (ageism).

Anyone deviating from the perceived norm of a population may be subject to social exclusion.

The outcome of social exclusion is that affected individuals or communities are prevented from participating fully in the economic, social, and political life of the society in which they live.

Social exclusion is a multidimensional process of progressive social rupture, detaching people and groups from social relations and institutions and preventing full participation in normatively prescribed activities of society.

Social exclusion and inclusion are a continuum on a vertical plane relative to the social horizon.

Ten social structures impact exclusion and fluctuate over time:

> race, geographic location, class structure, globalization, religion, social issues, personal habits and appearance, education, economics, and politics.

In an alternative conceptualization, social exclusion theoretically emerges at the individual or group level on four correlated dimensions:

> insufficient access to social rights,
>
> material deprivation,
>
> limited social participation, and a
>
> lack of normative integration.

Social inclusion or exclusion outcomes result from:

> *personal risk factors* (e.g., age, gender, and race)

> *macro-societal changes* (demographic, economic, and labor market developments, technological innovation, and evolution of social norms)

> *government legislation and social policy*

> *behaviors* of businesses, administrative organizations, and fellow citizens

Marginalized groups

However, an inherent problem with the term *marginalized groups* is the tendency of its use by practitioners who define it to fit their argument.

Social exclusion at individual levels results in exclusion from meaningful social participation.

Modern welfare system is based on entitlement to basic means as a productive member of society, as an organic function of society and compensation for socially useful labor.

For example, a single mother's contribution to society is not based on formal employment but on the notion that the provision of welfare for children is a necessary *social expense*.

In some career contexts, caring work is devalued, and motherhood is a barrier to employment.

Single mothers were marginalized despite their significant role in socializing children due to the attitude that an individual can only contribute meaningfully to society through *gainful employment*, as well as a cultural *bias against unwed mothers*.

Today, this marginalization of single mothers is primarily a function of *class conditions*.

Western feminist movement is a reaction to the marginalization of white women (although other races were affected and became represented more as the movement grew).

Women are still excluded from the labor force, and their work in the home is often undervalued.

Feminists argue that men and women should participate equally in the labor force, public and private sectors, and the home. At the beginning of the movement, there was a focus on labor laws to increase access to employment and recognize *child-rearing* as a valuable form of labor.

In many places today, women are still marginalized from executive positions and continue to earn less than men in upper management positions.

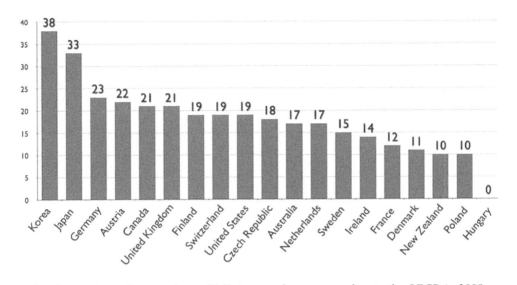

Gender gap in median earnings of full-time employees according to the OECD in 2008.

For example, individual marginalization is the exclusion of people with disabilities from the labor force. Studies have shown that employers may consider that hiring individuals with disabilities will jeopardize productivity, increase the rate of absenteeism, and result in more accidents in the workplace. They report concerns about the excessive cost of accommodating those with disabilities. The marginalization of individuals with disabilities is prevalent today despite legislation intended to prevent it in most Western countries.

There are exclusions of LGBTQ people because of sexual orientation and gender identities. The *Yogyakarta Principles*, established at a world meeting of human rights experts in Yogyakarta, Indonesia, require that states and communities comply with international human rights law standards for LGBTQ people and all gender identities.

Many communities experience social exclusion based on *race* (e.g., Black communities in the U.S.) or *economic status* (e.g., Romani, derogatorily named "gypsies," in Europe).

For example, marginalization of Aboriginal communities in Australia was a product of colonization. Aboriginal communities lost their land, were forced into destitute areas, lost livelihoods, and were excluded from the labor market. Additionally, Aboriginal communities lost their culture and values through forced assimilation and lost their rights in society.

Today, Aboriginal communities continue to be marginalized due practices, policies, and programs that meet the needs of white people. Poor people living in run-down council estates and areas with high crime suffer social deprivation.

Some intellectuals and thinkers are marginalized because of their dissenting, radical, or controversial views on AIDS, climate change, evolution, alternative medicine, green energy, religion, government administrations, women's rights, or politics.

Sometimes, their views are met with harsh responses. However, society often regards them as intellectual freethinkers and dissidents whose ideas and views are contrary to the mainstream, or their work may bolster a social movement.

At times, they are marginalized and abused, often systematically ostracized by colleagues, and in some cases, their work is ridiculed or banned from publication.

Health and Healthcare Disparities

Health determinants

Social determinants influence health:

> *cultural/behavioral* factors

> *materialist/structuralist* factors

Cultural/behavioral focus is that individuals' behavioral choices (e.g., tobacco and alcohol use, diet, physical activity) are responsible for their developing and dying from a disease.

Social determinants influence health: the *materialist*, *neo-materialist*, and *psychosocial*.

Materialist/structuralist focus emphasizes a person's material conditions (amenities, working conditions, and available food and housing quality). *Materialist approach* offers insight into the sources of health inequalities among individuals and nations, and the influence of social determinants of health. *Materialist framework* focuses on how health is shaped by living conditions and the social determinants of health that constitute these living conditions.

Neo-materialist framework extends the materialist analysis by asking how these living conditions come about. It analyzes how nations, regions, and cities differ and how economic and other resources are distributed among the population. This distribution of resources can vary widely from country to country.

Neo-materialist view directs attention to the effects of living conditions on health and the societal factors that determine the quality of the distribution of these social determinants of health. How a society chooses to distribute resources to citizens is critical.

Psychosocial framework considers how people compare themselves to others and how these comparisons affect their health and well-being. It maintains that the social determinants of health affect a person's interpretations of their standing in the social hierarchy. Individually, the perception and experience of status in unequal societies leads to stress and poor health.

For example, feelings of shame, worthlessness, and envy harm a person's autonomic, metabolic, neuroendocrine, and immune systems.

Comparisons to those of a higher social class can lead individuals to attempt to alleviate their feelings of inferiority by overspending, taking on additional employment threatening their health, and adopting health-threatening coping behaviors such as overeating and using alcohol and tobacco.

Widening community societal hierarchy weakens *social cohesion*, a *health determinant*.

Social comparison approach to health identifies the psychosocial effects of public policies that weaken the *social determinants of health*.

These effects may be secondary to how societies distribute *material resources* and provide *security to citizens*, processes of *materialist* and *neo-materialist approaches*.

Socioeconomic gradient in health

Wealth of a nation is a strong indicator of population health. Within nations, socioeconomic position is a powerful predictor of health with material advantages or disadvantages over time.

Personal material conditions of life strongly structure behavioral choices, and these behavioral risk factors account for a small variation in disease incidence and death.

Material conditions of life determine health by influencing the quality of personal development, family life and interaction, and community environments. They lead to differing likelihoods of:

> *physical* issues (e.g., infections, malnutrition, chronic disease, and injuries),

> *developmental* issues (e.g., impaired cognitive, personality, and social development),

> *educational* issues (e.g., learning difficulties and attrition), and

> *social* issues (e.g., socialization, inadequate preparation for work and family life).

Chronic stress induced by constant concerns regarding *income, housing,* and *food security* weakens the immune system, leading to increased insulin resistance, greater incidence of lipid and clotting disorders, and medical conditions that are precursors to adult disease.

Health-threatening behaviors are influenced by *material deprivation* and *stress*. Environments influence whether individuals use tobacco or alcohol, maintain poor diets, and engage in low levels of physical activity. Tobacco, excessive alcohol use, and carbohydrate-dense diets are means of coping with difficult circumstances.

Health status disparities

Health status disparities are the discrepancy in the disability and disease rates between groups.

Groups are distinguished by race, ethnicity, socioeconomic status, geographic location, sexual orientation, age, or disability.

Determinants of health influence an *individual's* or *population's* health.

U.S. Office of Disease Prevention and Health Promotion lists determinants as biology, genetics, behaviors, health services, socioeconomic status, physical environment, discrimination, literacy levels, racism, and legislative politics.

Health is determined by *availability* and *access* to high-quality education, nutritious food, sufficient and safe housing, affordable and reliable public transportation, culturally sensitive healthcare providers, health insurance, clean water, and non-polluted air.

Healthcare disparities

Healthcare disparities are differences in access or availability of health facilities and services.

Healthcare availability may fluctuate based on *geographical location* (e.g., remote facilities in rural areas or overcrowded facilities in urban areas) and *socioeconomic status* (e.g., poorer areas may not have the resources to build healthcare infrastructure, and poorer people may not live in areas with healthcare services).

Disparity in access to health care may be due to:

> *personal identity* such as *race, gender, sexual orientation* (discrimination and insensitivity by healthcare professionals and institutions), or

> *socioeconomic status* (inability to afford needed healthcare).

Disparities by class

Socioeconomic status is a social determinant of health. An individual's (or population's) class status may affect health outcomes. The link between class and health shows that those in lower socioeconomic classes are more likely to have health problems due to a combination of factors.

Low-income individuals are more likely to be in a perpetuating cycle of poor health, including detrimental personal health habits, frequent physical illness, lack of availability of or access to preventive care and treatment, and heightened emotional negativity.

Low income and insufficient education are strong predictors of physical and mental health issues, including respiratory viruses, arthritis, coronary disease, and schizophrenia. *Gallup-Healthways Well Being* Index of 2010 indicated that the highest rates of obesity, heart attack, diabetes, high blood pressure, high cholesterol, asthma, cancer, and depression diagnoses were among the lowest socioeconomic class population.

For example, socioeconomic class affects health through education; people in the lower class tend to have less education. Education in higher socioeconomic families is typically considered much more important within the household and the local community.

Education is devalued in poorer areas, where food and safety are priorities. Less education may prevent people from earning enough money to afford healthy foods, healthy living conditions, and healthcare.

Education affects individual behaviors, such as eating healthily, smoking, or taking drugs without proper information on the adverse health effects of these behaviors.

Lower-class youth are at risk for many health and social problems in the U.S. and Europe, such as unwanted pregnancies, drug abuse, and obesity.

Healthcare is limited by costs and access

Disparity of healthcare by socioeconomic class is analyzed through the barriers to accessing healthcare—lack of availability, high cost, lack of insurance, and limited language access.

Each barrier directly correlates to socioeconomics due to income, education acquisition, or living conditions (for instance, does the area have decent health facilities).

Individuals with lower socioeconomic status may have less education, which leads to decisions that adversely affect their health; lack of education may affect their employment without sick days and healthcare for employees and their families.

According to KFF Health News, in 2022, 15.7% of low-income families did not have health insurance. This figure was a significant improvement from 18.1% in 2019.

Hispanic and White people comprised the largest shares of the nonelderly uninsured population at 40.0% and 37.7%, respectively. Most uninsured individuals (75.6%) were U.S. citizens, while 24.4% were noncitizens in 2022. Nearly three-quarters live in the South and West.

Disparities by race

Racial health disparities can be examined from three perspectives:

> 1) disparity reflects inherited or biological variations in susceptibility to disease,
>
> 2) disparity in health by race as the disparity in health by class or
>
> 3) race and class disparities are separate but interact to influence health disparity.

Sociological analysis of racial health disparity examines social and biological reasons why, for example, Black populations have a much higher incidence of hypertension and diabetes.

Racial disparities in healthcare are examined cross-sectionally with *gender* and *class*.

For example, while men of color overall experience poorer healthcare services and outcomes than Caucasians, women of color are often the most underserved, receiving, on average, lower quality care than Caucasian or minority males.

Racial groups have different healthcare experiences. The Census Bureau reported that Hispanics were the ethnic group most often lacking health insurance coverage in the U.S. (at a rate of approximately one in four).

Among Hispanic immigrants, the lack of coverage was 39%, while natural-born Hispanic U.S. citizens' rate was 17%.

Legal status, language barriers, lack of culturally-specific outreach programs, lack of employer-provided (and affordable) healthcare plans, and economic hardships contribute to this disparity.

Likewise, the Black community suffers from similar disparities. Economic difficulties and the lack of affordable employer-provided health care plans were prime factors contributing to the rate of uninsurance among Black Americans, which in 2010 was reported at 21%. This coverage gap puts pressure on the high obesity rate among Black people, which exceeds the rates of whites in most states. As a result, existing diabetes, heart disease, and asthma problems are exacerbated by the lack of preventative care.

With poorer access to prenatal care (as indicated in 2005 data), Black women suffer higher maternal and infant death rates. This stems from greater difficulty attaining the needed childcare, transportation, work time off, and other support to meet their required prenatal care.

The higher rate of *maternal and infant deaths* is impacted by a decrease in the quality of their doctor's care that white women received; a higher percentage of black women in 2008 reported that their providers did not communicate well, respect what they had to say or devote enough time to their care than reported by white women.

Asian community healthcare reflects disparities. 82% of the Asian community was covered by health insurance as of 2010. Asians are less likely to seek cancer screenings than other ethnic groups. Asian women are less likely to receive pap smears compared to their white counterparts. Asian women also suffer the highest rates of obstetric trauma.

Asians, like Hispanics, have language and cultural barriers that can be obstacles to the adequate delivery of healthcare.

For inclusion in making care decisions, Asian women rates are much lower than white women.

Indigenous communities have poor access to adequate healthcare facilities due to geography and economic hardships. Sixty-eight percent of Indigenous people had health insurance, and preventative care is lacking. Indigenous women are less likely than other racial groups to have their cholesterol checked.

Indigenous women are less likely than women of other racial groups to receive proper prenatal care during the first trimester. Children suffer ailments stemming from a lack of healthcare; for example, they are at a much higher than average risk of losing all their teeth by age 18.

Disparities by gender

Health disparities between men and women and in the LGBTQ community exist all over the world. Differences in U.S. healthcare due to gender cover many experiences, including access to healthcare insurance, services offered or received, and the resultant outcomes.

The U.S. Department of Health and Human Services tracks these differences between men's and women's experiences with the healthcare system. They have found that while the uninsured rates of both men and women have decreased steadily since 2010, men historically are subject to greater rates.

In 2014, uninsured males were 12.9% compared to women's 10.5%.

Data for the uninsured is affected by age, with the uninsured rate for both genders peaking at age 26 (29% for men, 21% for women), when children stop coverage under parent's policies.

When insurance is obtained, women use primary care providers more than men, attributed to women's greater need for routine gynecological and prenatal care. Male gender roles contribute to men's higher rate of avoiding healthcare.

Delivery of healthcare services is affected by gender. Inherent cultural and societal influences could account for several of them, as can the lingering effects of the recent economic downturn. Others, however, are caused by different patient and provider factors. These disparities often arise in the diagnosis stage.

Women experience health discrepancies worldwide due to gender disempowerment, abuse and mistreatment, and inability to receive equal pay or opportunities in work and education.

Disparities are based on gender and other factors

Women have higher rates of sexual abuse and STDs, are more likely to experience violence and abuse, and there are still high rates of maternal mortality and female genital mutilation in many parts of the world.

Women are more likely to live longer and be less susceptible to diseases.

Male birth rates are slightly higher, but males tend to have higher mortality rates.

Despite women's lower uninsured rate, between 2002 and 2007, they were less likely to be able to receive needed dental work, prescription medication, or medical care.

Percentage of women receiving adequate dialysis is higher than that of men.

Adult females suffering from depression were more likely (68%) than men (57.8%) to receive treatment in the last 12 months, attributed to women's openness to talk about mental health.

Males were more likely than females to complete substance abuse treatment (47% to 41%).

Regarding weight, obese adult females were informed by a healthcare professional of their unhealthy weight 70.6% of the time, while obese males were informed 60.7%.

Obese adult females (63.3%) were advised to exercise more than men (54.9%).

The disparities present in these two obesity statistics are often attributed to the greater ingrained acceptance of male obesity versus female obesity in American society; it is more likely for the same weight in a man to be accepted as normal versus in a woman.

Rate of female patients receiving inappropriate prescriptions was 18.1% compared with men's 11.8%; studies point to social and societal dynamics as the primary explanation (e.g., different approaches men and women use to seek and provide care).

Males had a higher rate (1.8%) of developing postoperative sepsis than females (1.4%).

Males experienced a higher death rate (11.2%) after complications of care than females (9.9%).

Relationship matrix

Notes for active learning

Notes for active learning

CHAPTER 7

Research Methods

Sociology is an empirical discipline since knowledge is developed through conducting empirical research. Sociologists may use experimental and correlational research, surveys, observations and case studies. The phenomenon being investigated determines the research method to be used. Each method brings advantages and disadvantages and has the potential to contribute to the understanding of studied phenomena. Reasonable conclusions are derived through proper and quality research design, which establishes validity. The resulting data provides the grounds for theory development. Regardless of the chosen research method, professional sociologists must adhere to ethical guidelines that govern research design.

Social Science Research

Purposes of social science research

Social science research attempts to make sense of human behaviors and patterns.

Research isolates, defines, and explains the relationship between critical variables to understand and predict the underlying nature of reality.

Social science research observes and analyzes human and animal behavior.

Social science (e.g., psychology, sociology, and anthropology) is objective and uses research, observations, data collection, analysis, and conclusions.

Evaluation research guides social sciences and public policy by identifying specific and measurable relationships. It measures program effects against goals, outcomes, or criteria for decision-making and improves outcomes.

Policy analysis identifies actions (or inactions), causes, and consequences by studying:

>*proposals* (specified means for achieving goals),

>*programs* (authorized means for achieving goals),

>*decisions* (specified actions taken to implement programs), and

>*effects* (measurable impacts).

Results are categorized into *subgroups* (or *themes*), which help researchers interpret findings.

Theory and concepts

Theory-before-research model proposes that theory must occur *before* empirical research.

Research-before-theory model proposes that empirical research must occur *before* theory.

Theories are logical explanations for interrelated patterns, concepts, relationships, or events, explaining the relationship between variables (i.e., objects, concepts, or characteristics).

Theory organizes concepts, frames research, guides interpretations, and fosters decision-making. It addresses the *why* by defining parameters that measure and filter inputs people use to process complex phenomena.

Concepts are abstractions representing objects, properties, or features with a:

>*symbolic element* (i.e., word, term, or symbol) and

>*definitional element.*

For example, the concept of delinquency communicates the idea of a young person engaged in crime, truancy, or problems with parents and adults.

Concepts are abstractions:

> 1) assigned numerical values encompass *quantitative research* and

> 2) sensitizing ideas encompass *qualitative research*.

Propositions are statements about relationships between concepts.

Quantitative (*nomothetic approach*) and qualitative methods (*idiographic approach*) are used to generate and evaluate hypotheses (e.g., human behavior and cognition).

Paradigms and relationships

Paradigms are theoretical and methodological beliefs for evaluation. They organize reality into structures, frameworks, and perspectives.

Operationalization defines concepts by describing how they will be measured.

Operational definitions are conceptual meanings and criteria for measuring the empirical existence of a concept.

Objectivity is value neutrality (or dispassionate approach) to the subject.

Hypothesis specifies the proposed relationship between variables.

Deduction involves moving from a level of generalized theory to a specific hypothesis.

Cognitive reality consists of thoughts within a person's mind.

Induction involves inferring a whole group based on knowing about some cases.

Methodological fanaticism (*methodological narcissism*) is when methods overlook substance.

Knowledge is what people create symbolically to represent reality.

Sensory reality consists of substances and experiences of the external world.

Empathy is the willingness to put oneself in the role of another.

Research Methods Overview

Empirical research

Research methods answer questions about human cognition, behaviors, and emotions.

Researchers develop a hypothesis and use the research objective (i.e., question posed) to inform the research design.

Empirical research collects data by *observation and experience* (as opposed to theoretical).

Choosing the proper design is essential to valid and productive research.

Investigators must understand the design's *strengths*, *weaknesses*, and *purpose*.

Three research designs in social sciences:

> 1) *controlled experiments* (including *clinical trials*)
>
> 2) *correlational studies*
>
> 3) *survey research*

Each of these research designs has its advantages and limitations, and it is not uncommon in the field to use a mixed research design when testing complex hypotheses and developing theories.

Skilled researchers first develop their hypothesis and then let their question dictate and inform the most appropriate research design, depending on the goal of the question.

Research design terms

Null hypotheses state hypotheses of no difference based on independent variables.

Methodology is the collection of accurate facts.; it concerns *what is*.

Cross-sectional designs study one group and refer to a representative sample of this group.

Longitudinal studies focus on a group over time, and studies *change over time*.

Time-series designs involve measuring a single variable at successive points in time.

Pretest is an observation before treatment, and a *posttest* is a measurement after treatment.

Single-masked studies are when participants are unaware of the experiment.

Double-masked experiments are when investigators are unaware of the treatment and control group identities.

Experimental mortality is the expected loss (or *attrition*) of subjects during a study.

History is specific events occurring during the study and may have produced the results.

Maturation is biological or psychological changes unrelated to the experimental variable.

Multiple-treatment interference is when more than one predictor (i.e., treatment or independent variable) is used on the same subjects; the outcome may result from a specific combination of independent variables that can be uncovered only by more sophisticated research designs.

Reactivity (i.e., awareness of being studied) produces atypical behavior by subjects. Thus, an awareness of being studied, rather than the experimental treatment (i.e., *independent variable*), may become a factor in the outcome.

Replication is the repetition of experiments or studies utilizing the same methodology.

Replicability produces comparable results in replicating experiments; results should be the same when measured at separate times.

Statistical regression is the tendency of groups with extraordinarily high or low scores to *regress* (i.e., move toward) the mean (or average) on second testing.

Selection bias is when the researcher chooses *non-equivalent groups* for comparison, negatively impacting the ability to infer findings beyond the group studied.

Non-representative selection of groups invalidates attempts to generalize to larger populations.

Selection-maturation interaction is when factors other than the predictor variable are responsible for the results.

Single-subject designs are quantitative case studies using longitudinal (i.e., over time) dependent variable measurement on a single subject (or case).

Testing bias (or *pretest bias*) is knowledge introduced to respondents from pretesting; on a second test, they are no longer naïve regarding the subject and may use sensitivities, information, and attitudes garnered from the pretest.

Testing effect is when pretests eliminate naiveté of respondents to variables and alter awareness (or sensitivity), complicating the ability to generalize responses to a larger population.

Verification confirms the accuracy of findings (or *certitude in conclusions*) by observations.

Research Strategy and Design

Study designs

Research design is a study's plan and includes the investigations of who, what, where, when, why, and how.

Research designs control *invalidity* or resolve *causality problems.*

Investigators do not report a *control group* unless they for a *controlled experiment.*

Comparison groups (or *non-equivalence comparison groups*) have no random assignment. A variable may be manipulated but *without* random assignment. For example, studying the 10th-grade curriculum uses classes that cannot be assembled, so the investigator finds two comparable classes to study. Thus, *randomization* is an issue with inherent differences between the academic abilities of early risers (for 8:30 am class) versus late risers (for 1:00 pm class) and the representation of majors *vs.* non-majors.

Observational research studies are *qualitative* or *qualitative.* Methods include using observed data and recorded cases, ethnographic, and ethnological studies.

For example, a case study uses extensive notes based on client observations and interviews.

> *Advantages of experiments* include controlling factors that affect internal validity; the researcher controls for *causal factors* that invalidate findings. Researchers control the stimulus, environment, treatment time, and degree of subject exposure.

> *Disadvantages of experiments* include controls imposed by the researcher for *internal rival causal factors* that may create *atypical conditions*, impeding the ability to extrapolate to larger populations.

Replication in natural settings is complex since obtaining conditions with similar variable manipulation is difficult.

Investigators must answer how these differences are related and justify that the two groups are comparable.

Case study methods are in-depth, qualitative studies of illustrative cases. It includes oral and life historical recounts of events by participants.

Research design types

Experimental design includes:

controlled experiments vs. quasi-experiments vs. non-experiments.

Research design types:

1) *controlled experiments* (e.g., clinical trials)
2) *correlational research* (or non-experimental)
3) *quasi-experiments*

Research design considers:

random assignment

manipulation of variables

controlling extraneous factors

To design a study, investigators build from previous studies, explaining the merits of the proposed study.

Formulate *testable hypotheses* and *define concepts and variables*.

Methodological problem is isolating interventions' effects from *confounding causes* by identifying the intervention's effect through a controlled statistical design.

Confounding factors are not considered by statistical controls but by direct comparisons (e.g., intervention effects).

Confounding variables are minimized by evaluating the treatment and control groups similarly (e.g., both measured during the summer or during the winter, but not differently), eliminating time as a variable (a *confounding variable*).

Qualitative research

Qualitative and *quantitative* methods are used, but the data obtained differs.

Qualitative research requires a broad spectrum of observational methods, including exploratory statistics, structured interviews, and participant observation, to gather rich information unattainable by classical experimentation.

For example, if a researcher wants to measure students' level of satisfaction with their teachers, they may ask open-ended questions like *"What do you like and dislike about Mr. Patel's teaching style?"* Responses will include many descriptive words offering insight and feedback. Information analysis can be used to increase student retention and satisfaction, inform teachers about strengths and weaknesses, and be used in promotion decisions.

Quantitative research

Quantitative research uses numbers to describe data.

For example, a researcher might be interested in how long adolescents watch television daily. Thus, they might ask a local high school: *"How many hours per day do you watch television?"*

Instead of providing students with an open-ended question, they provide the following options: 1 hour, 2 hours, 3 hours, 4 hours, or 5 or more hours per day. Students select one response, and researchers quantify each student's television viewing habits.

Quantitative research provides numbers that can be analyzed. For example, investigators might study demographic information (e.g., age, number of family members or pets).

Notes for active learning

Controlled Experiments

Establishing cause and effect

Controlled experiments are preferred for empirical research.

Controlled experiments are the only research design using *random assignment* to treatment and *control groups* where an *independent variable* is manipulated to observe outcomes (*dependent variable*).

Controlled experiments establish a *cause-and-effect* relationship between two variables.

For example, a social scientist wants to study whether playing violent video games causes aggression in children. The investigator studies whether video games (*independent variable*) cause aggression (*dependent variable*) in children. The independent variable (e.g., video games) is manipulated in the treatment and control groups, and the outcome (i.e., dependent variable) is measured to evaluate cause and effect.

Investigators chose two video games (*Hitman* and *Call of Duty*) and recruited children ages ten through twelve to participate in the study, and eighty children signed up. As each signed up, they were randomly assigned to a category: A) *Hitman*, B) *Call of Duty*, or C) Control group (children playing a non-violent video game Tetris).

After playing three hours of *Hitman*, *Call of Duty*, or *Tetris*, the investigator measured each child using the *Video Aggression in Children Inventory*, rating aggression on a scale of 1-5. The researcher obtains child and parent-report data regarding the number of violent acts (e.g., hitting, kicking, biting, or intentionally causing pain to another) the child engages in throughout the week after playing the video games.

Controlled experiment includes the Wolfer and Visintainer study (1975), which examined the effects of systematic preparation and support on children scheduled for minor inpatient surgery.

Alternative hypothesis was that such preparation would reduce the amount of psychological upset and increase the amount of cooperation among three young patients. Eighty children were selected and randomly assigned to the treatment or control group.

During their hospitalization, the *treatment group* received the *intervention* (i.e., independent variable), and the *control group* received the *placebo*.

Measures (i.e., dependent variable) included heart rates before and after blood tests, ease of fluid intake, and self-report anxiety measures.

The study demonstrated that systematic preparation and support reduced these kids' difficulties of being in the hospital.

Variables in experimental design include the following:

> *independent* (or treatment),

> *dependent* (outcomes), and

> *confounding* (unstudied) *variables*.

Researchers can control (*independent*) variables and examine outcomes (*dependent variable*).

Independent variable is the attribute manipulated.

Controlled experiments methods

Variables are operationalized concepts that change in response to other factors.

Random assignment is when each subject has an equal probability of selection for treatment or control groups.

Controlled experiments test subjects *similarly* and use a *double-masked* design. Imposing experimental controls is easier with laboratory studies.

Controlled experiments

> 1) *variables* are *manipulated* and *monitored* (i.e., subject to change)

> 2) *random assignment* of participants into experimental or control groups.

Experimental (or *treatment*) group receives the treatment (*independent variable)*, and the control group does *not*.

Independent variable is manipulated to examine its *influence on the dependent variable*.

Independent variable is the *predictor variable* that causes (or precedes) the dependent variable.

Dependent variables are outcome variables.

*Dependent variable*s are measured, and the experimenter does not control it.

Dependent variable evaluates if treatment (*independent variable*) has a statistically significant (not chance) effect.

Control group compares the outcomes (i.e., *dependent variable*) due to the *independent variable* (treatment).

For example, clinical trials evaluate the efficacy of a treatment by using carefully designed studies. Clinical trials randomly assign the treatment (*independent variable*) and control (or *placebo*) groups. They are *double-masked* experiments with neither patients nor clinicians knowing which patient receives the treatment or placebo (control).

Experimental design included:

>*Control group* to determine if outcomes (i.e., dependent variable) were due to treatment (i.e., independent variable) or other factors. Controls provided a comparison.

>*Independent variable* was the presence (or absence) of the stimulus (e.g., treatment).

>*Dependent variables* are outcomes (e.g., heart rates, fluid intake).

>*Random assignment* balances the participants between the control and treatment groups.

>For example, if *friendly* children were placed in the treatment group, investigators would not know whether they were less anxious and cooperative (i.e., dependent variable) because of the treatment (i.e., independent variable) or because they were *friendly*. (another variable).

Clinical research

Clinical research determines the effectiveness and safety of treatments or medications. The proposed treatment, whether to prevent a disease or treat a disorder, must be effective.

Clinical research differs from clinical practice because treatments are not yet established. It permits investigators to compare novel modalities for *efficacy* (i.e., effectiveness) and *safety*.

Clinical research is frequently conducted in medical schools or large hospitals.

Non-experimental studies have neither *random assignment* of subjects nor the ability to *manipulate variables*.

Experimental design limitations

Experimental design enables researchers to evaluate *cause-and-effect* between variables.

Experiments provide precision and a controlled environment but may lack *ecological validity*.

Ecological validity is how realistically the experiment represents human behavior.

Ethical limitations (e.g., physical violence or trauma) restrict research methods.

Furthermore, if laboratory manipulations generalize to real-world situations, it is unknown.

Each research design has advantages and limitations, so a *mixed research design* (qualitative and quantitative methods) is used when testing complex hypotheses or developing theories.

Quasi-experimental design

Quasi-experimental design has *one element missing* (i.e., random selection and assignment).

Quasi-experiments *do not* use random assignment but *manipulate variables*.

For example, quasi-experiments include studies of violence inside prisons; human behavior is studied in natural settings, providing *ecological validity* but less *internal validity*.

Quasi-experimental designs match (i.e., groups without randomization for equivalence) comparison groups on how similar the groups are to the treatment group on crucial variables.

Quasi-experiments require distinguishing what is experimental and what is non-experimental.

Quasi-experiments study naturally formed groups or use pre-existing groups.

For pre-existing groups not naturally formed, the variable manipulated between the groups is the independent variable (e.g., intervention). Except for *no random assignment*, study design is like *controlled experiments*.

For naturally formed groups, the variable under study is a subject variable.

Without random assignment, therefore, no causal statements can be made based on the results.

Quasi-experimental designs:

> *Comparison groups* (or *non-equivalence comparison groups*) *without* random assignment.
>
> *Variable manipulated*

For example, studying the 10th-grade curriculum uses classes that cannot be assembled, so the investigator finds two comparable classes to study. Thus, *randomization* is an issue with inherent differences in the academic abilities of early risers (8:30 am class) versus late risers (1:00 pm class), representing majors *vs.* non-majors. Investigators must answer how these differences (e.g., study groups) are related and justify that the two groups are comparable.

Correlational studies

Correlational research examines *covariation* (i.e., the relationship between independent and dependent variables) with empirical data.

Correlation research is *observational research,* as investigators *do not* manipulate variables.

Correlation research variables are *not manipulated* but merely correlated. Non-experiments (or *correlational research*) have no:

> 1) randomization or
>
> 2) manipulation of variables.

For example, controlled experiments studying violent video games are impractical; surveys and questionnaires are appropriate. Elicited data collected and answers correlated.

Reciprocal causation is prone with correlational research and mitigated with longitudinal *vs.* cross-section studies.

Correlational studies examine the association between two variables that cannot be controlled experimentally; variables are *not manipulated*, loosely describing relationships, and asserting behavior (or events).

Correlational studies use *random selection,* but variables are *not* manipulated.

Correlational research is *unrelated* to cause-and-effect conclusions. It is *not causal*, and no statements concerning *cause and effect* are valid because the:

      1) *direction of the cause* is unknown, and

      2) *unknown variables* may be involved (i.e., an unknown variable may affect the variables studied).

Correlation studies describe relationships and provide data to make predictions and examine (or create) hypotheses for further studies.

Correlational design cannot be used to determine causality (i.e., *cause and effect*) and can only provide insight into the magnitude and types of existing relationships.

For example, an unstudied variable may cause an observed relationship since not all variables can be controlled.

Causal relationships (i.e., *cause and effect*) are *not* established by correlational design because the *independent variable* (or *treatment*) is *not* controlled.

For example, a correlational study evaluates the association between morning caffeine intake and reported higher levels of focus in college students. Since each student's caffeine intake is not controlled, only an association (or tentative relationship) between alertness and caffeine intake is proposed, *not* a cause-and-effect relation.

Another example of correlation research is when an investigator wants to determine if people's weight is related to height. They use a correlational design because they cannot randomly assign people their weight. One hundred participants were randomly selected and asked to report weight and height. Data (e.g., self-reporting results) are examined, and a *systematic relationship* is found between two variables: people who weigh more tend to be taller.

Correlational research is often exploratory to *identify variables* for controlled experiments.

For example, initial studies on smoking tracked the number of cigarettes smoked. Data was collected on smoking (i.e., independent variable) and lung disease (i.e., dependent variable) without controlling other factors (e.g., number of daily cigarettes). Smoking research examined *covariation* (not *cause and effect*) of smoking and lung disease.

For example, low levels of norepinephrine are associated with increased levels of clinical depression. The two variables *covary* (i.e., a relationship exists), but investigators *cannot* conclude a causal relationship (i.e., causation).

It is unknown whether a depletion in norepinephrine neurotransmitters causes depression or depression causes a depletion in neurotransmitters. Subsequently, other investigators determined that the number of postsynaptic neuron receptors increases in depression, which may be responsible for the relationship between neurotransmitter levels and depression.

Cause-and-effect statements *cannot* be based on *correlational research*.

Survey research

Survey methods are used in social science research.

Survey research uses *self-report questionnaires* or *interviews* to assess beliefs, feelings, values, and attitudes.

Likert Scale asks respondents to rate answers on a 5-point scale (from 1 to 5), with 1 being the weakest and 5 being the strongest agreement (or disagreement) with the statement prompt.

Survey research methods include a true *vs.* false response paradigm.

Survey research includes *focus groups* and *qualitative interviews*, where open-ended questions elicit information from the participants about a specific topic.

For example, the U.S. Census, which occurs every ten years and describes the demographics of the entire American population, is survey research. The government asks about age, family size, employment, and residence. This data helps policymakers allocate funding and resources.

Another example is a clinical psychologist who wants to know how many immigrants have PTSD (post-traumatic stress disorder). Since many countries have underdeveloped mental health care systems, she developed a questionnaire for newly arrived immigrants about PTSD symptoms. The questionnaire asks whether they experienced traumatic events, have flashbacks, etc. She determines whether their symptoms meet PTSD based on established criteria.

Questionnaires and interviews

Surveys involve questionnaires or interviews and are often classified as observational research.

Verbal surveys are *interviews* and *written surveys* are *questionnaires*.

Survey questions must be short and straightforward, without skips or open-ended questions.

Participant reactivity can be minimized by social desirability scales (i.e., "Do you always?").

Interviews can be structured or unstructured and allow for probing.

Descriptive survey research may use *statistical probability* to assess sampling error.

Analytic survey research explores *cause-and-effect* questions like experimental research.

Investigators utilize research design before the fact to remove the effects of *rival causal factors*. Survey researchers try to remove these rival factors after the fact using *statistical analysis*.

Survey research includes *errors* in the interpretation of findings. In most instances, surveys record either expressed attitude or claimed behavior, seldom the behavior itself.

Survey research answers questions to address problems, establishes baselines against which comparisons can be made, analyzes trends across time, and describes what exists, in what amount, and in what context.

Independent and dependent variables define the study's scope but cannot be explicitly controlled by the researcher.

Before conducting the survey, the researcher must predict and identify expected relationships among variables. The survey is constructed to evaluate the hypothesis by observations.

Three distinguishing characteristics of survey research.

1) Quantitatively describes aspects of a population, examining relationships among variables.

2) Data is collected from people and is, therefore, subjective.

3) Uses a selected portion of the population with findings generalized to the population.

Surveys suffer from "*no responses*" and "*refusals*" to respond.

Survey number must allow for no response and unusable, illegible, and incomplete responses.

Too many *unusable responses introduce bias*.

Strengths and limitations of survey research

Survey research allows social scientists to collect descriptive information inexpensively.

Survey designs provide data from many people. However, this may cause sampling errors, such as *oversampling* of a particular subpopulation (e.g., age, income, religion, ethnicity), distorting (or skewing) the results.

Questions may be misunderstood, and participants may guess the answer.

Participants' *response bias* (specific answers) may influence the results.

People may rush and answer questions without reading the choices or entire questions.

For example, a participant consistently picks the middle option, regardless of the question.

Surveys can elicit information about attitudes challenging to measure with observations.

In contrast to survey research, a survey is a data collection tool for social science research.

Surveys gather information about many people's characteristics, actions, or opinions and assess needs, evaluate demand, and examine impact. They are well suited for demographic data describing the sample's composition.

Statistics

Descriptive statistics

Statistics may seem intimidating initially, but descriptive statistics are straightforward.

Descriptive statistics are:

      1) *central tendency*

      2) *measures of variability*

      3) *correlation coefficients*

Statistical power

Statistical power is the probability that the researcher *rejects the null hypothesis* when the alternate hypothesis is true.

Statistical power is determined, in part, by *effect size* and *sample size*.

Effect size is a determinant of statistical power evaluating *the overall importance of a result.*

Surveys use a sample of participants within the population; each random sample has a *mean* and *variance.*

Effect size is the extent to which the distributions of means for the *null and alternate* hypotheses *do not* overlap.

The greater the difference in the distributions of means, the *higher the power.*

Distribution of means is the distribution of *possible population means*, given *null hypothesis.*

> *Sample distribution* (representing the alternate hypothesis) is compared to the *distribution of means* (representing the null hypothesis) to determine whether the *sample distribution* differs significantly from the null hypothesis.

As the sample size increases, the distribution of means becomes narrower, and variance decreases, thereby reducing overlap between the null and alternative hypothesis distributions and increasing power.

Correlation coefficients

Correlation coefficient is *co-relationship strength* between variables; *not* implying causation.

Correlation coefficients measure the *relationship between variables*, ranging from +1.0 to –1.0.

Correlation of +1.0 or –1.0 is the strongest correlation, but rare.

Positive correlation means that the variables both increase or decrease together.

Negative correlation means that one variable decrease while the other increases.

+ and – signs indicate a *positive* (related) or *negative correlation* (inversely related).

Numeric value (i.e., magnitude) is the *strength* (i.e., predictability) of the correlation.

Strong correlations predict the strength of the relationship (i.e., correlation).

Weak correlation (+0.03) might result from people's height *vs.* IQ, unrelated variables.

Stronger correlation (+0.83) for the relationship between variables.

Central tendency

Central tendency uses the mean, the median, and the mode to describe the scores most representative of the entire group of numbers.

For example, four friends are asked how long they studied for a statistics exam; their responses in hours are 1, 3, 3, 5.

Median (or *midpoint*) values assigned to each item are taken as its score or weight.

Weighted values at intervals along the scale are retained for the final scale administered to respondents.

Means and medians are represented with line graphs, bar graphs, or histograms, depending on purpose and measurement scale.

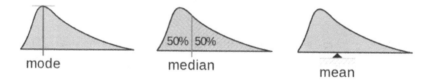

Mode

Mode is used for nominal and ordinal interval/ratio.

    Most common category or score value.

    Can have multiple modes (bimodal, trimodal, etc.).

    Not necessarily reflective of "*central*" in the distribution of a quantitative variable.

Mode is the score in the distribution that occurs most frequently. For example (1, 3, 3, 5), 3 occurs most frequently. Thus, 3 is the mode.

Distributions can have one or more modes. For example, everyone in class was asked what their favorite color was, and the results were 10 blue, 10 green, 9 pink, 8 orange, 5 red. The data is a bimodal distribution because both blue and green occur most often.

Mode reports data collected using a *nominal scale* (i.e., favorite restaurants, college majors).

Median

Median is used for ordinal and interval/ratio (espesially if skewed); the middlemost score.

Median finds the midpoint of scores and divides the group into two equal-size groups.

Median is the score in the middle of the distribution, equally divided, so 50% of subjects scored at or below the median.

Odd number of scores; the median is the middlemost.

Even number of scores, halfway between two in the middle.

Odd number samples are arranged in ascending order (e.g., 1, 3, 3, 5). For example, 3 is the median because 2 values (i.e., 1 and 2) are below it, and 2 (i.e., 4 and 5) are above it.

Even number samples are arranged in ascending order (i.e., 1, 3, 3, 5), identify the middle two numbers and divide by 2. For example, 1 + 3 + 3 + 5; use (3 + 3/2 = 3). Thus, 3 is the median.

Median offers several *advantages over the mean* and is preferable for *ordinal scale data.*

Not necessarily "*central*" in a distribution of quantitative variables.

Median should be used if the distribution has an extreme or *skewed score* because the *mean is susceptible to disproportional scores.* For example, 5 people report their income, and one is a billionaire; their income is an extreme score that *skews* (or *slants*) the data.

However, the median will identify the group's middle number, so an *outlier* (i.e., statistically different value) does not distort the descriptive statistic.

Mean

Arithmetic mean is used for interval/ratio and requires interval data (or at least equal-appearing ordinal scores)

Mean may be distorted by skewed distributions. Cutting extremes produces trimmed mean.

Sum of arithmetic means is the arithmetic mean of a sum. For example, SAT scores (verbal + quantitative). Permits linear transformation.

Geometric mean – used for data of ratios, proportionate growth, and percentage change.

Lessens the impact of positive skewness.

Geometric mean of ratios is the *ratio of geometric means*.

Mean of a group of numbers is the mathematical *average*.

Mean (denoted *M*) is calculated by summing scores in the distribution and dividing by the total number of scores. For example, add $1 + 3 + 3 + 5 = 12$. Then, 12 is divided by 4 since the sample has four numbers. $(12 / 4 = 3)$, mean is 3.

Mean has characteristics that should be noted. Since the mean includes all scores in a distribution, changing one number changes the mean.

If a constant value is added (or subtracted) from each score, the same value must be added (or subtracted) from the mean. Similarly, the mean changes by multiplying (or dividing) scores by a constant.

These rules are helpful to change the units of measurement (e.g., hours into minutes).

Variability

Measures of variability include *range*, *interquartile range*, and *standard deviation*.

Measures of variability describe how close (or far apart) scores are in distribution. If scores in a data set were the same, there would be *no variability*.

It is uncommon to have no differences in research data. Some phenomena have little variability (e.g., the number of hands each person has), while others vary greatly (i.e., response time in answering test questions).

Variability describes differences in distribution and explains the degree to which a score is representative of the sample.

Range

Range is the difference between the highest and lowest values in the data set. For example, if someone asked everyone in a room to report their ages, they would identify the lowest value (e.g., youngest) and the highest value (e.g., oldest person) as the range.

Range describes the spread of scores in a distribution; it does not account for middle values. For example, a room chose to poll at a birthday party for a grandmother turning 100. Her niece is one and the youngest. The range is $100 - 1 = 99$; there is no information on the average age of people present.

Range uses the two extreme scores (youngest and oldest) and ignores others; this is problematic for outliers in a distribution and does not accurately describe the variability.

Range is *unreliable* for measuring *variability* since it uses two extreme values.

Interquartile range

Interquartile range, unlike range, ignores extreme scores and focuses on numerical values covered by the middle 50% of the distribution.

For example,

> Data for the number of jeans each participant owns: 1, 2, 3, 4, 5, 6, 7, 8.

> Identify the boundary at which 25% of the scores fall below to locate the *interquartile range* and *label Q1* (or *quartile 1*). A line is drawn between the 2 and the 3.

> Identify the boundary at which 25% of the numbers fall above, *labeled Q3* (or *quartile 3*). The line is drawn in between 6 and 7.

> Thus, the middle 50% would be between 3 and 6.

Calculate the interquartile range by drawing a *histogram* (graph).

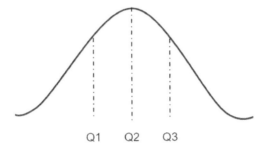

Quartile range where Q1 has 25% below, Q2 is median and Q3 has 25% above

Standard deviation

Standard deviation (SD) is a measure of *variability* (or *dispersion*), showing the variation from the "*average*" (or mean).

Standard deviation informs investigators how far the data points are from the mean.

Low standard deviations indicate that the data points are close to the mean.

High standard deviations indicate that the data are spread over a broad range of values.

Standard deviation of a statistical population (or complete population), data set, or probability distribution is the *square root of the variance*:

$$\sigma = \sqrt{\frac{(x_1 - \mu)^2 + (x_2 - \mu)^2 + \cdots + (x_N - \mu)^2}{N}}$$

where σ is the standard deviation, $x_1, x_2, \ldots, x_N$ are values from a finite data set, μ is mean, and N is the number of values in the data set.

Sample standard deviation is used when the data is obtained by random sampling from some parent population, and the denominator is reduced by one:

$$s = \sqrt{\frac{\sum_{i=1}^{N}(x_i - \bar{x})^2}{N-1}}$$

where s is the sample standard deviation, $\{x_1, x_2, ..., x_N\}$ are the observed values of the sample, x is the mean value of observations, and N is the number of observations in the sample.

Standard deviation has the *same units* as the data points.

For example, the average height of adult males in the US is about 70 inches, with a standard deviation of 3 inches.

One standard deviation: most men (about 68%, assuming a normal distribution) have a height within 3 inches of the mean or between 67 and 73 inches (i.e., one standard deviation above and below the mean).

Two standard deviations: most men (about 95%) have a height within 6 inches of the mean or between 64 and 76 inches (i.e., two standard deviations above and below the mean).

Three standard deviations account for 99% of the sample, assuming a normal distribution (bell-shaped curve).

Zero standard deviation means all men would be 70 inches tall.

If the standard deviation were as large as 10 inches, then men would have much more variable heights, with a typical range of about 60 to 80 inches within one standard deviation.

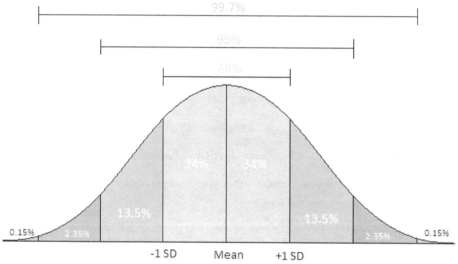

Bell-shaped curve for standard deviation (SD) of normal distribution curve with 1 SD at 68%, 2 SD 95% and 3 SD at 99.7%

Statistically significant differences

Inferential statistical information from the sample is generalized to the populations.

Samples (i.e., a limited number of subjects) are used to investigate questions since it is impractical (i.e., too costly or time-consuming) to include the entire population.

For example, to evaluate the efficacy of an anxiety medication, investigators select a sample from the population, administer the *independent variable* (i.e., medication) to the treatment group, and *simulate* the treatment (i.e., placebo) with the control group.

Data is generated and analyzed to determine whether the groups have a *statistically significant difference* (unrelated to random change) between the *dependent variables* (i.e., effects).

> *Statistically significant difference* is when the *independent variable* has influenced the treatment group compared to the control group.

Statistically significant differences are evaluated by probability using *z-score* statistics.

z-score around 0 (or *population mean*) is representative of the population.

Extreme scores (e.g., +2.00 or –2.00) are statistically different (not due to chance).

Therefore, the *null hypothesis* (i.e., no expected difference) is *rejected*, and the *alternative hypothesis* (there is a difference) is *accepted*.

Notes for active learning

Visual Representation of Data

Graphing

Data visualization is essential for social scientists to present, analyze, and share information to make data more accessible and understandable.

Data visualization is the *graphical representation* of information and data.

Visual elements like charts, graphs, and maps are data visualization tools that provide an accessible way to identify and understand trends, outliers, and patterns in data.

Visual elements present data to non-technical audiences without confusion.

Data visualization techniques are essential to analyze massive amounts of information for *data-driven decisions*.

Advantages of data visualization are sharing information and visualizing relationships.

Disadvantages of data visualization include biased or inaccurate information; correlation does not mean causation, and the core messages can be obscured.

Charts

Charts represent data in a *graph*, *diagram*, or *tabular format*, with data displayed along two axes as a *graph, diagram*, or *map*.

Familiar charts include *scatterplots*, *bar charts*, *line graphs*, and *pie charts*.

These chart types, or a combination, address questions for relational data.

Charts draw points using cartesian coordinates (e.g., X, Y, Z) based on dimensions and measures.

Dimensions (e.g., categories, dates) and measures (e.g., deaths, temperature) are analyzed.

Measures are then rendered with coordinates to create a visualization.

Some visualizations favor displaying many dimensions (e.g., ordered bar charts), while others support few with clarity (e.g., pie charts).

Each chart type has its strengths and weaknesses.

Aesthetic conventions combine form and function to affect the perception of the data.

Scatter plots

Scatter plots represent the relationship between *two variables*.

Three scatter plots:

Positive correlation

Negative correlation

Null correlation

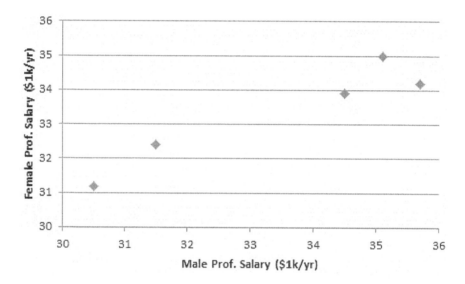

Scatter plot showing a strong positive correlation

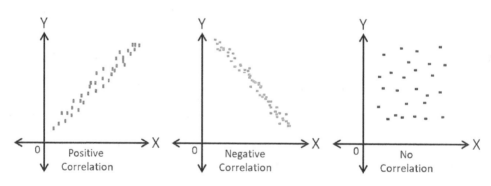

Scatter plots and correlation examples

Tables and graphs

Table: a set of figures displayed in rows and columns.

Graph: a diagram of points, lines, segments, curves, or areas representing variables in comparison, usually along two axes at a right angle.

Geospatial: a visualization in map form using shapes and colors to show relationships between pieces of data and specific locations. These visualizations focus on the relationship between data and its physical location to create insight. Any positional data works for spatial analysis. Scale makes geospatial visualizations unique is the scale.

Geospatial visualizations primarily use maps, highlighting the physical connection between data points.

Geospatial maps are susceptible to common pitfalls that may introduce errors:

> *Scaling* - changes in the size of the map can affect how the viewer interprets the data.

> *Auto-correlation* may create an association between data points *appearing* close on a map, even for unrelated data.

Infographics combine visuals (e.g., charts or diagrams) and words to represent data.

Dashboards collect visualized data displayed in one place to analyze and present data.

Area maps are geospatial visualizations with specific values set over a map of a country, state, county, or other geographic location.

Choropleths and *isopleths* are common types of *area maps*.

Bar charts

Bar charts represent numerical value comparisons (e.g., integers, percentages), with the bar's length representing each variable's value. For example, bar charts show variations in categories scaling width or height across simple, spaced bars or rectangles.

Bar charts have quantitative measures vertically, on the y-axis, or horizontally, on the x-axis. The style depends on the data and the questions the visualization addresses.

Qualitative dimension is plotted against the *quantitative measure*.

Bar charts typically have a baseline of zero. If another starting point is used, the axis should be clearly labeled to avoid misleading the viewer.

Bar charts have many variations. For example, stacked bar charts, side-by-side bar charts, clustered bar charts, and diverging bar charts.

Labels and legends help the viewer determine the details included in these charts.

Bar charts show a comparison of subcategory values. For example, bar charts may plot what a small business spends by expense type or how many different items each department sells across a consistent interval of time.

For example, bar charts can show the effectiveness of strategies to achieve a goal. Partition five strategies applied to the same subcategories, then compare the results for each method.

Stacked bar charts show extra detail within the overall measure.

For example, an office supplies store uses colored blocks in a bar representing revenue to represent sales opportunities. Blue blocks represent the contribution from office furniture, while green blocks represent electronics.

Bar charts show measures over a specific (discrete) length of time, while other chart types can show a continuous amount of time.

Well-designed bar charts:

> start at zero
>
> have labeled axes
>
> legend is consistent and defined
>
> image does not have too many bars

Poorly designed bar charts have bars with different widths, too many bars with subcategories, and unlabeled axes.

Box and whisker plots

Box-and-whisker plots (or *box plots*) show ranges (the box) across a set measure (the bar).

Box and whisker plots show the distribution of data points across a selected measure. These charts display ranges within the variables measured and include outliers, the median, the mode, and where most of the data points lie in the "box."

Box and whisker plot visuals compare the distribution of many variables against each other.

Box and whisker plots portray data distribution, outliers, and the median.

Box within the chart displays where around 50% of the data points fall and summarizes a data set in five categories.

Category with the greatest value is the *maximum* and likely falls far outside the box.

Category with the lowest value is the *minimum* and likely falls outside the box on the opposite side as the *maximum*.

Box itself contains the lower quartile, the upper quartile, and the median in the center.

Median separates the higher half from the lower half of a data sample, a population, or a probability distribution. The median is "the middle" value in a set of numbers based on a *count of values* rather than based on a *numeric value*.

Box and whisker plot sections help viewers see where the median falls within the distribution.

Lower quartile is the 25th percentile, while the *upper quartile* is the 75th percentile.

Whiskers are lines extending from each side of the box.

Range (the box) is the boundary for outliers.

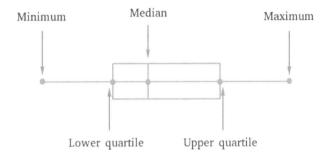

Box and whisker plot with median, lower, and upper quartiles, and minimum and maximum values

Gantt chart depicts timelines and tasks and is typically used in *project management*.

Heat map is a geospatial visualization displaying specific data values in distinct colors.

Highlight table uses color to categorize data, allowing viewers to read it easily and intuitively.

Histogram is a bar chart splitting continuous measures into vertical lines per distribution.

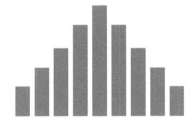

Histogram with heights indicating relative values for separate categories

Pie charts

Pie chart is circular with triangular segments that show data as a percentage of a whole.

Pie charts organize and show data as a percentage of a whole using a circle to represent the whole and slices to represent categories.

Pie charts help users compare dimensions' relationships (e.g., products, individuals, countries) within a specific context. Usually, the chart splits numerical data (measure) into percentages of the total. Slices represent proportions.

Pie charts show relationships of parts to the whole and should have a limited number of categories. They draw attention to values if one section of the whole is overrepresented (or underrepresented) and are less valuable when comparing exact numbers.

Well-designed bar charts have 2 to 5 categories, one more prominent than the others.

Poorly designed pie charts have too many categories, similar values for the chosen dimensions, do not represent a uniform whole (or percentages do not add to 100), and there are negative values (or complex fractions) for reported values.

Each pie slice should be labeled with the correct number (or percentage) attached to the slice.

Slices should be ordered by size (e.g., biggest to smallest) to make slice comparisons evident.

Limit legends and external references as they make it harder to focus on the dimensions. A 3-dimensional pie chart is much harder to analyze.

Labels should be attached to the slices whenever possible.

Consider a different chart type for more than *five slices*; use a legend, list, or table for context.

Do not complicate the visual display; complicating the chart with graphics can overwhelm it.

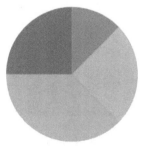

Pie graphs are valuable for comparisons among five or fewer categories

Graphing distributions

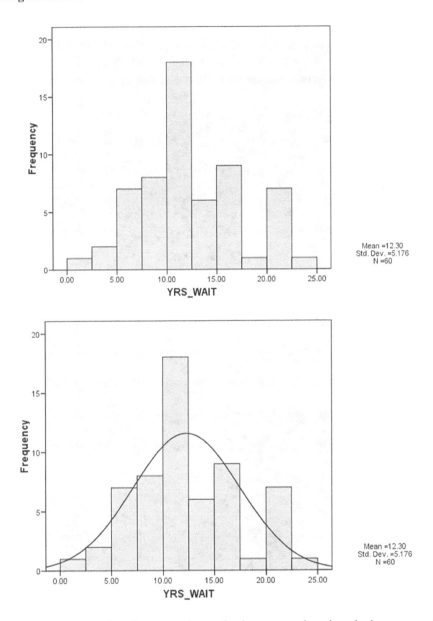

Histogram showing distribution, with standard curve overlayed on the bottom graph

Graphing selective variable

Data selected to graph can influence the viewer's perception.

Plotting specific data can influence the observer's interpretation of the data. For example, highlighting specific regions by reporting *the highest or lowest kidney cancer rates.*

Highest kidney cancer death rates

Lowest kidney cancer death rates

Ethics in Research

Principles of ethics

Ethics rely on values and morals, as opposed to facts, so it can be challenging to differentiate right from wrong.

Ethical *vs.* unethical behavior is often within a gray area.

General Principles require researchers to respect and protect people's civil and human rights.

Historically, guidelines became necessary after the unfair treatment of humans was discovered. Humans have been subjected to dangerous medical and psychological research without their consent. For example, during World War II, the Nazis forced prisoners to undergo cruel experiments.

Social science (e.g., psychological, or sociological) research ethics include:

   1) *Ethical treatment* of humans and animals participating in research studies.

   2) *Accurate and fair research conduct* and *reporting of findings*.

Ethics guidelines and practices help investigators distinguish ethical *vs.* unethical research. Principal instigators must train and oversee research teams to maintain high ethical standards.

Federal Department of Health and Human Services (DHHS) issues guidelines for ethical research. State and municipal boards may promulgate regulations for human research.

Ethical guidelines are issued by professional organizations, government, and institutional review boards (IRB). Professional organizations promulgate detailed documents describing an investigator's role in protecting the welfare of human and animal subjects.

Academic and clinical investigators take specific training required by *institutional review boards* (IRB) at universities or hospitals. Ethics and Institutional Review Boards are committees that oversee human research. Institutional Review Boards (IRBs) oversee research projects so investigators neither physically nor emotionally injure research subjects.

Academic and clinical research is guided through IRBs, which often consist of at least five members, including one community member with a non-scientific interest.

IRBs require research proposals to include a method description, whether human or animal subjects will be involved, informed consent, and debriefing information. IRBs request copies of literature or forms used (e.g., questionnaires, survey questions, and participant info).

During debriefing, participants are allowed to ask questions about the information, nature, and results

Researchers must obtain approval for the research before commencing human studies and agree to conduct their research study without changing the approved protocol. Investigators must not change approved methods without obtaining approval to ensure research oversight and that the researcher cannot decide what is ethical.

Expedited reviews are read and determined by the designated IRB committee member rather than the full committee. Studies entitled to expedited review are evaluations of educational institutions examining organizational effectiveness, instructional techniques, curricula, or classroom management strategies.

Ethical issues in research

Ethical issues inform and constrain social science research studies, including:

> *informed consent*
>
> *respect for privacy*
>
> *confidential data*
>
> *research team training*
>
> *accurate results reporting*

Honor commitments to respondents and respect reciprocity.

Reciprocity involves a mutual trust and obligation between the researcher and subjects.

Risk-benefit assessment considers maximal benefits balanced with minimal harm and used for the subject's protection; potential benefits must exceed hazards to respondents; some risks are justified if the knowledge gained exceeds the potential harm.

Paramount is avoiding procedures that harm participants. Researchers should not conduct studies that may harm subjects, particularly if the potential harm has not been explained and without informed consent.

Objectivity and professional integrity are required when performing and reporting research. The researcher should attempt to maintain a value-free, po0litically indifferent approach to the subject matter.

Confidentiality and privacy of respondents must be protected. Researchers should avoid deliberate misrepresentations of their identity when entering the private realm of subjects' lives, which otherwise would be barred to the researcher.

Confidentiality removes elements that might indicate a subject's identity from research records.

Anonymity means that the subjects remain nameless.

Data collection and storage require *confidentiality* and *precautions* when storing sensitive data (e.g., de-identifying information if stolen). Researchers may use codes instead of names to decrease the likelihood of identification.

Power differential exists between participants and researchers, with this disparity pronounced for underrepresented groups, such as non-native speakers, children, and minorities.

Informed and implied consent

General Principles require informed consent from research participants. Researchers must inform prospective participants about the research's purpose, length, and procedures.

Qualitative relationships differ from quantitative approaches as most conventional procedures for *informed consent* and *protection of human subjects* amount to little more than ritual.

Researchers must inform participants of the right to refuse participation, decline any portion of the study, or withdraw after it begins. Participants receive contact information for questions about their involvement or rights.

Researchers must disclose factors that may influence a participant's willingness to be in the study (e.g., medical procedure, loss of confidentiality, uncomfortable questions).

Informed consent is the *knowing and willing* agreement (i.e., free choice) to participate, absent fraud, deceit, duress, unfair inducement, or manipulation. Subjects must be made aware of the study's intentions.

Informed consent includes *potential benefits and risks* given to research participants. It must be written to make the procedures understandable, and participants' questions should be addressed.

Informed consent must be obtained *before* beginning research unless the study uses only observation in public places or archival data, avoiding identifying or harming individuals.

Implied consent may be indicated, for example, when a subject signs a completed questionnaire.

Active consent is the *formal written permission* by an informed parent or legal guardian that allows a child to participate in a research project.

Active consent requires *informed consent, which is* too stringent for many qualitative research.

Passive consent assumes parental permission is granted if parents do not return a refusal form after being informed about the study's purpose. The moral question is whether passive procedures inform parents about the research or provide sufficient opportunities to refuse participation.

Researchers must obtain informed consent from prospective participants

Deception in research

Deception is an issue in research and should be avoided if another research design is available.

If a non-deceptive procedure is unavailable, deception is allowed only if significant value is to be gained from the study.

For deception, researchers must inform participants and permit them to withdraw their data.

Deception is not allowed if physical pain or elevated levels of emotional distress are possible.

Compensation to participants for time and travel is permitted, but excessive financial inducements are avoided.

Researchers must debrief research participants, and participants must be allowed to ask about the study's information, nature, and results. Researchers should correct the participant's confusion regarding their role or the study's aims.

If investigators become aware that research has harmed someone unforeseeably, they must minimize the harm and report the unforeseen harm to a governing board (e.g., IRB).

Ethics violations

Lucifer effect transforms human character and causes good people to engage in evil actions.

Fraud occurs when researchers purposely fabricate or misrepresent their findings.

Plagiarism is fraud in which a writer presents the ideas or work of someone else as their own.

Scientific misconduct includes negligence, deception, cover-ups of misconduct, reprisals against whistleblowers, malicious allegations of misconduct, and due process violations in addressing misconduct.

Misbehavior includes sexual or other harassment, misuse of funds, gross professional negligence, tampering with the experiments of others, and violation of government research regulations.

Researchers must remain objective and '*value-free*' in approaching and reporting their findings.

Guiding ethical principles

Belmont Report has three principles:

> 1) *Respect for persons* requires autonomy and protection.
>
> 2) *Beneficence research* must not harm subjects.
>
> 3) *Justice* requires benefits and burdens to be distributed equitably.

Shield laws constitute prosecutorial immunity as state-guaranteed confidentiality for researchers if subpoenaed.

Research areas excluded from review:

> Information obtained is recorded so the participants cannot be identified.
>
> Disclosure of the participant's responses outside the research cannot reasonably identify the subject.
>
> The study and results do not place the participant at risk of criminal or civil liability, nor will they damage their financial standing, employability, or reputation.

Research conducted on preexisting data, documents, records, pathological specimens, or diagnostic specimens publicly available or investigator records if subjects cannot be identified.

Ethical concerns

Voluntary participation may conflict with the methodological principle of representativeness.

In 1958, Gold proposed the typology of a researcher's four roles as a *field researcher*:

> Complete participant
>
> Participant as observer
>
> Observer as participant
>
> Complete observer

Qualitative research may have the relationship between researcher and subject ongoing and evolving.

Ethical relativists propose that they have a scientific right to study any group, whether it is interested in being studied or not, provided this researcher furthers scientific understandings.

Ethical absolutists propose that researchers have no right to invade people's privacy for scientific research and that deliberate deception regarding the researcher's intentions can harm subjects.

Ethics shape which treatment conditions are used, administration frequency, and duration.

Ethical experimenters rely on a randomized experiment only if the relative effectiveness of treatments is unknown; one of the treatments may be a control.

Ethical compromise

Ethical compromise includes:

> Simple dose-response experiment with strong and weak treatments compared.
>
> Deployment of treatment so that
>
> > 1) everyone gets the treatment at some point, and
> >
> > 2) treatment is delayed randomly for some recipients to form a temporary control group.
>
> Recognizing that a no-treatment control does not exist in many settings and, in some cases, should not.
>
> Consider the need and supply for effective treatment.

People confuse the idea of the random allocation of eligible individuals from a specified eligible sample to alternative treatments with a random selection of ineligible individuals from a sample within an undefined target population.

Assign randomly to treatments those who are marginally needy or deserving (i.e., a continuum of need or merit).

Alter eligibility requirements to meet standards of human ethics and evidence in experiments, recognizing that subsets of eligible individuals might be randomized even if the primary target population cannot.

Avoid ethically objectionable imbalances in the characteristics of individuals assigned to different treatments; people are randomly assigned to treatments in randomized trials.

Individual Privacy and Confidentiality of Research Records

Privacy is an attribute of the individual.

Confidentiality is an attribute of records.

Research acquires information to understand the effectiveness of programs, notably in randomized experiments.

Relationship matrix

Topic

Notes for active learning

Notes for active learning

Appendix

Important Figures in Sociology (in alphabetical order)

Mary Ainsworth (1913–1999) was an American-Canadian developmental psychologist best known for her work on *attachment theory*. Ainsworth devised a particular situation design to study the emotional attachment of infants to their caregivers. In these experiments, a child would play in a room for twenty-four minutes while caregivers and strangers entered and exited. Children were observed based on the amount of exploration they engaged in, their reactions to the departure and return of their caregiver, and their level of stranger anxiety. The children were then categorized based on their behaviors as either secure, anxious-avoidant, or anxious-ambivalent/resistant.

Solomon Asch (1907–1996) was a Polish-American social psychologist. Asch was a Berlin School of Experimental Psychology member and emphasized the role of the "whole" in his research. Asch is best known for his research on conformity. He found that group pressure can change the opinions of individuals.

Albert Bandura (1925–2021) was a Canadian-American psychologist. He is best known for developing social *learning theory* and his Bobo doll experiment. In this experiment, Bandura found that children who had seen an adult playing aggressively with a Bobo doll were more likely to play aggressively with the same doll than children who had seen an adult playing gently with the doll.

Howard Becker (1928–2023) was a prominent American sociologist who studied interactionism, labeling theory, crime, and deviance. Dr. Becker is best known for his groundbreaking book *Outsiders: Studies in the Sociology of Deviance* (1963), in which he used action-focused sociology to demonstrate that deviance is not innate as an act but instead results from how others perceive the act. Becker's ideas gained much traction in France, and his book became a staple in the French social science curriculum.

Pierre Bourdieu (1930–2002) was a French sociologist, anthropologist, and philosopher known for social stratification based on aesthetic taste. Bourdieu theorized that social classes pass their aesthetic preferences to the younger generation. These passed-down aesthetic dispositions are intended to distance oneself from other social groups. He contributed to sociological theory and the link between education and culture. He pioneered the terms habitus, symbolic violence, and cultural capital and is known for his work entitled "*Distinction: A Social Critique of the Judgment of Taste.*" He developed theories about forms of capital and their importance in contemporary society.

John Bowlby (1907–1990) was a British psychologist, psychiatrist, and psychoanalyst known for his childhood development and attachment theories. Bowlby's work emphasized the importance of having a warm and nurturing mother or mother figure. He theorized that children and infants who had the presence of a warm caregiver in their lives would develop a secure base from which to learn and explore. He called this a secure attachment.

Noam Chomsky (born 1928) is an American cognitive scientist, historian, linguist, logician, (analytical) philosopher, political activist, and social critic. He contributed to developing a new cognitivist framework for studying language and the mind, creating *universal grammar theory*, *generative grammar theory*, Chomsky hierarchy, and the minimalist program.

Albert Cohen (American sociologist, 1918–2014) put forth a hypothesis regarding the increase in *antisocial behavior* in Western Societies. According to Robert Merton's *Strain Theory*, he elucidated *status frustration*.

Patricia Hill Collins (American sociologist, b. 1948) is a feminist and race theorist who popularized intersectionality, race, class, gender, and sexuality as systems of oppression. Books and articles include Black Feminist Thought and Learning from the Outsider Within: The Sociological Significance of Black Feminist Thought (1986).

Auguste Comte (French philosopher and mathematician, 1798–1857) founded the doctrine of *positivism* and coined the term *sociology*. He shaped and expanded sociology with *systematic observation* and *social order*. Comte is often regarded as the first philosopher of science, and his ideas were fundamental to the development of sociology, the discipline he considered to be the crowning achievement of the sciences.

Charles Horton Cooley (1864–1929) was an American sociologist known for his concepts of the looking-glass self, primary and secondary groups. He was a founding member and eighth president of the *American Sociological Association*. According to Horton's *looking-glass self-theory*, individuals' identities are formed through the perceptions that others have of them. He developed concepts of *primary* and *secondary relationships* and identified primary groups as closely-knit groups that exert tremendous influence on their members, with secondary groups being less influential and more temporary social groups.

William E. Cross, Jr. (born 1940) is a psychologist and theorist known for his work on ethnic and racial identity development, particularly his *Nigrescence model*. This model proposes five stages people of color go through when forming their racial identity. The first stage is the pre-encounter stage when the individual is unaware of their race. The second stage is the encounter stage, when individuals have some experience that makes them conscious of their race. In the third immersion/emersion stage, individuals strongly identify with their racial identity and disparage the dominant racial culture. The fourth stage is the internalization stage, when individuals stop disparaging the dominant racial culture and can establish relationships with whites. The fifth stage is the internalization/commitment stage, in which individuals advocate for the concerns of people of color and have a positive sense of their racial identity.

Charles Darwin (1809–1882) was an English naturalist and geologist. By far, Darwin is best known for his *theory of evolution*, which claims all of Earth's species (both current and extinct) are connected, over time, to shared common ancestors. The branching pattern of species from these common ancestors is the product of natural selection, the condition by which only the most successful members of a species are the ones to survive and successfully reproduce, passing on their phenotype.

Alexis de Tocqueville (French sociologist, 1805–1859) is known for his book *Democracy in America*. He published in comparative and historical sociology and was active in politics and political science.

Dorothea Lynde Dix (1802–1887) was an American activist for the more humane treatment and provision for poverty-stricken mentally ill people. The United States' first mental asylums were created mainly due to her vigorous and successful lobbying of state legislatures and Congress, actions inspired by her abhorrence of the mentally ill being largely confined in cruel, makeshift fashion around the country.

W.E.B. Du Bois (American sociologist, pan-Africanist, and civil rights advocate, 1868–1963) researched race and racism after the U.S. Civil War. He was the first African-American to earn a doctorate from Harvard University. He headed the National Association for the Advancement of Colored People (NAACP) in 1910. His works include The Souls of Black Folk, which advances his *double consciousness* theory focused on U.S. social structure in *Black Reconstruction.*

Emile Durkheim (French sociologist, 1858–1917) is the *"father of sociology."* and positioned sociology as a science and academic discipline. He significantly impacted the growth of anthropology and sociology. Durkheim wrote several books about morality, religion, and education. *"Suicide: A Study In Sociology"* describes the characteristics of people who commit suicide. *The Division of Labor in Society* is crucial, as it provides insight into how society functions and regulates itself.

Friedrich Engels (1820–1895) was a German philosopher, historian, political theorist, revolutionary socialist, and businessman. Engels was also Karl Marx's close friend and collaborator, serving as a leading authority on Marxism. Marx and Engels co-authored many works, including *The Holy Family*, *The German Ideology*, and *The Communist Manifesto*. They were organizers and activists in the Communist League and First International. Engels financially supported Marx for much of his life, and after Marx died in 1883, Engels compiled Volumes II and III of Marx's *Das Kapital* (1885 and 1894).

Leon Festinger (1919–1989) was an American social psychologist best known for his work on cognitive dissonance and *social comparison theory*. Festinger's research on cognitive dissonance revealed that inconsistency is psychologically uncomfortable, and individuals experiencing dissonance will try to reduce it by changing their behaviors or cognitions. Social comparison theory proposes that humans evaluate their opinions by comparing them to those close to them.

Michel Foucault (French social theorist, philosopher, historian, intellectual, and activist, 1926–1984) revealed through his method of "*archaeology*" how institutions wield power by creating discourses that control people. He is one of the most widely read and cited social theorists, and his theoretical contributions are still relevant in the 21st century.

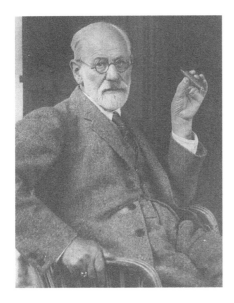

Sigmund Freud (1856–1939) was an Austrian neurologist best known for his psychoanalysis and psychosexual development theories. Freud is known for his conceptualization and articulation of critical mental functions of the mind comprising the id, the ego, and the superego. Freud proposed that a libido (or energy) exists that drives human behavior. Freud argued that libido is expressed in different ways depending on what stage of psychosexual development a person is in. The five stages that Freud identified are the oral, anal, phallic, latent, and genital stages.

Clifford Geertz (1926–2006) extensively influenced the field of symbolic anthropology. He finished an interdisciplinary course at Harvard University before starting an academic career. He published theoretical papers and essays on *symbolic anthropology*, significantly impacting contemporary anthropology and communication studies.

Anthony Giddens (British sociologist, b. 1938) developed theories of *structuration*, his holistic view of modern societies, and his political philosophy called the *Third Way*. Giddens is a prominent contributor with 34 published books in over 28 languages. He developed the theory of structuration. He has served as a political consultant for various administrations.

Erving Goffman (1922–1982) was the 73rd president of the *American Sociological Association* and the sixth most-cited intellectual in humanities and social sciences by *Times Higher Education Guide*. Creator of the *symbolic interaction perspective* and *dramaturgical perspective*, he pioneered *face-to-face interaction* studies. Books include *The Presentation of Self in Everyday Life* and *Stigma: Notes on the Management of Spoiled Identity*. According to Goffman, individuals vary their behavior based on the "stage" they are currently in. The front stage refers to engaging with people and a performance tailored for them. Backstage refers to times when we do not need to put on a show and can act like ourselves. Goffman is also known for *impression management*; individuals use strategies to portray themselves to others in a certain way.

Antonio Gramsci (Italian political activist and journalist, 1891–1937) wrote prolific social theory while imprisoned by Mussolini's fascist government from 1926–1934. He advanced Marx's theory by focusing on the roles of intellectuals, politics, and media in maintaining bourgeois dominance in a capitalist system. *Cultural hegemony* was Gramsci's essential contribution.

Jurgen Habermas (German sociologist, critical theorist, and pragmatist philosopher, b. 1929) developed the *theory of rationality* and the *concept of modernity*. He is one of Germany's most influential philosophers and a prominent public intellectual. In 2007, Habermas was the 7th most-cited author in humanities by the *Higher Times Education Guide*.

Alfred Kinsey (1894–1956) was an American biologist, entomologist, sexologist, and zoologist known for his contributions to the field of sexology. In 1948, he published *The Kinsey Reports on Human Sexual Behavior*, two widely cited volumes discussing the sexual behaviors of males and females. Kinsey gathered information through face-to-face interviews, believing they were the best way to get accurate data. Kinsey was also known for his heterosexual/homosexual rating scale, a measure still sometimes used today.

Harriet Martineau (British writer, social theorist, and political activist, 1802–1876) is among the earliest Western sociologists and founders. Martineau was the first female sociologist, a pillar of British feminism, and essential to the development of sociology. Her scholarship was on the intersections of politics, morals, and society, and she wrote prolifically about sexism and gender roles from a sociological, holistic, religious, and feminine perspective, translated works by Auguste Comte, and, rarely for a woman at the time, supported herself from her writings.

Karl Marx (German political economist and socialist revolutionary 1818–1883) developed the theory of *historical materialism*, focusing on how social order (e.g., class structure and hierarchy) emerges from a society's economic system. He theorized this relationship as a dialectic between the base and superstructure of society. He published a three-volume *Das Kapital* and *The Communist Manifesto* (co-written with Friedrich Engels) with theories that internal tension in capitalism will result in the socialist mode of production eventually replacing other systems. Marx is among the most influential figures in human history, and a 1999 BBC poll voted him *"thinker of the millennium"* by people worldwide.

Abraham Maslow (1908–1970) was an American psychologist known for his *Hierarchy of Needs* diagram. This model states that individuals must fulfill their most pressing needs before moving on to higher needs. According to Maslow, physiological needs are the most pressing, followed by safety, belonging, esteem, and self-actualization. Maslow was also known for his work on "peak experiences." He believed that self-actualized individuals would experience profound moments of happiness, termed *peak experiences*.

George Herbert Mead (American psychologist and sociologist, 1863–1931) pioneered *pragmatism* and *symbolic interactionism*. His *social self* is based on the self as a *social emergent*. He pioneered *symbolic interactionism*, a theory exploring relationships between people in societies. He developed the "*I*" and "*Me*" concept and founded *social psychology*. His theories became referred to as the *Chicago School of Sociology* while a professor at the University of Chicago. Books based on his famous lectures were not released until his passing.

Robert K. Merton (American sociologist, 1910–2003) was an influential social scientist. He developed theories of *deviance* and the concepts of *self-fulfilling prophecy* and *role models*. Merton had a keen interest in the *American Dream*, the conviction that success is possible for anyone who puts in the necessary effort.

Robert Michels (1876–1936) was a German sociologist and student of Max Weber. He is best known for his theories that contributed to *elite theory*. Michels also proposed the *iron law of oligarchy*, a political theory claiming that rule by an elite is inevitable within any democratic organization.

Stanley Milgram (1933–1984) was an American social psychologist and educator best known for his research on obedience. In his famous experiment, volunteer participants were told they were partaking in a study examining memory. Participants were instructed to administer shocks to Milgram's confederate (pretending to be a volunteer) whenever he answered a question incorrectly. The confederate was not receiving shocks. Whenever participants seemed disturbed by the confederate's acted "pain" and wanted to stop, the experimenter provided strong verbal encouragement to continue. Milgram found that 65% of participants would persist until they had administered the final "shock" of 450 volts. Milgram concluded that most individuals lack the cognitive resources to resist authority.

C. Wright Mills (American sociologist, 1916–1962) is known for his controversial critiques of contemporary society and sociological practice in his book *The Sociological Imagination* (1959). He studied power and class in the U.S. in his book *The Power Elite* (1956).

Ann Oakley (British sociologist, b. 1944) is a notable female sociologist who discusses issues affecting women, including division of labor, domestic duties, and experiences of motherhood. She has written numerous academic works, many focusing on the lives and roles of women in society as well as several best-selling novels.

Talcott Parsons (1920–1979) was an American sociologist and Harvard professor who is regarded as one of the most influential figures in 20th-century sociology. He established the foundation for the modern *functionalist perspective* and social action theory. Parsons's theories are concerned with the stability and order of social life, and he drew on ideas from cybernetics and systems theory. His work also influenced the intellectual bases of other disciplines of modern sociology, including German sociology.

George Ritzer (born 1940) is an American sociologist an American sociologist, professor, and author who studied globalization, metatheory, patterns of consumption, and modern/postmodern social theory. He is best known for his concept of "McDonaldization." Ritzer identified four dimensions of McDonald's that have influenced society. These characteristics are efficiency, calculability, predictability, and control.

Julian Rotter (1916–2014) was an American psychologist. Rotter is best known for developing the locus of control concept and his contributions to *social learning theory*. Rotter identified that some individuals believe they can control events affecting them, and some believe outside forces cause these events. Individuals who believe they can control events affecting them are said to have an internal locus of control. In contrast, those who do not believe they have any control over them are said to have an external locus of control.

Hans Selye (1907–1982) was an Austrian-Canadian endocrinologist best known for his work on stress and the stress response. He coined the term "stress" and found that the physical stress response was the same for positive and negative stressors.

Muzafer Sherif (1906–1988) was a Turkish-American psychologist considered the founder of modern social psychology. He is best known for his *social judgment theory* and *realistic conflict theory*. *Social judgment theory* is a framework for studying human judgment that proposes that people weigh new ideas at the instant of perception. They then categorize these ideas based on their preferred position, the alternatives, and the level of ego involvement with issues. *Realistic conflict theory* proposes that deviance and hostility result from competition over resources.

Georg Simmel (German sociologist, philosopher, and critic 1858–1918) used a neo-Kantian approach to lay the foundations for sociological *antipositivism* and *structuralist styles of reasoning*. He wrote on the philosophy of Schopenhauer and Nietzsche and broadly rejected academic standards. He had a son with philosopher Gertrud Kinel while married.

B. F. Skinner (1904–1990) was an American behaviorist, inventor, social philosopher, psychologist, and innovator of radical behaviorism. Skinner developed the principle of reinforcement and the term operant conditioning.

Herbert Spencer (British sociologist, 1820–1903) was among the first to regard social life as a social system. He viewed societies as organisms progressing by evolution, like living species. Spencer was essential in the development of the *functionalist perspective*.

Charles Spearman (1863–1945) was an English statistician and psychologist known for his critical role in promoting factor analysis, developing Spearman's rank correlation coefficient, and researching models for human intelligence.

Max Weber (1864–1920) was a German economics professor, historian, and lawyer. Along with Karl Marx, Auguste Comte, and Émile Durkheim, he was one of the founders of sociology, even though he did not identify as one. Weber is regarded as one of the most influential theorists who have significantly impacted social theory and research. He is known for his thesis on the Protestant ethic and his model of bureaucracy. Weber identified six characteristics of an ideal bureaucracy and believed that bureaucracies were the ideal model for government agencies.

Philip Zimbardo (born 1933) is an American psychologist and professor best known for his Stanford "prison" experiment. In this experiment, 24 students declared sane were randomly assigned to the roles of prisoner or guard. The guards were not given instructions on how to treat the prisoners. After only six days, the experiment was stopped due to the guards' cruel behavior. Zimbardo concluded that situational influences could make people act in cruel ways.

Notable Sociologists by Field

Positivism	**Auguste Comte**
	Herbert Spencer
	Emile Durkheim
	Charles H. Cooley
Functionalism	Talcott Parsons
	Kingsley Davis
	Robert K. Merton
	Wilbert E. Moore
	Albert Cohen
Marxism	Karl Marx
	Louis Althusser
Interactionism	Howard Becker
Weberian theory	Max Weber
Structuration	Anthony Giddens
Urban sociology	Robert E. Park
	George Murdoch
	W.E.B. Du Bois
	Pierre Bourdieu
	Stuart Hall
	Ulrich Beck
	Jeffrey Weeks

Feminism   Harriet Martineau

Jessie Bernard

Judith Stacey

Ann Oakley

Nancy Chodorow

Judith Butler

Catriona Mirrlees-Black

Annotated Glossary of Sociology Terms

A

Ableism – discrimination of disabled people based on the belief that non-disabled people are superior and assumptions that able-bodied experiences are natural and universal.

Absolute monarchy – a political system under which a king or queen controls a country.

Absolute poverty – the condition of having too little income to buy the necessities (e.g., food, shelter, clothing, and health care). Defined in terms of the minimum requirements necessary to afford minimal food, clothing, health care, and shelter standards.

Academic dependency – the dependence of scholars and intellectuals from the Global South on the institutions and ideas of Western social science.

Access – creating, measuring, and redesigning opportunities to enhance participation by underrepresented groups.

Achieved status – social status based on an individual's effort rather than traits attributed to biological factors. *Examples of achieved status include veteran, graduate, or doctor.*

Acid rain – the increased acidity of rainfall is caused by emissions of sulfur dioxide and nitrogen oxides, the primary sources of which are power plants and automobiles.

Acquired Immune Deficiency Syndrome (AIDS) – a disease, often passed on through sexual contact, that attacks the body's immune system.

Actor-network theory – perspective holding that reality comprises networks of interrelated, interacting elements, including non-human elements such as objects and ideas. *Actor-network theorists seek to trace the associations between these elements.*

Acute disease – a short-term disease (such as influenza or pneumonia) from which a person dies or recovers.

Adaptation – the ability of a sociocultural system to change with the demands of a changing physical or social environment. The process by which cultural elements change in form or function in response to changes in other parts of the system.

Adult socialization – the process of learning new roles in maturity.

Affective action – individual action motivated by emotions; it is one of Weber's four action types. See *traditional action, Wertrational*, and *Zweckrational*.

Affirmative action – action favoring those who tend to suffer from discrimination. Organizational policies intended to assure minorities and women of equal hiring or admission opportunities. *Requires employers to make special efforts to recruit, hire, and promote qualified members of previously excluded groups, including women and minorities.*

Age cohort – a group born around the same time.

Age discrimination – the differential treatment of people based solely on their age.

Age grades – a system, in some traditional cultures, in which the population is grouped by sex and age. Age grades go through rites of passage, hold similar rights, and have similar obligations.

Age-sex pyramid – see *age-sex structure.*

Age-sex structure (or *age-sex pyramid)* – the relative proportion of different age-sex categories in a population. Often depicted using a bar graph, the age-sex structure of society shows the proportion of males to females in each designated age category and the proportional relationship between each age category and the population overall. Pre-industrial societies have a pyramid-shaped age-sex structure, with younger age cohorts forming a broad base; because of a declining birth rate and an aging population, modern industrial societies have a vastly different age-sex structure.

Ageism – prejudice against a person on the grounds of age in the belief that unequal treatment is justified because the age category to which he or she belongs is inferior to other age categories. *Discrimination or prejudice against a person on the grounds of age.*

Agency – the capacity to act in a chosen manner, shaping individual and social patterns.

Agents of socialization – people, groups, and experiences that influence behavior and self-image. A group or institution within which socialization processes occur. See *social reproduction.*

Aggregate – a collection of people in the same place at the same time but have no other connection to one another. *For example, a crowd of people crossing a city street.*

Aging – the combination of biological, psychological, and social processes affecting people as they age.

Agencies of socialization – groups or social contexts within which socialization processes occur. Family, peer groups, schools, media, and the workplace are all arenas in which cultural learning occurs.

Agrarian society (or *agricultural society)* – a society whose mode of production is based on agriculture (crop growing) primarily using human and animal energy. 1. subsistence based on agricultural production (e.g., crop-growing). 2. a society that raises crops by using animal-drawn plows. *Large-scale cultivation using plows and draft animals is the primary means of subsistence.* See *traditional state.*

Agribusiness – the mass production of agricultural goods through mechanization and rationalization.

Agricultural society – see *agrarian society.*

Air pollution – the contamination of the atmosphere by noxious substances. See *depletion*, *environment*, and *pollution.*

Alienation (*Marxism*) – the process by which workers are separated or estranged from the products of their labor. Marx holds that in the capitalist production system, workers lose control over their labor and its products; as a result, their labor becomes something foreign to them.

Alienation – the sense that one has lost control over social institutions that one has participated in creating; often characterized as estrangement from the self and from society. Marx believed that general alienation is rooted in the loss of control on the part of workers over the nature of the labor task and the products of their labor.

Alienation – workers in a bureaucracy feel they are being treated as objects rather than people. *The separation or estrangement of individuals from themselves and others. The sense that our abilities, as human beings, are taken over by other entities.*

Altruistic suicide (*Durkheim*) – suicide performed for the good of a group or for accomplishing a political or social cause.

Amalgamation – the biological and cultural assimilation (merging) of racial or ethnic groups.

Ambivalence – a contrasting feeling or opposing commitments towards an entity or event.

American Dream – the belief that all Americans, regardless of conditions of birth, have an equal chance to succeed.

Americanization – the spread of American cultural elements—products, lifestyles, customs, institutions, and ideologies—around the globe.

Androgyny – the blending of traits traditionally regarded as feminine or masculine.

Animism – a religion based on the belief that the activities of spirits often cause events. The belief that the activities of spirits mobilize events in the world.

Anomalies – science observations or problems that cannot be explained or solved in a prevailing paradigm.

Anomia – a condition of anxiety and confusion experienced by individuals without adequate social guidance by clearly defined social norms.

Anomic suicide (*Durkheim*) – suicide performed because the egoistic individual is not given clear guidance from the social order.

Anomie (*Émile Durkheim; strain theory*) – feeling disconnected from society can occur when people lack the institutionalized means to achieve their goals. A structural condition in which social norms are weak or conflicting. A breakdown or confusion in a group or society's norms, values, and culture. A condition of relative normlessness. Lack of societal values shared by the rest of one's society. *Describes feelings of aimlessness and despair provoked by the rapid social change in the modern world, which results in social norms losing their hold.*

Anomie (*Durkheim*) – a social state characterized by dramatic shifts in individual status, typically due to rapid, unregulated economic change. Feelings of anomie are associated with frustration, uncertainty, and unhappiness and may cause *anomic suicide*.

Anomie theory (or *structural strain theory*, *Robert Merton's theory of deviance*) – forms of deviance are caused by a disjunction between society's goals and the approved means to achieve those goals. Deviance and crime occur when there is an acute gap between cultural norms and goals and socially structured opportunities for individuals to achieve those goals.

Anthropology (*social sciences*) – intricately linked to sociology that concentrates (although not exclusively) on studying traditional cultures (particularly hunting-and-gathering and horticultural societies) and the evolution of the human species.

Anti-Semitism – prejudice or discrimination against Jews. It defines the Jewish people as inferior and targets them for stereotyping, mistreatment, and acts of hatred.

Anticipatory socialization – the process of taking on the attitudes, values, and behaviors of a status or role one expects to occupy in the future, learning new roles and attitudes in preparation for joining a group or *a future role*.

Antipositivism – the view that social researchers should strive for subjectivity as they work to represent social processes, cultural norms, and societal values.

Apartheid – a social system in which the races are separated. The system of strict racial segregation established in South Africa and dismantled in the early 1990s. *A policy of racial separation in South Africa was enforced by legal political and military power.*

Appearance – the way we look physically to other people.

Applied social research – aims not just to understand a social problem but also to contribute to solving it. *Much criminological research, for example, is applied research aiming to reduce crime levels. Applied social research is a feature of all social science disciplines and often demands the involvement of multi-disciplinary teams.*

Applied sociology – using sociological theory and methods to solve social problems. Trained researchers, community workers, and activists who use sociology methods, theories, and concepts beyond academia to answer questions of clients and community groups in policy, not-for-profit work, and industry.

Appropriate technology – designed with the user's needs, values, and capabilities in mind.

Archaeology – studying human activity and culture in the past on the basis primarily of the discovery and analysis of material remains.

Arms race – a competition between nations in which each side attempts to achieve or maintain military superiority.

Arms trade – the international selling of armaments for profit by governments and private contractors worldwide.

Arranged marriage – arranged by family members, usually parents, based on factors other than the couple's personal preferences, such as family connections or the desire for social status or economic gain.

Artisan (or *craftsman*) – a skilled manual worker.

Ascribed status – a social position given at birth based on such characteristics as race or sex.

Ascribed status – 1. one's societal status at birth, an unearned social status. 2. a trait or characteristic people possess because of the circumstances of birth. *Social status based on biological factors like race, sex, or age.*

Assimilation – the process whereby group members give up parts of their own culture to blend into a new one. A minority group's internalization of the values and norms of the dominant culture. The minority group becomes socially, economically, and politically absorbed into the wider culture. *The acceptance of a minority group by a majority population, in which the group takes on the values and norms of the dominant culture. The merging of minority and majority groups into one group with a common culture and identity.*

Association – people bound by common goals and rules but not by close personal ties.

Athletics – a form of sport closer to work than to play.

Attachment – one's ties to their social groups (e.g., family, friends, community)

Augmented reality (*Jurgenson*) – the merging of material reality and digital technologies.

Augmented selves (*Jurgenson*) – self-identities combining physical and digital aspects or are developed through online and offline interaction.

Authoritarian personality – distinctive personality traits, including a demand for conformity and an inability to tolerate diversity or accept ambiguity. *Such personalities desire security, structure, and clear lines of authority.*

Authoritarianism – a political system that does not allow citizens to participate in government.

Authority – power attached to a position that others perceive as legitimate. *Power regarded as legitimate.*

Autocatalytic process – a positive feedback cycle between two variables (e.g., A and B) such that an increase in A causes an increase in B, which then causes a further increase in A. *An example of such a relationship is between the production and reproduction modes.*

Autocracy – rule or government concentrated by a single ruler or group willing to use force to maintain control.

Autocratic rule – authority by a specific leader who concentrates power.

Automation – the replacement of workers by machines and the monitoring and coordination of workers by machines with minimal human supervision. *Production processes are monitored and controlled by machines with only minimal supervision from people.*

B

Baby boom – the people born in the United States between 1946 and 1965. This group represented a sharp increase in birth rates and the absolute number of births compared to pre-1946 levels.

Back region (*Erving Goffman*) – an area away from *front region* performances, where individuals can relax and behave informally.

Balance of power – the theory that military conflict can be avoided if both sides have equivalent military power.

Base (*Marxism*) – the economic foundation of a society, including the relations and materials of production.

Beliefs – specific ideas that people feel to be true. *Shared ideas held collectively within a sociocultural system.*

Bias – a scientist's values and attitudes influence scientific observations and conclusions.

Bicultural – the capacity to understand and function well in multiple cultural groups.

Big data – a large amount of data generated by digital commerce and social media channels.

Biodiversity – the assortment of species of life forms on Earth.

Biographical research (*research methods*) – elicits individual lives or life histories as its primary focus. Involves oral histories, life stories, autobiographies, biographies, and more.

Bilateral kinship – tracing of descent through the mother and father (as in most of the Western world).

Bioethics – ethical questions relating to life and the biological well-being of the planet.

Biological determinism – the view that biology (nature, genetics) determines complex social behavior.

Biological drives – physiological needs for human survival, such as food, water, love and affection, and sex for reproduction.

Biological racism – *a* belief that certain racial or ethnic groups are superior based on intrinsic factors of biology.

Biopower (*Foucault*) – how modern nation-states regulate citizens' behaviors and life processes. *Biopower involves the control of the population through practices of public health, risk regulation, control of reproduction, etc.*

Bio-psychological constants – Marvin Harris's four predispositions, or drives, that all humans share: 1. the need for food, with a general preference for foods high in calories and proteins; 2. the need to conserve human energy; 3. the need for love and affection; and 4. the need for sexual expression. While these needs are universal, how a socio-cultural system satisfies them varies widely.

Bioterrorism – the threat or the actual dispersal of biological or chemical agents to cause widespread disease or death to further a group's political, economic, or social agenda.

Birmingham School – Centre for Contemporary Cultural Studies at the University of Birmingham in England: *Scholars have developed an approach to the sociological study of cultures and subcultures.*

Birth rate – the number of births per year per 1,000 women 15 to 44 years old.

Bisexual – an orientation of sexual activities or feelings towards other people of either sex.

Black-White Paradigm – studying race that only examines relationships between White and Black people rather than including non-Black people of color.

Black feminism – focuses on the experiences of Black women and the intersection of racial and gender inequality. Feminist thought highlights the multiple disadvantages of gender, class, and race that shape the experiences of non-white women. *Black feminists reject single unified gender oppression experienced by women and argue that early feminist analysis reflected the specific concerns of white, middle-class women.*

Black feminist thought – focuses on the assumptions and ideas of Black feminism.

Blackface – exaggerated stage makeup used to ridicule and subjugate African people and their descendants in comedy acts, plays, and movies. *Americans adopted these conventions in minstrels (racist musical acts and skits) in the early 1800s. Around the same time, blackface was imported to Australia, targeting Aboriginal and Torres Strait people, with instances continuing in the present day in racist "costumes" and popular culture acts and "satire."*

Blasé attitude (*Simmel*) – a detached attitude towards events and people required to navigate life in a city. A flatting and homogenization of spontaneity, unpredictability, and, ironically, individuality that the city appears to afford.

Blended family (or *stepfamily*) – consisting of two adults, both with children from previous relationships, plus their children.

Blue-collar – another term for the *working class.*

Body language – how bodies consciously and unconsciously communicate.

Bonding social capital – networks of similar individuals in some vital way. Bonding social capital typically unites people *within* some specific group.

Border thinking – draws on the perspectives, knowledge, and forms of expression marginalized by colonial domination and focuses on experiences, lives, and structures' intersections of different borders.

Bourgeoisie (*Marxism*) – the class which owns and controls the means of production within the capitalist system. Historically, the merchant class in feudal societies. Today, the term is a synonym for the middle class. The owners of the means of production (i.e., factories, businesses, and equipment) needed to produce wealth.

Bricolage – new cultural forms via combining, reworking, or altering existing cultural forms.

Bridging social capital – networks of people dissimilar in some vital way. Bridging social capital typically relates people within a group to those *outside* of this group.

Bureaucracy (*Weber*) – administrative organization characterized by hierarchy, chain of command, division of labor, formal procedures, and impersonal interaction. An organization of a hierarchical sort takes the form of a pyramid of authority. A type of formal organization uses a rational approach to handle large tasks. According to Weber, bureaucracy is the most efficient type of large-scale human organization. *As organizations grow, Weber argued, they inevitably tend to become increasingly bureaucratized.*

Bureaucratization – the third stage of a social movement, in which the social movement becomes an established organization, often with a formal hierarchy and paid staff. *Bureaucracies tend to refine their procedures to attain their goals more efficiently. More generally, the process of secondary organizations taking over functions performed by primary groups.* See *intensification* and *rationalization*.

C

Calling (or *vocation*) – employment or occupation someone is emotionally or morally drawn towards or to which they are exceptionally resolute, qualified, or well suited.

Calling – certain branches of ascetic Protestantism live acceptably to God by fulfilling the obligations imposed by one's secular position.

Canon – a collection of classic works considered especially important and influential.

Capital – any asset, including money, property, and machines, which produces commodities for sale or invested in a market to achieve a profit. *Money or other assets (e.g., land, buildings, machinery) used to start a business or develop it to produce wealth. Karl Marx titled his three-volume critical analysis of political economy Das Kapital.*

Capital punishment (or *death penalty*) – the state-sanctioned execution of a person convicted of a crime that is punishable by death.

Capitalism – a system of economic enterprise based on market exchange. The economic system in which the means of production are owned privately, and individuals are free to keep their profits. *An economic system in which the means of production are held privately and operated for profit. Private individuals accumulate and invest capital by owning the means of production and controlling profits. Common features of capitalist systems include private property, wage labor, competitive markets, and voluntary exchange.*

Capitalists – those who own companies, land, or stocks and shares, using these to generate economic returns.

Capitalist class (or *elite*) – in industrialized societies, the rich and powerful and the owners of the means of production. Those who own companies, or stocks and shares in companies, and use them to generate economic returns or profits.

Captive mind (*Alatas*) – a mode of thought in which the perspective of an external source is adopted in an uncritical and imitative manner. *Alatas proposes that the external source is Western social science and humanities.*

Carrying capacity – the population of a species that a particular ecosystem can support without suffering irreversible deterioration. A closed form of stratification in which an individual's status is determined by birth and cannot be changed. See *ecology*.

Cash-crop production – growing and harvesting crops for world markets rather than consumption by the local population.

Cash-nexus – defining human relationships in terms of monetary exchange.

Caste – social stratification in which an individual's social position is fixed at birth and cannot change. *Virtually no intermarriage between the members of different caste groups.*

Caste system – social stratification in which prestige and social relationships are based on hereditary position at birth. *A system of stratification based on ascribed statuses.*

Category – a collection of people who share a particular characteristic but have nothing else in common.

Cathedrals of consumption (*George Ritzer*) – commercial displays meant to inspire awe, wonder, and enchantment in the consumer, such as shopping centers, casinos, and sports stadiums.

Causal relationship – when one situation (the effect) is brought about by another (the cause).

Causation – the causal influence of one factor on another. Relationship in which a change in one variable (*independent variable*) induces a change in another (*dependent variable*). Causal factors in sociology include individual motivation and many external influences on human behavior that often go unrecognized. Causal factors in sociology include individuals' reasons for their actions and external influences on their behavior.

Census – a population count, often including a detailed population profile.

Centralization – power and authority concentrated in a few offices.

Centrally planned economy – an economic system that includes public ownership of or control over all productive resources and whose activity is planned by the government.

Charisma [*the gift of grace*] – the exceptional mystical or even supernatural quality of personality attributed to a person by others. *A personal quality attributed to leaders who arouse popular support and enthusiasm.*

Charismatic authority (*Weber*) – rests on the extraordinary characteristics of leaders attributed to them by followers. See *rational-legal authority* and *traditional authority*.

Charismatic leadership (*Weber*) – authority depends on the leader's charisma as experienced by the followers. *An individual enlisting strong emotional support from followers through personal and seemingly supernatural qualities. Charismatic leaders possess exceptional abilities or qualities, setting them apart from other individuals.*

Charter – the capacity of certain schools to confer special rights on their graduates.

Chronic disease – of long duration, often not detected in its initial stages, from which the patient will not recover. *Examples include high blood pressure and diabetes.*

Church – a formally organized, institutionalized religious organization with formal and traditional religious doctrine, beliefs, and practices. A religious group integrated with society. A large body of people belonging to an established religious organization. Churches typically have a formal structure, with a hierarchy of religious officials, and {also used for the building where their religious ceremonials are held.

Cisgender – *personal* identity and gender corresponds with their birth sex.

Citizen – a member of a state, having rights and duties associated with that membership.

Citizens United – a US Supreme Court decision (2010) that awarded labor unions and corporations the same First Amendment free speech protections as natural persons, allowing them to spend unlimited sums of money on advertising related to political campaigns.

City – a permanent settlement of many people who do not grow or gather food.

Civil disorder – social conflicts (such as riots) where the government becomes involved in restoring public order.

Civil law – addressing wrongs against the individual (e.g., torts and contracts).

Civil religion –(*Bellah*) –an institutionalized collection of beliefs with a quasi-religious or sacred character. Secular forms of ritual and belief like those involved in religion, such as political parades or ceremonies. *Interweaving religious and political symbols in public life.*

Civil rights – legal rights held by all citizens in a given state.

Civil society – a sector of society that lies outside of the state or the market.

Civilizations – distinct cultural groupings sharing foundational values, typically spanning several politically independent societies (e.g., *Western civilization*).

Civilizing process (*Elias*) – the long-term historical process by which manners and behavior became increasingly refined in European societies.

Clan – a broad extended kin group in many pre-industrial societies.

Class – categorizations of individuals based on economic status. Class members have been conceptualized as similar in wealth, occupational type, and lifestyle. Socio-economic differences between groups of individuals create differences in their life chances and power. Marx differentiates classes by their relationship to the mode of production (owner/non-owner). *Position in a social hierarchy based on prestige or property ownership.*

Class ceiling – barriers impeding upward class mobility.

Class consciousness – an objective awareness of the class system, including the common interests of people within one's class.

Class conflict – struggle between societal classes (e.g., socioeconomic classes) that engage in conflict theory. *The struggle between competing classes, specifically between the class that owns the means of production and the class or classes that do not.*

Class consciousness (*Karl Marx*) – recognition by workers of their unity as a social class in opposition to capitalists and capitalism. Awareness of one's class, interests, and relationship to the means of production. *The sense of common class position and shared interests held by members of a social class.*

Class system – a system of stratification based primarily on unequal ownership and control of economic resources. A multi-dimensional phenomenon in which populations are ranked by occupation, education, property, racial or ethnic status, age, and gender. Each of these dimensions is a class system. Gerhard Lenski (1966) states that a class system is "*a hierarchy of classes ranked in terms of a single criterion.*" Thus, "*working class*" is a particular class within the occupational class system; terms such as *African American*, *Latino*, or *French-Canadian* designate groups existing within a racial-ethnic class system. *Social stratification is based on individual achievement (i.e., status).*

Clerical worker – a low-prestige and low-paid white-collar worker who performs office tasks such as keeping files and checking forms.

Clergy – the middle stratum of the estate system of stratification, composed of Roman Catholic priests.

Climate change (or *global warming*) – changes in Earth's climate caused by the accumulation of gases in the atmosphere, especially carbon dioxide and methane, which absorb some of the sun's energy being reflected into space and radiate it in all directions, thus exacerbating the natural greenhouse effect and increasing Earth's temperature. See *greenhouse effect*.

Clique – an internal cluster or faction within a group.

Closed system – in organizational theory, the degree to which an organization is isolated from its environment.

Closet (*Sedgwick*) – *coming out of the closet* is a metaphor for power shaping sexuality in Global Northern societies and the limitations of a heterosexual and homosexual binary.

Coalescence – the second stage of a social movement, when people organize around issues.

Co-constituted – two processes or outcomes are co-creating or reinforcing each other. Structure and agency in sociology are not separate or opposed forces but structures enabling agency and agency recreating structures.

Coercion – social interaction in which one is made to do something through social pressure, threats, or force.

Cognition – human thought processes, including perceiving, reasoning, and remembering.

Cognitive ability – to think in abstract terms.

Cognitive development – the systematic improvement of intellectual ability through a series of stages.

Cognitive development theory – individuals try to pattern their lives and experiences to form a consistent picture of their beliefs, actions, and values.

Cohabitation – living in a sexual relationship permanence without being legally married.

Cohort – people sharing something in common (e.g., born in the same year or period).

Collective effervescence (*Durkheim*) – a feeling of excitement and group unity aroused by participating in communal gatherings and rituals.

Collective – groups of people that make up a society.

Collective action – social action undertaken spontaneously by many people.

Collective behavior –

Collective behavior – activities of people and social groups that emerge spontaneously (e.g., crowds and riots) rather than arising from processes of socialization leading to conformity to social rules and norms. *Spontaneous behavior shared by a large group that does not reflect social norms and structure (e.g., riots, mass hysteria, trends). Occurs in crowds and mobs when the usual norms are suspended.*

Collective conscience (*Durkheim*) – common beliefs and values that guide human behavior. *A conscience is necessary for maintaining social order.* Sometimes translated as *"collective consciousness."*

Collective violence – social behavior perpetuated by many people engaging as a mass.

Colonialism – a nation establishing political and economic rule over less powerful nations.

Colonialism – the process by which some nations enrich themselves through political and economic control of other countries. *The tendency for a powerful country to invade a weaker country to exploit its resources by making it a colony.*

Colonization – the process by which a nation establishes control over another territory or people, typically to prove economic benefits for the colonizer.

Color-line (*Du Bois*) – racial segregation, social and legal barriers separating people based on perceived race.

Coming out – the act of openly declaring oneself as gay.

Command economy (or *planned economy*) – an economic system in which government agencies plan investment, supply, prices, and the distribution of goods. *Examples include the former Soviet Union and contemporary North Korea.* See *market economy.*

Commercialization – the organization of an activity around the goal of making a profit.

Commitment – willingness of group members to do what is needed to maintain the group.

Commodification – the process by which goods and services previously exchanged through primary group ties come to be exchanged through the mechanisms of a market economy.

Commodity – equivalent goods (e.g., coffee beans) bought and sold.

Commodity chain – the raw material, production, and labor network responsible for the fashioning of a product. *These chains often span the globe, with some countries profiting from contributing to the chain and others being exploited.*

Commodity riot – the focus of violence is the destruction of property.

Communal riot – the target of violence is another group (usually based on race or ethnicity).

Communication – the transmission of information from one individual or group to another.

Communication technology – used to extend the transmission of information between individuals and groups over both distance and time. *Examples include language, writing, printing, telegraph, telephone, and the Internet. The development of such technology quickens and intensifies the pace of sociocultural change.*

Commoners – the lowest stratum of the estate system of stratification, composed of the masses of people who spent their lives engaged in hard physical labor.

Communism (*Marxist theory*) – a stateless society created in the wake of the revolution in which workers seize the forces of production. In this society, the forces of production will be fully developed, and goods and services distributed according to the needs of the people. *However, communism, as developed by Lenin and institutionalized throughout Eastern Europe (until 1990) and in China, bore little resemblance to Marx's vision. In such "communist" countries, the means of production and distribution were (and are) controlled by an authoritarian state with the expressed goal of industrial development and eventual creation of an egalitarian social order. An aspirational economic system like socialism in which all means of production are owned by everyone and all profits are shared equally. An economic and political system in which all members of a society are socially equal.*

Community – a social structure (including *culture*, *norms*, *values*, and *social status*). A collection of people in a geographical area may include the idea that the collection has a social structure and a sense of community spirit or belonging; follows a larger social structure. They may organize social life within a place, or a sense of belonging sustained across time and space. Communities are *imagined,* and *ideas* shape the meaning of communities.

Comparable worth (or *pay equity*) – the idea that jobs dominated by women and jobs dominated by men should be evaluated based on training, skills, and experience to equalize wages. The principle is that people should be paid equally for jobs of comparable worth. *A policy of equal pay for people doing similar work, even if the jobs are labeled differently by sex.*

Comparative and Historical Sociology (CHS) – a sociological research approach that involves studying current and historical patterns of behavior and transformative breaks in societal behavior.

Comparative research (*research methods*) – compares one set of findings on one society with the same findings on other societies.

Competition – a goal-directed social interaction in which the goals or objects pursued are limited, so not all competitors can attain them. *Competitive behavior is governed by rules and limitations (or restraints).*

Complementary marriages – when a husband and wife take distinctly separate family roles.

Concentrated Animal Feeding Operation (CAFO) – as defined by the US Environmental Protection Agency, an Animal Feeding Operation (AFO) is a facility that confines and feeds animals for forty-five days or more out of twelve months. Animals are not allowed to graze normally; feed is brought to them to fatten them before slaughter artificially. AFOs that exceed a specific size are formally assigned the "Concentrated" label by US government agencies if they confine more than 1,000 "animal units" (equivalent to 2,500 swine, 100,000 broiling chickens, 700 dairy cows, or 1,000 beef cattle). *Apart from their impact on the animals confined, these operations pose a serious environmental and public health hazard, chiefly because they produce millions of tons of manure each year and an array of other pollutants, which, if not responsibly managed, can threaten water quality.*

Concentric-zone theory – a theory of urban development holds that cities grow around a central business district in concentric zones, with each zone devoted to a different land use.

Concept – a formal definition of what is being studied. *Any abstract characteristic that can potentially be measured; mental construct representing part of the world, inevitably in a simplified form.*

Conflict – social interaction involving a direct struggle between individuals or groups over commonly valued resources or goals. A clash of interests (sometimes escalating to active struggle) between individuals, groups, or societies. *It differs from competition because individuals are more interested in defeating an opponent than achieving a goal.*

Conflict approach – one of the major theoretical perspectives in sociology: emphasizes the importance of unequal power and conflict in society. *Weberian conflict theorists* stress inequality and conflict based on class, status, and power; *Marxian theorists* emphasize conflict and inequality based on ownership of the means of production.

Conflict theories (*Karl Marx*) – analyses social phenomena by examining their role in creating or maintaining group power. A sociological perspective that focuses on the tensions, divisions, and competing interests in human societies. Conflict theorists believe that the scarcity and value of resources produce conflict as groups struggle to access and control resources. The writings of Marx have strongly influenced many conflict theorists. *Society exists due to the eternal struggle between those who have and need resources. In any capitalist society, there is an eternal conflict between the owners of the means of production and the workers.*

Conflict theory (*sociological theory*) – emphasizes the role of power, authority, and manipulation in sociocultural change and stability.

Conflict view of deviance – purports that equality in a capitalist society is an illusion. The owners of the means of production have a vested interest in maintaining the status quo by keeping the working class in a disadvantaged position.

Conformity – human behavior that follows the established norms of a group or society. Going along with the norms or behaviors of a group. Most human behavior conforms, as people accept and internalize their culture's or subculture's values. Conformity is one of the five modes of adaptation in Robert K. Merton's anomie theory. See *innovation, rebellion, retreatism*, and *ritualism*.

Conformists (*Merton's theory of goals and means*) – those who accept cultural goals and the institutionalized means of achieving them.

Conglomerate – a large corporation comprising separate companies producing or trading several products and services. A conglomerate is usually the result of a merger between companies or a takeover of one firm by another.

Conjugal family – a family organization centered around the husband-wife relationship rather than around blood relationships.

Consensus – agreement on fundamental social values by a group or society members.

Consolidated Metropolitan Statistical Area (CMSA) – a supercity with more than one million people. *There were 181 such cities in the United States in 2023.*

303

Conspicuous consumption (*Thorstein Veblen*) – the idea that many people consume goods and services to display their wealth, status, and taste publicly. Spending money on goods or services primarily designed to signal status, taste, and economic power.

Constitutional government – a system constrained by a written document that defines the organizational structure of that government and sets forth the authority and rules of conduct of the various offices within that structure.

Constitutional monarchy – the reigning royal family member is the symbolic head of state, but elected officials govern.

Consumerism – philosophy of seeking happiness through the consumption of goods and services. An extension of symbolic interaction theory, which proposes that reality is what humans cognitively construct it to be.

Consumer society – promotes mass-produced product consumption. Consumer societies also generate an ideology of consumerism, which assumes that ever-increasing mass consumption is beneficial.

Consumption – the utilization of goods or services.

Contact hypothesis – people of different racial groups who became acquainted are less prejudiced toward one another.

Contagion theory (*Bon*) – the anonymity people feel in a crowd makes them susceptible to the suggestions of fanatical leaders, and emotions can sweep through such a crowd. *The idea that individuals in crowds are suggestible and take on a single way of acting.*

Content analysis – a research method used to describe and analyze objectively and systematically the content of literature, speeches, or other media presentations. Cultural meanings through artifacts such as books, documents, songs, and other communication products. *The method helps identify cultural themes or trends.*

Content of socialization – the ideas, beliefs, values, knowledge, and so forth presented to people being socialized.

Contest mobility – the educational pattern in which selection for academic and university education is delayed and children compete throughout their schooling for high positions.

Context of socialization – the setting or arena within which socialization occurs.

Contingent inclusion – how racial minorities become included in communities based on other characteristics.

Contingency work – temporary, part-time, or contracted employment for the duration of a project. Contingency work is one of the fastest-growing employment sectors in many industrialized countries. *It enables employers to expand and contract their workforce with the vagaries of the market and avoid costly fringe benefits and other commitments related to long-term employment.*

Continued subjugation – using force and ideology by one group to retain domination.

Contradiction (*Marxism*) – mutually antagonistic tendencies within an institution or broader society, such as between profit and competition within capitalism.

Contradictory class location – a position in the class structure that shares characteristics of the class positions above and below. *The classic position would be a supervisor in a factory or a department chair in academics.*

Control group – a group not exposed to the independent variable of interest to a researcher but whose members' backgrounds and experience are otherwise like those of the experimental group exposed to the independent variable.

Control theory (*Walter Reckless*) – posits that when a person is tempted to engage in deviance, inner controls and outer controls can prevent him or her from doing so.

Controlling for (*research design*) – the effort to hold constant factors that might influence observed changes in the dependent variable.

Convenience sample (*research methods*) – the arbitrary selection of respondents for a study based on simple opportunity rather than a rigorous quest for representativeness and used in much applied social research with practical applications.

Convergence theory – modernizing nations resemble one another over time. *In collective behavior, a theory suggests that certain crowds attract people who may behave irrationally.*

Conversation analysis (*research methods*) – the empirical study of conversations, employing techniques drawn from ethnomethodology. *Conversation analysis examines details of naturally occurring conversations to reveal the organizational principles of talk and its role in the production and reproduction of social order.*

Convivial culture (*Gilroy*) – the lively, friendly interaction between different racial groups.

Cooperation – social interaction involving collaborative effort to achieve a common goal.

Cooptation – a social process by which people who might otherwise threaten an organization's stability are brought into the organization's leadership or policy-making structure.

Core country – occupies a central position on the world stage, such as the advanced industrial societies of North America, Western Europe, and Japan. *According to world-systems theory, the most advanced industrial countries take the lion's share of profits in the world economic system.* See *peripheral countries* and *semi-peripheral countries*.

Corporate crime – criminal or deviant behavior committed by a corporation. Offenses committed by large corporations in society. *Examples of corporate crime include pollution, false advertising, and health and safety regulations violations.*

Corporate culture – a branch of management theory that seeks to increase productivity and competitiveness by creating a unique organizational culture involving firm members. *A dynamic corporate culture - involving company events, rituals, and traditions - is thought to enhance employee loyalty and promote group solidarity.*

Corporation – a legally recognized organization set up for profit in which the powers and liabilities of the organization are legally separate from the owners or the employees. In the United States, corporations have the same legal status as a person. See *Citizens United.*

Correlation (*statistics*) – a relationship between two variables that vary. *For example, a correlation between parents' income and reading ability among primary school children. Statistical correlation can vary from –1 to 1. (Zero indicates no correlation between the variables.) A positive correlation between two variables exists where a high score on one is associated with a high score on the other; a negative correlation exists where a high score on one variable is associated with a low score on the other.*

An observed association between a value change in one variable and another. A regular relationship between two dimensions or variables, often expressed in statistical terms. Correlations may be positive or negative.

> *Positive correlation* between two variables exists where a high rank on one variable is regularly associated with a high rank on the other.

> *Negative correlation* exists where a high rank on one variable is regularly associated with a low rank on the other.

Correlation coefficient – a measure of the degree of correlation between two variables.

Cost-benefit decision-making – based on analyzing and weighing a decision's benefits against the associated costs.

Counterculture – a subculture whose norms and values sharply contradict the dominant norms and values of the society in which it occurs. *Cultural patterns opposed to the dominant cultural patterns of a society. A way of living that opposes the dominant culture.*

Coup d'état – an armed government takeover by a small group of conspirators, often military officers. See *rebellion* and *revolution.*

Craftsman (or *artisan*) – a skilled manual worker.

Created environment – human constructions such as buildings, roads, factories, and private homes.

Creationism – a theory that sees all major types of living things, including people, as having been made by the direct creative action of God in six days.

Creative destruction – a revolutionary process of capitalism described by Joseph Schumpeter in which innovative technologies and industries incessantly destroy old ones, causing great turmoil in the economy.

Credential – the educational degree or certificate used to determine a person's eligibility for a position.

Credentialism – the tendency for jobs to require increasingly formal education, even though the skill or knowledge requirements for the job have not changed.

Crime – any action that contravenes the laws established by a political authority. *The violation of a written law. A behavior prohibited by law.*

Crime against the person – an act of violence either threatened or perpetrated against a person.

Crime against property – the theft of property or damage to another's property.

Criminal law – enacted by recognized political authorities that prohibits or requires certain behaviors.

Criminology – a social science discipline focusing on crime and the criminal justice system.

Crip theory – an approach playing on the term *cripple*, reclaimed by the disability rights movement. Crip theory resists able-bodied heteronormativity as a taken-for-granted ideal.

Crisis medicine (or *curative medicine*) – medical treatment focusing on curing illness rather than preventing it.

Criteria for inferring causality – evidence that two variables are correlated. *The hypothesized cause preceded the effect in time, and that evidence eliminates rival hypotheses.*

Critical theory – explicitly concerned with discovering and critiquing social injustices.

Cross tabulation (or *crosstabs*) – a table illustrating the relationship between two variables, such as sex (male and female) and years of education.

Crowd – a temporary gathering of people with a common focus of attention and whose members influences one another.

Crude birth rate – statistical measure representing the number of live births per year for every thousand people in a population.

Crude death rate – the number of deaths yearly for every thousand people in a population.

Cult – an organized group acting out religious feelings, attitudes, and relationships that may focus on unusual worship or belief. A fragmentary religious group that lacks permanent structure. *A religious organization outside a society's cultural traditions.*

Cultural appropriation – the adoption of elements in one culture, typically a minority culture, by another culture, typically a dominant culture. *Cultural appropriation is typically seen as negative when cultural elements are misused or divorced from their original meaning.*

Cultural capital (*Bourdieu*) – non-economic resources allow one to advance one's position in a field. Such resources include dispositions, tastes, behaviors, credentials, and skills. *Types of knowledge, skills, and education confer advantages to those who acquire them. Cultural capital can be embodied (in forms of speech or bodily comportment), objectified (in cultural products such as works of art), or institutionalized (in educational qualifications).*

Cultural change – modifications or transformations of a culture's customs, values, ideas, or artifacts.

Cultural determinism – society's nature is shaped primarily by the ideas and values of the people living in it.

Cultural diffusion – the process whereby an aspect of culture spreads throughout or from one culture to another. *Transmission of cultural elements between sociocultural systems.*

Cultural division of labor – when a person's place in the occupational world is determined by cultural markers (e.g., ethnicity).

Cultural dupes – criticize theories treating individuals as blind followers or consumers of cultural trends or products. Such theories are thought to see individuals as cultural dupes.

Cultural identity – one's sense of belonging to a cultural group.

Cultural imperialism – the process by which one society's culture, values, and norms are imposed on another. *Typically used for global dominance of Western culture and ideals.*

Cultural imposition – forcing members of one culture to adopt the practices of another.

Cultural integration – the close relationship among various elements of a cultural system

Cultural interface (*Nakata*) – cross-cultural interactions are '*layered and very complex entanglement of concepts, theories, and sets of meanings of a knowledge system.*' Relates to Indigenous people's complex lives and social connections across cultural formations.

Cultural lag – a dysfunction in the sociocultural system that results when a change occurs in one part of the system, but another part fails to adjust. Failure often causes conflict until adjustment is made. *An example is the engagement of married women in outside employment and the continuance of the traditional domestic division of labor. Cultural elements change at different rates and may disrupt a cultural system.*

Cultural materialism – a macro social theory that attempts to account for the similarities and differences between sociocultural systems by focusing on the environmental constraints to which human action is subject.

Cultural pluralism – 1. the peaceful coexistence of multiple subcultures within a society. 2. the coexistence of several subcultures within a society on equal terms.

Cultural racism – a belief that the culture of one 'race' or ethnic group is superior. Cultural racism typically involves the belief that certain ethnic cultures are fundamentally incompatible. Contrast *multiculturalism*.

Cultural relativity – judging culture by that culture's standards rather than ours. Rather than thinking other people's customs are strange or threatening, understand that this behavior makes sense for people with local history and social context. Contrast *ethnocentricity*.

Cultural relativism – judging a culture by its standards. The idea that a cultural item can be judged or understood only in relationship to the entire culture in which it is embedded. The attitude that to understand the traits of another culture, one must view them within the context of that culture.

Cultural reproduction – the process by which a society transmits dominant knowledge from one generation to another.

Cultural revolution – repudiation of existing cultural elements and substituting of new ones.

Cultural sociology – interpreting meanings and significance of cultural forms and patterns.

Cultural superstructure (*sociocultural materialism*) – the shared symbolic universe within a sociocultural system, including such components as art, music, dance, rituals, sports, hobbies, and accumulated knowledge base. See *mental superstructure* and *superstructure*.

Cultural transmission – the socialization process whereby individuals internalize the norms and values of the group. *The process by which one generation passes culture to the next.*

Cultural universals – features (e.g., use of language) shared by human societies. *Traits that are part of every known culture.*

Culture – the common heritage shared by the people of a society, consisting of customs, values, language, ideas, and artifacts. The values, ceremonies, and ways of life characteristic of a group. Like the concept of society, the notion of culture is widely used in sociology and social sciences (particularly anthropology). *Social practices, materials, and symbols guide human interaction and shape our sense of meaning. It includes language, dress, values, and way of life. Beliefs, values, behavior, and material objects constitute a people's way of life. Everything made, learned, and shared by members of society. Culture is one of the most distinctive properties of human social association.*

Culture industry (*Adorno and Horkheimer*) – how popular culture in capitalist societies is produced in an industrial, standardized manner. *For Adorno and Horkheimer, the culture industry products promote docility and passivity in citizens.*

Culture lag – the time difference between introducing material innovations and resulting changes in cultural practices. *The tendency for changes in material culture to occur at a more rapid rate than changes in nonmaterial culture.*

Culture pattern theory (*sociology of sports*) – explains aggression and violence in sports as learned behavior that mirrors the degree of aggression and violence in society.

Culture of poverty (*Oscar Lewis*) – a social theory proposing that the economically disadvantaged have a different value system contributing to their poverty. As poor children are socialized into this value system, the inability to escape poverty is perpetuated. The idea that poor people do not learn the norms and values that can help them improve their circumstances and hence get trapped in a repeated pattern of poverty. *A distinctive culture thought to develop among poor people and characterized by failure to delay gratification, fatalism, and weak family and community ties.*

Culture shock – disorientation resulting from experiencing a new and different culture or rapid social change in one's culture. Personal disorientation from encountering an unfamiliar way of life. *The surprise, disorientation, and fear people experience when encountering a different culture.*

Cumulative change – a distinctive change associated with complex systems composed of multiple, interrelated parts. Within these systems, some parts change, while others remain unchanged. *Cumulative change combines elements of continuity with elements of change: many parts of the system persist for extended periods while new parts are added, and others are replaced or transformed. Evolutionary change tends to be cumulative.*

Curative medicine (or *crisis medicine*) – medical treatment focusing on curing illness rather than preventing it.

Custodial care – health care, which focuses on the institution's needs (e.g., convenience and efficiency) rather than the patient's needs.

Cybercrime – criminal activities using electronic networks or new information technologies. Electronic money laundering, personal identity theft, electronic vandalism, and monitoring of electronic correspondence are all emergent forms of cybercrime.

Cyberspace – electronic network of interaction between individuals at different computer terminals, linking people at a level (and in a dimension) without regard for territorial boundaries or physical presence.

Cyberterrorism – the threat of hacking or hacking into computer networks causes widespread disruption to further a group's political, economic, or social agenda.

Cyborg – an entity fusing elements of humans and machines.

Cyclical theories – suggest that societies follow a particular life course, from vigorous and innovative youth to more materialistic maturity and then to decline.

D

Data (*research methods*) – a collection of observations gained through *methods*. Systematically measured information. With data, *theories* are developed or tested.

Data analysis – the organization of data to detect patterns and uniformities.

Decline – the final stage of a social movement when change is successfully brought about or resisted or when the movement fails due to repression, co-optation, or a lack of support.

Deduction – reasoning from the general to the specific.

Deductive reasoning – the process of reasoning from general theory to specific hypotheses. See *inductive reasoning* and *generalization*.

***De facto* segregation** – separating social groups not by law but in observed reality (i.e., as a matter of fact). Housing patterns in North America often reflect de facto segregation. See *de jure segregation*.

Defensive medicine – the healthcare practice of ordering multiple medical tests as a precaution against overlooking a condition, thus opening the physician up for a lawsuit.

Defining the situation – the socially created perspective people apply to a phenomenon.

Deforestation – the destruction of forested land, often by commercial logging. Removal of trees from an area. See *depletion*, *desertification*, and *environment*.

Degradation ceremony (*Garfinkel*) – the process whereby an individual with a spoiled identity is expelled from a group and stripped of his or her membership.

Dehumanization – depriving people of their human qualities; treating people like animals or things, as if they have no feelings or intrinsic dignity or worth.

Deindustrialization – the loss of manufacturing capacity.

Deinstitutionalization – moving people with a mental health condition out of hospitals and into communities.

***De jure* segregation** – the separation of social groups by law. See *de facto segregation*.

Democracy – a political system in which the people exercise power. A form of government that recognizes the right of citizens to participate directly in political decision-making or to elect representatives to government bodies. *A political system in which citizens periodically choose officials to run their government.*

Democratic-collective organization – when authority is placed in the group, rules are minimized, members have considerable control over their work, and job differentiation is minimized.

Democratic socialism – an economic and political system combining significant government control of the economy with free elections.

Demographic transition – stabilizing the population level in an industrial society once economic prosperity has been reached. *Population is thought to stabilize because of economic incentives for families to limit the number of children.* For example, the demographic change experienced in Western Europe and North America since the Industrial Revolution in which the birth rate has declined so that it is about equal to the death rate.

Demographic transition theory – linking population patterns to a society's level of technological development. *An interpretation of population changes holds that a stable ratio of births to deaths is achieved once economic prosperity has been reached.*

311

Demography – the scientific study of human populations, including size, composition, distribution, and patterns of change in those features. The study of the characteristics of human populations, including their size, composition, and dynamics.

Denomination – a religious sect that has lost its revivalist dynamism and has become an institutionalized body, commanding the adherence of significant numbers of people. One of several religious organizations in a society with no official state church, it has some formal doctrines, beliefs, and practices but tolerates diverse religious views. *A church independent of the state that accepts religious pluralism.*

Dependency theory (*Marxism*) – social development linked to unequal power relationships between a *periphery* of poor and *core* wealthy states, and the latter had developed at the expense of the former. Arose in opposition to modernization theory. Economic development argues that poverty in low-income countries stems directly from exploitation by wealthy countries and transnational corporations based in wealthy countries. *A model of economic and social development that explains global inequality from the historically exploiting poor societies by rich ones.*

Dependent variable (*research methods*) – occurs or changes in a patterned way due to the presence of, or changes in, another variable or variables. A variable, or factor, causally influenced by another (the independent variable). A variable that another (independent) variable changes.

Descent – the system by which members of a society trace kinship over generations.

Density (or *population density*) – the number of people living in each area. This is usually measured by the number of people per square kilometer or square mile.

Dependency theory – the thesis that many countries of the Global South cannot control major aspects of their economic life because of the dominance of industrialized societies, which allows core nations to exploit peripheral nations in economic relationships.

Dependent variable (*research hypotheses*) – a value expected to vary following variations in another factor. *In the predicted relationship between education and income, for example, the level of income (the dependent variable) is thought to depend in part on the level of education (the independent variable).* See *independent variable.*

Depletion – the use of natural resources beyond sustainable limits. *The sustainable use limit is equivalent to their replacement rate for renewable resources like water and trees. In the case of non-renewable resources, such as fossil fuels, the final limit depends on the total amount of these resources available on the planet, our ability to access these resources, and the rate at which we consume them. These limits can be inferred based on existing knowledge and use patterns and can often be stretched (although not eliminated) through technological advances, conservation, and recycling.* See *intensification* and *pollution.*

Deregulation – the freeing of corporations from legal constraints. In the past, such constraints had a much more significant role in protecting the environment, workers, and consumers from exploitation. Deregulation advocates argue that such regulations are costly and ineffective and that corporations can self-regulate.

Descriptive study (*research methods*) – describes the social phenomena being studied.

Desertification – the process of a fertile region being rendered barren by the activities of human societies. Intense land degradation resulting in desert-like conditions over large areas. See *depletion* and *pollution*.

Deskilling – the process through which workers' skills are downgraded or, over time, eliminated and taken over by machines or managers. *Breaking down jobs into less complex segments that require less knowledge and judgment on the part of workers.*

Detailed division of labor (or *manufacturing division of labor*) – the breakdown of product manufacturing into simple discrete steps, with each task assigned to an individual worker. Because it leads to greater productivity, the detailed division of labor is also increasingly applied to service, administrative, and professional occupations. See *division of labor*.

Deterrence theory – armaments can prevent military conflict. It is based on ensuring that a potential aggressor would suffer too many losses to make the initiation of hostilities worthwhile. The view that certain qualities of punishment (i.e., certainty, swiftness, and severity) help prevent others from committing crimes that have been so punished. *Mutually assured destruction* (MAD) was based on this theory.

Determinism –individual action is determined (or constrained) by outside forces.

Deviance (or *deviant behavior*) – behavior that does not conform to significant norms most group members or society hold. Behavior that does not conform to social norms. A violation of a norm. *What is regarded as deviant is variable across societies.*

Deviant behavior – see *deviance.*

Deviant career – the regular pursuit of activities regarded by the individual and others as deviant.

Deviant community – a group organized explicitly around a form of social deviance.

Deviant identity – a person's self-identification as deviant.

Deviant subculture – a subculture whose members have values and norms that differ substantially from those of the majority. *A way of living that differs from the dominant culture in which members share a particular form of deviance.*

Dialectic – an interpretation of change that emphasizes the clash of opposing interests and the resulting struggle as an engine of social transformation.

Diaspora – a community living outside their shared country or region of ancestral origin. The dispersal of an ethnic population from an original homeland into foreign areas, often in a forced manner or under traumatic circumstances.

Dictatorship – a government in which one person exercises supreme power and authority.

Differential association (*Edwin Sutherland*) – posits that deviance is learned behavior. *A theory of crime and delinquency holds that deviance is learned because of long-term interaction with others. Attributes deviant behavior to learning from friends or associates.*

Differentiation – the development of increasing complexity and division of labor within sociocultural systems.

Differentiation, functional – the division of labor or of social roles within a society or an organization.

Differentiation, rank – the unequal placement and evaluation of various social positions.

Diffusion – the voluntary spread of inventions and discoveries from one group to another; a source of cultural change. Spread of cultural traits from one sociocultural system to another.

Disability studies – investigates the position of disabled people in societies, including the experiences, history, and campaigns of disabled people and their organizations.

Disciplinary power (*Foucault*) – power characteristic of modern societies in which social control is maintained using surveillance, socialization, and the instilling of routines and disciplines on the body.

Discourse (*Foucault*) – sets of widely accepted norms or ways of thinking about topics taken for granted in a particular period or locale.

Discovery – uncovering something that existed but was unknown, a source of cultural change.

Discrimination – unfair treatment of an individual or group based on their characteristics. Activities that deny the members of a particular group resources or rewards that others can obtain. *Treating others unequally due to social background. This is an exercise of power by dominant groups who impede the social mobility or progress of minorities, such as by denying children fair and equal access to education or deciding not to hire minority women due to racial and gender bias.*

Disenchantment (*Weber*) – change by which individuals develop a more rational, scientific understanding of the world. *Disenchantment is associated with the devaluation of religious ideas and practices. The retreat of mysticism (i.e., belief in the supernatural) and awe from social life, with these elements being replaced by secular values, rationality, and scientific understanding.*

Disgusted subject (*Lawler*) – a gendered and classed self-definition through condescension and even disgust towards those who cannot maintain middle-class feminized ways of acting.

Disintegration – the weakening of the social bond within a society. *Disintegration allows various groups to fragment and break away from the whole.*

Disneyfication – the process whereby something (such as religion) is transformed into a diluted or simplified, trivialized, and sanitized version of its original form to create an inoffensive neutral product.

Disorganization – the disturbance of a system from a state of order and predictability to chaos and unpredictability.

Displacement – transferring ideas or emotions from their source to another object.

Disruptive power (*Piven*) – political influence based on disruptive actions (e.g., strikes, boycotts, and sit-ins).

Distinctions (*Bourdieu*) – how groups differentiate themselves from others, typically to establish superiority.

Diversity – encompasses three distinct concepts: *equity*, *access*, and *inclusion*.

Divine right of kings – an ideology developed by the nobility during the Middle Ages that posited that the authority of the nobility came directly from God.

Division of labor – separation of tasks in a productive system. Work is separated into several parts or roles dispersed throughout society, generally divided into the division of labor in *manufacture* (i.e., specialization within organizations or manufactories) and division of labor in *society* (i.e., an increase in occupational distinctions). *The specialization of work tasks or occupations and interrelationships. All societies have some division of labor based on age and sex. However, with the development of industrialism, the division of labor becomes far more complex, affecting many parts of the sociocultural system. The division of labor is the most underrated concept in sociology.* See *detailed division of labor*.

Docile bodies (*Foucault*) – individuals who have internalized disciplinary power or been trained to behave in ways that preserve and maintain the present social order.

Documentary research (*research methods*) – the study of written texts, including personal diaries, government policies, fictional works, and mass media output.

Domestication – a process of human selection of successive generations of animals or plants for desirable characteristics such as size, taste, or ease of care. *This process eventually alters animals and plants at the genetic level.*

Domestic economy – in the cultural materialism of Marvin Harris, the structural components of sociocultural systems are organized around primary production, exchange, and consumption within domestic settings (e.g., houses, camps, families, and small communities).

Domestic labor (or *housework*) – unpaid work done in and around the home, such as cooking, cleaning, and shopping. Studies show that most of this labor is carried out by women despite the predominance of dual-income families.

Domestic violence – behavior directed by one household member against another.

Dominant culture – beliefs and values of the dominant group within a sociocultural system. *Held by the majority or most powerful group in society.*

Dominant status – one social position overshadowing an individual's other social position.

Domination – the control of one group or individual by another.

Double consciousness (*Du Bois*) – a feeling of internal conflict and estrangement arising from oppression. Double consciousness occurs when one's identity is bifurcated into distinct sets of thoughts, strivings, and ideals, which the individual struggles to reconcile. *Coined by Du Bois, it was used when referencing African Americans' experiences.*

Double standard – a set of social norms allows one group greater freedom (e.g., sexual expression, particularly before marriage) than another group. *Code of behavior restrictive based on some factors.*

Doubling time (*populations*) – when the population doubles. A reasonably accurate doubling time estimate can be computed by taking the annual growth rate and dividing it by seventy. At 2 percent annual growth, the world population (5.5 billion in 1996) will double in size (to 11 billion) in about thirty-five years (2031), assuming the annual growth stays constant. See *exponential growth.*

Dramaturgical model – a sociological perspective that sees the social world as a stage, with all the people playing their roles in the social order.

Dramaturgy (*Erving Goffman's concept of dramaturgy*) – life is like a never-ending play in which people are actors. The process of analyzing people's day–to–day interactions as if they were actors on the stage. *Likens social behavior to a dramatic performance.*

Dramaturgical analysis (*Erving Goffman*) – an approach to social interactions examined as theatrical productions. *Studying social interaction based on theatrical metaphors.*

Dual-career families – when both spouses are in the outside labor force.

Dual-career responsibilities – the responsibilities of wives and workers used to explain why women earn less.

Dual economy – the conceptual division of the economy's private sector into monopoly (*core*) and competitive (*periphery*) sectors.

Dual labor market – the hypothesis that people have differential earnings because they work in distinct parts of the labor market. *For example, men dominate the field of engineering (high pay, high prestige), while women dominate the field of social work (low pay, low prestige).*

Dual welfare system – includes disguised forms of welfare that go to the middle class and the rich. See *welfare.*

Dyad – a group composed of two people.

Dynamic equilibrium – a stable state in which all parts of a healthy society work together.

Dysfunction – social patterns with undesirable consequences for society. A part of the sociocultural system that has a negative impact (or harmful effect) on other parts of the system or the system. *Features of social life that challenge or create tensions in a social system. Any consequence of a social system that disturbs or hinders the integration, adjustment, or stability of the system.*

E

Eating the other – popular culture portraying Black and Indigenous cultures as primitive, exotic, uncivilized, violent, and threatening. Addresses how popular culture repackages and exploits Indigenous religions in reductionist and insensitive ways.

Eclecticism – a conceptual approach that lacks commitment to a single paradigm or theoretical strategy. Eclectics draw upon multiple theories (sometimes contradictory in their assumptions) to explain physical, biological, or social phenomena.

Ecological-evolutionary theory – sociocultural systems stress their origin, maintenance, and change by focusing on the relationships of the system to their social and physical environments.

Ecological paradigm – a theory of land use and living patterns that examines the interplay among economic functions, geographical factors, demography, and the replacement of one group by another.

Ecological succession (*urban sociology*) – the replacement of one group by another over time.

Ecological view – studying culture or social phenomena by emphasizing the importance of examining climate, food and water supplies, and existing enemies in the environment.

Ecology – studying the system of relationships between organisms and their environment. *Studies how organisms relate to one another and their environments.*

Economic core (or *monopoly sector*) – characterized by large, very profitable, oligopolistic national or multinational firms.

Economic growth – an increase in the amount of goods and services produced with the same labor and resources.

Economic institution – the pattern of roles, norms, and activities organized around a society's production, distribution, and consumption of goods and services.

Economic interdependence – the outcome of specialization and the division of labor when self-sufficiency is superseded, and individuals depend on others to produce many or most of the goods they need to sustain their lives. Individuals depend on others to produce most of the goods needed to sustain life. Auguste Comte and Durkheim note that economic interdependence is greater in societies with a high division of labor.

Economic periphery (*competitive sector*) – characterized by small, local, marginally profitable firms.

Economic power (*Mann*) – power derived from satisfying human needs through resource production, distribution, exchange, and consumption.

Economic surplus (*Gerhard Lenski*) – the amount of goods and services produced in a sociocultural system over and above what is needed to keep productive classes alive and industrious.

Economic system – management of a society's goods and services through a social institution; examples include capitalism and socialism.

Economy – the system of production and exchange providing for the material needs of individuals in each society. *The organization of production and distribution of goods and services within a sociocultural system. Institution responsible for producing and distributing goods and services.*

Ecosystem – a system formed by interacting a community of organisms with its environment. *A self-sustaining community of plants and animals within a natural environment.*

Education – the transmission of knowledge to members of society. The knowledge passed on comprises technical and cultural knowledge, technical and social skills, and the norms and values of society. The process, in school or beyond, of transmitting a society's knowledge, skills, values, and behaviors. A social institution promoting and enabling the transmission of knowledge and skills across generations. *Institutions responsible for preparing young people for a functional place in adult life and transmitting culture between generations.*

Education system – formalized transmission of knowledge and values within a society.

Educational deflation – the devaluing of education because of the forces of supply and demand.

Egalitarian family – when both partners equally share power.

Egalitarian marriage – a family with spouses sharing equally in family decision-making.

Ego (*Freudian theory*) – a concept referring to the conscious, rational part of the personality structure, which mediates between the impulses of the id and the rules of society. *The part of the self that represents reason and common sense. The part of the mind that resolves conflicts between the id and the superego.*

Egoistic suicide (*Durkheim*) – suicide performed by an individual who has not sufficiently integrated into the social order.

Elder abuse – acts of violence or neglect directed at the elderly, often by family members.

Elderly dependency ratio – the mathematical relationship between the number of elderly (i.e., 65 and over) and working-aged people (i.e., 18 to 64).

Elective affinity – a relationship between cultural elements in which each reinforces, supports, or affirms the other.

Elite – people occupying the highest positions of the dominant institutions of a society and who consequently hold enormous power. See *power elite*.

Elite crime – criminal behavior of elites as their regular activity, such as evading taxes, hiring illegal immigrants as domestics, or engaging in insider trading.

Elitist – attitudes that some are better than others and have a right to the extraordinary privilege, power, and wealth accorded them. Alternatively, one subscribes to the theory that, by their placement at the top of highly centralized and enlarged bureaucracies, a small, powerful elite can effectively control an advanced industrial society.

Emancipatory movement – concerned with freeing groups from oppression, discrimination, and exploitation.

Embodiment – how social influences manifest in bodily dispositions and behaviors.

Emergence – the first stage of a social movement, in which the movement begins to form around a particular issue or source of inspiration. *Movements in this stage have little organization; instead, their feelings of discontent begin to crystallize.*

Emergent norm theory – collective behavior suggesting that people form a shared definition of situations in typical circumstances.

Emigration – the movement of people from their native land to other countries.

Emotion work – an individual's effort to change an emotion or feeling to one that seems more appropriate to a given situation.

Emotional labor – managing the feelings or emotions of the customer and worker.

Empathy – the ability to understand and help others leads to positive social interactions.

Emphasized femininity – idealized norms about female behavior, encouraging women to conform to men's needs and desires. *Emphasized femininity encourages traits like submissiveness, attractiveness, and sexual availability.*

Empire – a group of states under a single government.

Empirical – data or facts based on systematic observation or measurement.

Empiricism – a philosophy that knowledge comes from observation and experience.

Encoding and decoding (*Stuart Hall*) – a communication model. *Encoding* is the production of a message in which a sender attempts to convey information via symbols, gestures, and other means. *Decoding* is the recipient's attempt to reconstruct the message's meaning or interpret what the sender intended to convey with the chosen means.

Encounter – a meeting between individuals in a situation of face-to-face interaction.

Endogamy – the forbidding of marriage or sexual relations outside one's social group. A system in which individuals may only marry within their social group. *Marriage between members of the same category, class, or group.*

Enlightenment – the seventeenth- and eighteenth-century European philosophical and cultural movement with great faith in science and human reason in dealing with social issues.

Entrepreneur – a person who starts or organizes a business. Someone who starts or owns a business venture and takes personal responsibility for the risks involved and the potential rewards gained.

Entropy – gradual decline into disorder. The entropy law, or the second law of thermodynamics, states that energy can only be transformed from ordered to disordered in one direction.

Environment – the physical, biological, and chemical constraints to which action is subject.

Environmentalism – a concern with preserving the physical environment in the face of the impact of industrialism.

Epidemiology – studying biological, social, and economic factors associated with disease and health.

Epistemology – the theory and study of knowledge, including what can be known and how.

Equality of opportunity – individuals competing on the same terms (i.e., *level playing field*).

Equilibrium (*functionalist theory*) – the view that society's parts fit into a balanced whole.

Equity – barriers, issues, and solutions to structural disadvantages.

Essentialism – group members possess intrinsic and essential traits that make them members.

Estate system – the three-tiered stratification system used during the Middle Ages.

Estates – the three groups into which the population in medieval Europe was divided: the *First Estate* comprised the clergy; the *Second Estate*, the nobility; and the *Third Estate*, everyone else (or *commoners*).

Estate system – a form of stratification established by law in which land ownership monopolizes power.

Ethnic group – people who share a cultural identity, separating them from other groups around them.

Ethnic group – a group that shares a common cultural tradition and sense of identity.

Ethnicity – one's ethnic group, cultural values, and norms distinguish group members from others. An ethnic group is one whose members share a distinct awareness of a common cultural identity, separating them from other groups around them. *Shared values, cultural practices, and ideas distinguish one group from another. Aspects of ethnicity include rituals, religious beliefs, languages, social norms, etc. A cohesive community with a shared language, religion, race, culture, customs, and place of origin.*

Ethnocentrism – judging cultures by standards, values, and ideas that are culturally familiar. The tendency to judge other cultures by the standards of one's own culture, often with the feeling that one's own is superior. Seeing one's culture as superior. *Ethnocentrism occurs when one evaluates the world from one's cultural perspective and ignores the perspectives of others. The tendency to judge another culture by the standards of one's culture.*

Ethnocentricity – judging culture by self-standards rather than considering other people's cultural practices within that specific culture, values, and norms. Contrast *cultural relativity.*

Ethnography – a qualitative mode of inquiry that studies systematic descriptions of cultural systems, social groups, or organizations based on direct observation. Studying people firsthand using participant observation or interviewing. A detailed study based on actual observation of the way of life of a human group or society. *Studying a specific group by immersing them in their culture and observing their lives.*

Ethnomethodology (*Garfinkel*) – the study of the methods used by individuals to communicate and make sense of their everyday lives as members of society. *Many ethnomethodologists focus on the study of language and everyday conversation. The study of how people negotiate and make sense of their daily lives. A theoretical perspective examines how people's background assumptions help them make sense of everyday situations. Ethnomethodology concerns humans who sustain meaningful interchanges with one another.*

Eugenics – a philosophy and social movement holding that populations or societies can be improved by encouraging certain groups to breed while discouraging others. A social movement in the early twentieth century that sought to apply genetic selection to "improve" humanity. *Eugenicist ideas have often been implemented by force.*

Eurocentrism – ethnocentrism with European culture or society perspective prioritized.

Euthanasia – killing a person who is terminally ill (active euthanasia) or allowing them to die by withholding treatment (passive euthanasia). Usually, claimed to be an act of mercy.

Eutrophication – the process by which an aquatic system becomes overfertilized. *One negative environmental consequence is the overgrowth of microscopic plants, leading to oxygen depletion, which causes certain aquatic species to die.*

Evaluation research (*social research*) – aims to assess the effectiveness of a particular policy or social program.

Evangelicalism – Protestantism stresses preaching the gospel of Jesus Christ, the validity of personal conversion, the Bible as the basis for belief, and active preaching of faith.

Evolution – the change of biological organisms through adaptation to the demands of the physical environment. *Genetic variation is random. Some mutations are beneficial and allow organisms to adapt to their environment and pass on their genes to future generations, thereby changing the species.*

Evolutionary theories – social change that sees societies evolving from simpler forms to more complex ones. In biology, living organisms develop new traits that may aid their adaptation or survival.

321

Exchange – social interactions involving the trade of tangibles (*objects*) or intangibles (*sentiments*) between individuals.

Exchange reciprocity – rough equality in exchanging goods and services between groups or sociocultural systems.

Exchange theory – an interpretive perspective that explains social interaction based on exchanging tangible or intangible rewards.

Exogamy – marriage between members of dissimilar categories, classes, or groups. A system in which individuals may only marry outside their social category or group.

Experiment (*research design*) – a carefully controlled experience where the independent variable is manipulated while other attributes are constant, determining whether the dependent variable changes. (*research methods*) when variables can be analyzed with carefully controlled conditions, usually within an artificial situation constructed by the researcher. An experiment can potentially determine whether a variable affects another independently.

Experimental group (*research design*) – individuals exposed to the independent variable the experimenter introduces.

Explanatory study – a research study to explain how or why things happen the way they do in the social world.

Exponential growth – a geometric rate of progression that produces a swift rise (or *explosion*) in a population. See *doubling time*.

Expressive – involves showing emotions or preferences in interpersonal relationships.

Expressive leader – a group leader whose role is to help maintain stability through joking, mediating conflicts, and otherwise reducing tension.

Expressive role (*Parsons*) – a specialized role in groups, primarily concerned with providing emotional support for group members. *In family groups, the expressive role is oriented towards the emotional needs of family members and caring for the young.*

Expropriation – the confiscation of property or labor from an individual.

Extended family – consists of close relatives extending beyond a couple and their children living within the same household or in a close and continuous relationship. More than two generations of the same kinship line living within the same household or as is more common in the West, very close to one another. *Several generations or branches of a family.*

Extroversion (*Amin*) –an economy oriented to the development of other national societies rather than its development. *Hountondji extended this to intellectual extroversion, oriented to the ideas and problems of other societies or cultures rather than their own.*

F

Face work (*Goffman*) – the actions individuals take to make their behavior appear consistent with the image they want to present.

Fad – collective behavior involving a novel, often frivolous, and usually short-lived activity. Striking behaviors that spread rapidly and, although embraced enthusiastically, remain popular for only a brief time.

False and true needs (*Marcuse*) – institutions (e.g., the media or advertising) manufacture false needs. *True needs* are the intrinsic psychological needs of individuals. *Marcuse argued that advanced industrial societies fulfilled false needs at the expense of actual needs.*

False consciousness (*Marxism*) – an ideology of the subordinate class that the ideology and control of elites within society have fashioned. *Marx's term for explanations of social problems grounded in individuals' shortcomings rather than society's flaws.*

Family – a group of individuals related to one another by blood ties, marriage, or adoption who form an economic unit, the adult members responsible for raising children. Two or more people related by blood, marriage, adoption, or serious long-term commitment to each other and living together. A group of individuals related to one another by blood ties, marriage, or adoption. *Members of families form an economic unit, the adult members of which are responsible for the upbringing of children. While societies involve families, the form varies. In modern industrial societies, the primary family form is the nuclear family, although various extended family relationships exist. They usually form an economic unit, and adult members care for the dependent children. Known societies involve some form of family system, although the nature of family relationships is widely variable. While the main family form in modern societies is the nuclear family, various extended family relationships exist.*

Family of choice – people with or without legal or blood ties who feel they belong together and wish to define themselves as a family.

Family of orientation – the family into which an individual is born and socialized.

Family of procreation – the family an individual creates when children are born or adopted.

Family unit – a group related by blood, marriage, or adoption, who usually live together.

Family violence – emotional, physical, or sexual abuse of one family member by another.

Fashion – a socially approved but temporary style of appearance or behavior. A social pattern favored for a time by many people.

Fatalism (*Durkheim*) – a social state characterized by powerful norms (or *over-regulation*) in which freedom of behavior is constrained. Feelings of fatalism are associated with a sense of oppression and hopelessness and may cause *fatalistic suicide.*

Fecundity – the number of children a woman is biologically capable of bearing in her lifetime in a particular society. See *fertility.*

Feedback loop (*sociocultural materialism*) – the dynamic relationships between the different components of socio-cultural systems. *While the theory begins with examining infrastructural determinism, it recognizes that structure and superstructure can play an independent role in determining the system's character.* See *infrastructural determinism*.

Fee-for-service medicine – providing medical services in return for fees paid by patients.

Femininity – the characteristic behaviors expected of women in a given culture. *Attributes or behaviors characteristically associated with women.*

Feminism – the advocacy of social equality for the sexes in opposition to patriarchy and sexism. Advocacy of political, economic, and social equality of the sexes.

Feminist theories – analyze social phenomena by examining their role in creating or maintaining male dominance.

Feminization of poverty – a process by which increasing proportions of people experiencing poverty are women and children. Women represent an increasing proportion of people experiencing poverty. *The phrase describes the increasing number of female-headed households living at or below the poverty level.*

Fertility – the incidence of childbearing in a country's population. Factual questions – Questions that raise issues concerning matters of fact (rather than theoretical or moral issues).

Feudalism – an economic and social system in which those who owned land (or *lords*) granted control to others (or *vassals*) in exchange for service and labor.

Feminist theories – emphasize the centrality of gender in analyzing the social world, particularly the uniqueness of women's experiences. *There are many strands of feminist theory, but they share the desire to explain gender inequalities and work to overcome them.*

Fertility – the average number of live-born children produced by women of childbearing age in a particular society. See *fecundity*.

Fetishism – obsessive attachment or sexual desire directed toward an object.

Feudalism – a social system based on fealty between a lord and a vassal. Feudalism is characterized by grants of land (*fiefs*) in return for formal oaths of allegiance and promises of loyal service.

Field (*Bourdieu*) – a system of social positions organized around particular stakes. Individuals occupy these positions and *compete* over the field's stakes, following rules and norms to advance their positions. *For example, artists compete for status, prestige, and recognition.*

Field research – when an investigator is directly involved with the people being studied.

Figuration – the process of simultaneously analyzing an individual's behavior and the society shaping that behavior.

First-wave feminism – a social movement (late 19th and early 20th centuries) that sought legal equality between men and women, especially for voting and property rights.

First World – nation-states with mature industrialized economies and capitalistic production. Refers to the group of nation-states with advanced industrial economies, usually market based. See *Second World, Third World, Global North,* and *Global South.*

Flexible production – a process in which computers design customized products for a mass market.

Flextime – an arrangement that allows employees to set their schedules (starting and quitting times) whenever possible.

Flow – an experience of total involvement in one's present activity.

Focused interaction – individuals engaged in an everyday activity or a direct conversation with one another.

Folkways – widespread standards of behavior. Social norms to which people conform, although without pressure. Society's customs for routine, casual interaction. A *norm followed out of convenience or tradition.*

Forces of production – Marx's term for the technology, labor, and raw materials used to produce economic goods in a society.

Fordism – an approach to manufacturing developed by Henry Ford to improve productive efficiency in the automotive industry. Henry Ford pioneered the assembly line system of production. Although Fordism became widespread, not all industrial processes were based on the assembly line. *Fordism includes standardization via machines, assembly line methods, and payment of sufficient wages to facilitate consumption. An economic system based on mass assembly-line production, mass consumption, and standardized commodities.*

Formal organization – a large, secondary group organized to achieve its goals efficiently. Highly structured groups with specific objectives and usually clearly stated rules and regulations. A secondary group organized to achieve specific goals tends to be large and impersonal. See *secondary group.*

Formal rationality – using *Zweckrational* (i.e., *goal-oriented rational behavior*) to achieve a goal without considering broader social values, traditions, or emotions. A popular name for the phenomenon is "technocratic thinking." See *substantive rationality.*

Formal sanction – a social reward or punishment administered in an organized, systematic way, such as receiving a diploma or getting a fine.

Forms – the traditional, legal, or accustomed ways of government, characterized by respect for office, procedure, law, opposing parties, consultation, and open communication within executive agencies and between branches of government.

Forms of authority (*Max Weber*) – three types of authority (i.e., *charismatic, traditional*, and *legal-rational*) managing societies.

Fourth-wave feminism – a social movement that began around the early 2010s, focusing on women's empowerment and linking it with digital tools and platforms. *Fourth-wave feminism is primarily concerned with body shaming and rape culture.*

Front region – a setting of social activity in which individuals seek to put on a definite *'performance'* for others.

Frontstage and backstage (*Goffman*) – a distinction between two action contexts. People engage in '*frontstage*' behavior while watching and '*backstage*' behavior when their actions are less visible.

Function – the part a recurrent activity plays in social life and its contribution to structural continuity. *How a sociocultural trait contributes to the maintenance or adaptation of another component of that system or the entire system itself.*

Functional analysis – the use of functionalism to analyze a socio-cultural system or a part of that system.

Functional approach – a theoretical approach that analyzes social phenomena regarding their functions in a social system.

Functional equivalent – a feature or process in society with the same function (consequence) as some other feature or process.

Functional necessity – a social phenomenon considered necessary for society to exist or function properly.

Functionalism (or *structural functionalism*) – a theoretical perspective based on the notion that social events can best be explained in terms of the functions they perform and contributions they make to the continuity of society. A theoretical perspective that focuses on how various parts of the social system contribute to the continuity of society and the effects that the various parts have on one another. *A view of society as a complex system whose various parts work in a relationship to each other in a way that needs to be understood. Theory that society moves as a large, interconnected machine and that if society is functioning, everyone benefits (conversely, if part of society is dysfunctional, the rest of society cannot function correctly).*

Functionalist theory – analyses social phenomena by examining their role in creating or maintaining social order.

Functions – the consequences of social phenomena for other parts of society or society.

Fundamental innovation – an idea, invention, or discovery genuinely revolutionary in nature such that it stimulates many other innovations or changes the way of life of the socio-cultural system. The invention of the steam engine and the discovery of penicillin are fundamental innovations.

Fundamentalism – a commitment to and belief in the literal meanings of scriptural texts. Religious traditionalism is characterized by the literal interpretation of religious texts, a conception of an active supernatural, and clear distinctions between sin and salvation. *A belief in returning to the literal meanings of scriptural texts. Fundamentalism may arise as a response to modernization and rationalization, insisting on faith-based answers and defending tradition using traditional grounds.*

Futurist – a person who attempts to forecast the broad parameters of social life, usually by studying present-day trends.

G

Game – competitive or cooperative interaction in which the outcome is determined by physical skill, strength, strategy, or chance.

Game stage – the third of three stages of childhood socialization described by George Herbert Mead. In the game stage, the child becomes aware of many social roles and how they relate to one another and the self. See *imitation stage* and *play stage.*

Gang – an informal group engaging in shared activities, many of which are outside the law.

Gemeinschaft / Gesellschaft [German; *community* and *society*] (*Ferdinand Tonnies*) – a small, traditional, community-centered society in which people have close, personal, face-to-face relationships and value social relationships as ends in themselves. *Gemeinschaft* is social ties based on personal interaction (e.g., family and friendship). Social ties are based on impersonal interaction (e.g., commercial exchanges). In an urban industrial society, people have impersonal, formal, contractual, and specialized relationships and tend to use social relationships to an end. *A social organization by which people have strong social ties and weak self-interest.*

Gender – a classification by which certain traits or behaviors are masculine or feminine. It has typically been distinguished from *sex (*classification as male or female based on genetic and physiological characteristics). Social expectations about behavior are regarded as appropriate for the members of each sex. *Gender does not refer to the physical attributes in which men and women differ but to socially formed traits of masculinity and femininity. Classification of behaviors corresponding to traditional masculinity or femininity.*

Gender-based violence – motivated by or otherwise connected to gender norms.

Gender-conflict theory – the application of conflict theory to societal gender roles; describes the societal subjugation of women as the result of the struggle for dominance by men.

Gender differences – variations in the social positions, roles, behaviors, attitudes, and personalities of people in a society.

Gender gap – differences between men and women in political attitudes and behavior.

Gender identity – one's self-identification as a man or a woman. Subjective state: someone says, 'I am a man' or 'I am a woman.'

Gender inequality – the differences in the status, power, and prestige of people in groups, collectivities, and societies.

Gender order (*R. W. Connell*) – represents patterns of power relations between masculinities and femininities widespread throughout society. *Societies shape notions of masculinity and femininity by power relations. Ideas and practices define gender identities or roles in particular societies and determine their relationship to one another.*

Gender performance – how masculinities and femininities are acted out.

Gender relations – the societally patterned interactions between men and women.

Gender role – learning and performing the socially accepted characteristics of a given sex. *Social roles are assigned to each sex and labeled as masculine or feminine. A set of behaviors, attitudes, and personality characteristics expected and encouraged of a person based on their sex. Behavioral norms expected of each gender a community or group holds.*

Gender-role expectations – beliefs about how men and women should behave.

Gender socialization – the tendency for boys and girls to socialize differently.

Gender stratification – the hierarchical ranking of men and women and their roles in unequal ownership, power, social control, prestige, and social rewards. *A society's unequal wealth, power, and privilege between the sexes.*

Genderqueer – an individual who does not identify with or behave following traditional gender categories.

Generalization – a claim that a specific observation will apply to a broader population. See *inductive reasoning*.

Generalized other (*George Herbert Mead*) – widespread cultural norms and values used to evaluate ourselves. A general idea of a group's expectations, attitudes, and values. *The organized and generalized attitude of a social group. The internalization of the norms and values of a culture. Our sense of the general expectations of others in a community or social group about appropriate beliefs and behaviors.*

Generation – the interaction of changing social conditions, the life course, and people's actions, creating experiences for youth cohorts that shape their unfolding adult lives. Generational change is created by how young people navigate and create social change when older patterns of action and thought seem difficult, inappropriate, or impossible in the changing context.

Generational units (*Mannheim*) – subgroups within generations that form different responses to the historical situation based on differences other than age.

Genetic engineering – heritable manipulation of organisms to produce desirable characteristics.

Genocide – an organized, systematic, and coordinated effort to persecute and annihilate any human group or collectivity by another group with power. The systematic, planned annihilation of an ethnic, racial, or political group. *Destruction of an entire population.*

Gentrification – a process of urban renewal in which older, decaying housing is refurbished by affluent people moving into the area. *The movement of middle-class and upper-middle-class people (usually white) into lower-income, sometimes minority, urban areas. For example, the renovation of poor and working-class urban neighborhoods and the displacement of the original residents.*

Gesellschaft / Gemeinschaft [German; *community* and *society*] (*Ferdinand Tonnies*) – a social organization based on loose personal ties, self-interest, rationalization, and impersonality. *Gemeinschaft* is social ties based on personal interaction (e.g., family and friendship). Social ties are based on impersonal interaction (e.g., commercial exchanges).

Gig economy – an economic model with short-term, temporary, or freelance work.

Ghetto (*Elijah Anderson*) – a widely held, sometimes tacit, stereotype of the neighborhoods where African Americans live or grew up, embedded in popular culture. A section of a city occupied predominantly by members of a single racial or ethnic group, usually because of social or economic pressure.

Glass ceiling – the unspoken and unwritten limit that a woman (or a member of a minority group) may attain within an organization.

Global cities (*Sassen*) – large urban centers (e.g., New York, London, and Beijing) are key regional and global network nodes, becoming more important in late modernity. *Critical for globalization, people and multinational companies are drawn to them.*

Global economy – an economy in which one nation's economic activities depend on other nations. *Activity spanning many nations with little regard for national borders.*

Global North (or *Minority World* and *Developed Countries*) – countries with high levels of industrialization. Except for Australia and New Zealand, these countries are in the northern hemisphere, and most were formerly considered the "First World." Following the collapse of the Soviet bloc, several Eastern European countries were reclassified as part of the Global North. Using a geographic reference linked to the northern hemisphere to capture countries' political, economic, and social status advantages and power. Previously called *Developed Countries*, mainly in this hemisphere. Contrast *Global South, Developing Countries,* and *Majority World.*

Global South (or *Majority World* and *Developing Countries*) – countries with limited industrialization. Most of these countries lie in the southern hemisphere, and many were former colonies of industrial states. The political, economic, and social status of countries previously called *Third World* or *Developing Countries*, primarily in the Southern Hemisphere. Contrast *Global North, Minority World,* and *Developed Countries.*

Global stratification – the stratification of nations. Systematic global inequalities between nation-states are determined by a nation-state's position in the capitalist world-system.

Global village – a notion associated with Canadian writer Marshall McLuhan, who saw the spread of electronic communication as binding the world into a small community.

Global warming – the gradual increase in the temperature of Earth. Although the *greenhouse effect* occurs naturally as carbon dioxide traps the sun's rays and heats Earth, global warming implies an enhanced greenhouse effect because of human activity. *The effects of global warming include floods, droughts, and other changes to the world's climate.*

Globalization – an ongoing process of social change when regions and nations become increasingly interconnected, especially regarding economics, politics, or culture. Extensive worldwide economic, social, or political relationship patterns between nations. *Growing interdependence between different peoples, regions, and countries as social and economic relationships stretch worldwide.*

Globalization of capitalism – the adoption of capitalism by countries around the world.

Glocalization – the idea that globalization increases or interacts with the importance of local and regional factors rather than simply erasing them.

Goal displacement (or *goal replacement*) – a formal organization's displacement of one goal with another to continue to exist.

Goals and Means (*Robert Merton*) – examines how members of society adapt their goals to the means that society provides for achieving them.

Gore capitalism (*Valencia*) – violence as a commodity in contemporary economics.

Government – the institution responsible for making and enforcing society's rules and regulating relations with other societies. *Formal institutional structures of the nation-state that regulate internal and external relations.*

Governmentality (*Foucault*) – governing techniques (broadly, not just by governments) using practices that shape people's conduct, beliefs, and identities.

Governance – the exercise of political, economic, and administrative authority in the management of a country's affairs at all levels

Government – formal organizations that direct the political life of a society. *Officials within a political apparatus regularly enact policies, decisions, and matters of state.*

Grand theories (*Karl Marx*)– attempt to arrive at an overall explanation of social life or social development. Marx's theory of successive class conflicts as the driving force of history is an example of grand theorizing.

Great transformation (*Polanyi*) – the social and political changes associated with the rise of modern market societies.

Green Revolution – the improvement in agricultural production based on higher-yielding grains and increased use of fertilizers, pesticides, and irrigation. The tremendous increase in farming productivity began in the 1950s with the application of pesticides, herbicides, and chemical fertilizers and the development of plant varieties specifically bred to respond to these chemical inputs.

Greenhouse effect – a rise in the Earth's average temperature (i.e., global warming) due to increasing concentration of carbon dioxide in the atmosphere. Process, whereby certain atmospheric gases such as carbon dioxide and methane (i.e., greenhouse gases) absorb some of the sun's energy, reflect into space, and radiate it in all directions, thus preventing some of the sun's heat from leaving Earth's atmosphere. *In recent decades, the natural greenhouse effect has been exacerbated by human activities that have increased greenhouse gases, causing climate change. The build-up of heat-trapping gases within Earth's atmosphere. A natural greenhouse effect keeps temperatures comfortable, but the build-up of greenhouse gases has been linked to global warming.*

Greying – a term used to indicate that an increasing proportion of a society's population is becoming elderly.

Gross domestic product (GDP) – the total annual value of goods and services produced within the boundaries of a country. A country's GDP includes the value of the production of foreign-owned firms within that country but not the value of goods produced by that country's firms on foreign soil. *GDP is now the preferred measure of the wealth of nations. All the goods and services produced by a country's economy in a particular year, regardless of who owns the factors.*

Gross national product (GNP) – the total annual value of goods and services produced by nationals of a country. A country's GNP does *not* include the value of the production of foreign-owned firms within that country, but the value of goods and services produced by that country's firms abroad. *Although GDP is the preferred measure of wealth of nations, GNP is often used in historical comparisons.*

Group – individuals who communicate and interact regularly, sharing attitudes and beliefs—collections of people sharing common goals and norms and whose relationships are usually based on interactions. *Two or more people interacting over time have a sense of identity, belonging, and norms that nonmembers do not have.*

Group dynamics – thoughts and behavior are influenced by the groups of which we are members, and, in turn, we influence the thought process and behavior of the group.

Group size effect – the variable effects of different group sizes on the group's dynamics.

Groupthink (*Irving Janis*) – 1. the tendency of individuals to follow the ideas or actions of a group. 2. people in positions of power tend to follow the group's opinions to the point that there is a narrow view of the issue. Tendency for groups to reach a consensus on most issues.

Guerilla movement –the organized efforts of a non-government military organization in resisting the legally established government.

H

Habitus (*Bourdieu*) – a set of dispositions, tendencies, and preferences through which we understand and participate. *A lifetime process of socialization where people absorb and embody ideas about history and culture and reproduce them without a conscious appreciation of how their ideas of reality came to be formed.*

Halo effect – the assumption that a physically attractive person also possesses other good qualities.

Hate crime – an illegal act against a person or property by an offender motivated by racial or other bias. Assault or other violent acts aimed at individuals because they are members of a deviant or a minority group.

Hawthorne effect – a change in a subject's behavior caused simply by being studied.

Health – a state of complete physical, mental, and social well-being.

Health maintenance organization (HMO) – in the United States, an organization that provides health care to patients in return for a fixed annual fee. HMOs, therefore, are interested in limiting the cost of treatment per patient. See *managed care.*

Hegemonic masculinity – idealized norms about male behavior legitimize the subordination of women and non-hegemonic men. *The dominant or main ways of being a man in a society. Hegemonic masculinity encourages traits like competitiveness, dominance, independence, muscularity, homophobia, and the devaluation of women and femininity.*

Hegemony (*Marxism*) – cultural domination in which the worldview of a ruling class becomes widely accepted as usual or correct, legitimizing their power and justifying the *status quo*. A nation-state's predominant political, economic, or social influence over others. The term *hegemon* refers to the dominant leader itself. *How a ruling or dominant group wins over a subordinate group through ideas. Domination by elite and powerful groups using ideology with consent rather than violent coercion. Hegemonic control is how the social order becomes accepted through lifetime socialization, influencing ideas, consciousness, and perception of reality. Historical relations, including past violence (e.g., colonialism and institutions), maintain the status quo. For Gramsci, hegemony involves a mix of consent, coercion, and some compromise.*

Herding societies (or *pastoral societies*) – when raising and herding animals such as sheep, goats, and cows are the primary means of subsistence. Subsistence derives from rearing domesticated animals; there is often a need to migrate between different areas according to seasonal changes or seek fresh grazing. *Relies on the domestication and breeding of animals for food.*

Heteronormativity – heterosexuality as the social norm, preferred or assumed default category of sexual orientation, and the social privileges attached to having this orientation.

Heterosexual – a person whose preferred partner for erotic, emotional, and sexual interaction is someone of the opposite sex.

Heterosexual matrix (*Butler*) – a rigid set of linked social categorizations linking sex, gender, and sexuality to make normative combinations seem natural.

Heterosexuality – an orientation in sexual activity or feelings towards people of opposite sex.

Hidden curriculum – rules and lessons taught at schools outside of explicit curriculum and school policies, including 'cultural' expectations around gender, class, or race. Behaviors or attitudes learned at school are not part of the formal curriculum. *For example, aspects of classism can often be "unintentionally" conveyed in learning materials.*

Hierarchy – the arrangement of positions in rank order, with those below reporting to those above.

Hierarchy of credibility – a hierarchy that some journalists observe by attaching the greatest importance to the views and opinions of those in positions of power, such as government ministers, political leaders, senior police officers, or wealthy and influential individuals.

Higher education – beyond high school level, often in college or university.

High-trust system – a work setting where individuals have much autonomy and control.

Hispanics – refers to Spanish-speaking persons, including many distinct ethnic groups.

Hipster racism – performing behaviors typically racist in an ironic, self-aware, or satire.

Historical materialism (*Marxism*) – the processes of social change are determined primarily (but not exclusively) by economic factors.

Holistic medicine – a medical approach that involves learning about a patient's physical environment and mental state.

Holistic – characterized by an emphasis on the entire system and the interdependent nature of the parts of that system.

Holistic medicine – treatment aimed at the whole person, including physical and mental aspects and the person's social environment.

Holocaust – genocide of European Jews by Nazi Germany during the Second World War.

Homo duplex (*Durkheim*) – humans have a dual nature, the *angel*, and the *beast*, with the beast being the stronger. The first and "lower" part of that nature is the "will," an id-like nature focused on the individual satisfaction of wants and desires. The other "higher" part is the "collective conscience," which is social in origin. This conscience is based on a collective moral system, a reality separated from the individual and comprised of ideas and values.

Homo sapiens – the species of modern humans that evolved in Africa 200,000 years ago during a time of great environmental change.

Homogamy – the tendency for individuals to select mates from similar social backgrounds.

Homogeneity – a collection of elements that are each identical to one another.

Homogenization – the process of becoming more uniform, with parts of a whole alike.

Homophobia – a fear or disdain of homosexuals.

Homosexual – someone emotionally, erotically, and physically attracted to same-sex persons.

Homosexuality – an orientation of sexual activities or feelings towards others of same sex.

Horizontal mobility – movement from one social status to another equal social hierarchy rank.

Horticultural societies – cultivating plants with hoes is the primary means of subsistence. *Hand tools are used to grow crops.*

Hospice – care for the terminally ill, emphasizing pain relief and emotional and spiritual counseling within the home. An organization designed to provide care and comfort for terminally ill persons and their families.

Household – a census term for a collection of people occupying a housing unit.

Housework (or *domestic labor*) – unpaid work done in and around the home, such as cooking, cleaning, and shopping. Studies show that most of this labor is conducted by women despite the predominance of dual-income families.

Human-capital explanation – worker's earnings vary because of differences in education or experience.

Human context – the connections that form a group of people rather than a collection of individuals (e.g., genetics in a family, shared interests between friends)

Human ecology – studying the relationship between humans and their environments.

Human resource management (HRM) – a branch of management theory that regards employee enthusiasm and commitment as essential to economic competitiveness. HRM seeks to develop the sense that workers invest in company products and the work process.

Humanitarian – a person devoted to human welfare and social reform.

Human relations management – the interdisciplinary study of worker relations in the workplace. The goal is to maximize productivity by improving worker-management relations by promoting social events and other activities to improve worker morale. Many sociologists (especially Mills and Braverman) consider human relations management simply an exercise in manipulation.

Hunting-and-gathering society – when subsistence is based primarily on hunting animals and gathering edible plants. Subsistence is gained from hunting animals, fishing, and gathering edible plants. Obtaining food by hunting animals, fishing, and gathering fruits, nuts, and grains. *These societies do not plant crops or have domesticated animals. People acquire food by hunting games and gathering edible plants.*

Hybrid economy – an economic system blending features of centrally planned and capitalist (or *market*) economies.

Hybridity – in post-colonial studies, the creation of new transcultural forms within the zone of cultural contact produced by colonization.

Hyper consumption – goods and services to the point of abnormal excess.

Hyper industrialism – a societal condition in which virtually all social institutions (government, family, education) have adapted to the demands of the industrial economy. Many scholars favor *hyper industrialism* over *post-industrial society* to refer to complex industrial societies (e.g., Canada and the United States). Prefix *hyper-* denotes "over and above," even to the point of "abnormal excess." To describe contemporary North America as "hyper-industrial" is to stress both its continuity with the past and rapidly changing nature—even to abnormal excess.

Hyperinflation – extreme inflation.

Hypothesis – a tentative statement about a given situation that predicts a relationship between variables, usually used as a basis for empirical testing. An idea, or an educated guess, about a given situation put forward in exact terms to provide the basis for empirical testing. A tentative statement asserting a relationship between one factor and another (based on theory, prior research, or general observation). *A testable proposition.*

I

I and me (*Mead*) – a distinction with 'me' for influencing or learning through interaction with others. 'I' is the individual's responses to 'me' (i.e., responses to the attitudes of others).

"I" portion of self (*George Herbert Mead*) – the spontaneous or impulsive portion of self.

Iatrogenic – a disease caused by a physician while examining or treating the patient.

Id (*Freudian theory*) – the first part of the mind to develop and responsible for satisfying physical states. The part of the self-representing human drives such as sexuality and hunger. *Refers to the unconscious instinctual impulses (e.g., sexual or aggressive impulses).*

Ideal type (*Max Weber*) – s theoretical model of how a formal organization should function. Weber's construct of a "*pure type*," an analytical tool created by emphasizing logical or consistent traits of a social item. Traits are defining but not necessarily desirable. *Ideal types do not exist in reality; they serve as constructs for comparing social phenomena. One example is Weber's ideal type of bureaucratic organization (anything but desirable). Widely used and understood examples include "ideal democracy" and "ideal capitalism."*

Ideal values – the characteristics (or traits) people say are essential, whether their behavior supports them.

Idealism (or *idealistic strategy*) – a perspective that human ideas shape society. *The pursuit of one's values and beliefs often to the exclusion of practical reality.*

Idealist – one who is influenced more by ideals than by practical considerations. Alternatively, one subscribes to the hypothesis that ideas are prime movers (important causal agents) in sociocultural systems.

Idealist strategy (or *idealism*) – a perspective that human ideas shape society.

Identification theories – children learn gender roles by identifying with and copying their same-sex parent.

Identity – the distinctive characteristics of a person's character or the character of a group that relate to who they are and what is meaningful to them. Some primary sources of identity include gender, sexual orientation, nationality or ethnicity, and social class.

Identity politics – political action in which political alliances form around specific identity categories. *For example, the categories of gender or race. Groups based on identity politics prioritize their identity group's concerns, needs, or demands.*

Ideological power (*Mann*) – power derived from the human need to find meaning. Ideological power involves control over meaning, ritual, symbolism, and values.

Ideology – beliefs, attitudes, and cultural patterns justifying existing social institutions and hierarchies. *It is linked to power and the maintenance of inequalities.* Shared ideas or beliefs justifying and supporting the interests of groups or organizations. A system of ideas that reflects, rationalizes and defends the interests of believers. *Shared ideas or beliefs that justify the dominant groups' interests. Ideologies are in all societies with systematic and ingrained inequalities between groups. The concept of ideology is intricately connected with power since ideological systems legitimize the differential power held by groups.*

Idiographic – characterized by a concern with unique historical events. See *nomothetic*.

Illegitimate opportunity structures (*Cloward and Ohlin*) – opportunities for crimes as a basic part of society.

Illusion (*Bourdieu*) – a commitment to participating in a particular field and the belief that the stakes of the field are worth competing over.

Imagined community – nations are socially constructed entities facilitated by a national media based on individuals believing they are part of the national group.

Imitation stage (*George Herbert Mead*) – the first of three stages of childhood socialization. In the imitation stage, the child mimics the behavior of others but without much understanding of the social meaning of the behavior. See *game stage* and *play stage*.

Immigration – the settlement of people in a country where they were not born. *The movement of people into one country from another for settlement.*

Impairment – abnormal functioning of the body or mind, either born with or arising from injury or disease.

Imperialism – establishing a colonial empire in which domination is political or economic.

Impression management – selective control of how others perceive us.

Impression management (*Erving Goffman*) – people manage, or control impressions others have of them by choosing what to conceal or reveal when interacting. The tendency of individuals to manipulate other's impressions of them. *Attempting to influence other's perceptions of us, typically to achieve certain ends. Describes the efforts of individuals to influence how others perceive them.*

In-group – a social group commanding a member's esteem and loyalty. *A group to which one belongs and feels loyalty.*

Incest – sexual activity between close family members.

Incest taboo – the prohibition of sexual intercourse between fathers and daughters, mothers and sons, and brothers and sisters.

Inclusion – actively seeking out, valuing, and respecting differences.

Income – the sum of money, wages, and salaries (earnings) plus income other than earnings. Payment of wages earned from work or investments, usually measured by year.

Indentured servitude – a system of stratification in which an individual agrees to sell his or her body or labor to another for a specified period.

Independent variable (*research methods*) – the value that an investigator believes affects another variable. *For example, in the posited relationship between education and income, education is the independent variable, and income is the dependent variable.* See *dependent variable. A variable that causes a change in another (dependent) variable. The variable whose occurrence (or change) results in another variable's occurrence (or change); the hypothesized cause of something else.*

Index crime. – street crime such as robbery, rape, and other serious offenses.

Indigenous culture – the native or original culture of a particular region.

Indigenous peoples – with ties to the land, water, and wildlife of their ancestral domain.

Indigenous standpoint – the perspective on social phenomena afforded to an individual by their experience as an Indigenous person.

Individualism – a belief in individual rights and responsibilities. A belief in the centrality and primary importance of the individual and the importance of self-sufficiency and independence.

Individualization – a general social trend evident in many contemporary societies, which affords people greater options and more choices regarding how they live their lives but also new responsibilities to manage structural contradictions personally.

Induction – reasoning from the particular to the general.

Inductive logical thought – reasoning that transforms specific observations into a general theory.

Inductive reasoning – the process of reasoning from specific observations to general statements. See *deductive reasoning* and *generalization*.

Industrial democracy – an employment system with democratic participation in the workplace.

Industrial production – economic production using machinery driven by inanimate power sources.

Industrial reserve army (*Karl Marx*) – the legions of unemployed within a capitalist-dominated society. The existence of an industrial reserve army keeps wages down. A disadvantaged section of labor supplied for extra demand.

Industrial Revolution – a series of production and manufacturing changes from the mid-18th century. The broad spectrum of social and economic transformations surrounds the development of modern industry and the transformation of technology based on human and animal labor to technology based on inanimate energy sources. It refers to the transformation in England in the second half of the eighteenth century and the first half of the nineteenth century. *Like many historical designations, the "Industrial Revolution" is an arbitrary construct used by social scientists and lay people to break the continuous world of reality into manipulable pieces. No one event marks the Industrial Revolution's beginning or end except as defined by social consensus. The Industrial Revolution included greater use of machines, organization of labor in factories, and the use of new materials (e.g., iron and steel).*

Industrial society – uses advanced energy sources, rather than humans and animals, to run large machinery.

Industrialism – a mode of production characterized by the large-scale manufacturing of goods (including agriculture). As with any mode of production, industrialism imposes severe constraints upon the rest of the sociocultural system. *Technology that powers sophisticated machinery with advanced sources of energy.*

Industrialization – the continually expanding application of sophisticated technology designed to efficiently draw energy and raw materials out of the environment and fashion them into human-use products. The shift within a nation's economy from a primarily agricultural base to a manufacturing base.

Industrialization of war – applying industrial production and bureaucratic organization to warfare.

Industrialized societies – rely on mechanized production, rather than human or animal labor, as the primary means of subsistence.

Industrializing nations – countries in the process of becoming industrialized include most of the countries of the former Soviet Union.

Infant mortality rate – the number of infants dying during the first year per 1,000 live births.

Infanticide – the intentional killing of infants. According to Malthus and others, one of history's secrets is the widespread practice of infanticide to control population level throughout human history.

Infant mortality rate – the number of infants who die during the first year of life per thousand live births. Infant mortality rates have declined dramatically in industrial societies.

Inflation – an increase in the supply of money in circulation that exceeds the economic growth rate, making money worth less in relation to the goods and services it can buy.

Informal economy – economic transactions outside orthodox paid employment.

Informal relations – relations in groups and organizations developed based on personal connections and ways of doing things that depart from formally recognized modes of procedure. Organizational relations are developed based on personal connections. These ties are often used instead of the formally recognized procedures to pursue organizational goals.

Informal sanction – a social reward (or punishment) given informally through social interaction, such as an approving smile or a disapproving frown.

Information age – the present historical age, especially in *post-industrial economies*. The growing economic importance of information technology marks the information age.

Information technology – forms of technology based on information processing and requiring microelectronic circuitry.

Infrastructural determinism – the central principle of cultural materialism asserts that production and population variables "probabilistically determine" the rest of the sociocultural system (Harris 1979, 55–58). Sociocultural materialism states the principle: The mode of production and reproduction probabilistically determines primary and secondary group structure, which in turn probabilistically determines the cultural and mental superstructure (Elwell 1999, 157–59). See *primacy of the infrastructure*.

Infrastructure – the interface between a sociocultural system and its environment. In sociocultural materialism, infrastructure constitutes the principal mechanism by which society regulates the amount and type of energy from the environment.

In-group – a social group that an individual belongs to and identifies with.

Inner city – the central neighborhoods of industrial cities, which are subject to dilapidation and decay, the more affluent residents have moved to outlying areas.

Innovation – introducing a recent technology, product, or technique into a sociocultural system. the discovery or invention of ideas, things, or methods; *a source of cultural change.* Alternatively, the behavior of individuals who have accepted the culturally approved goal but have not fully internalized the culturally approved means to attain this goal. These individuals, therefore, adopt a different (and often deviant) method for attaining the goal. Innovation is one of the five modes of adaptation in Robert K. Merton's anomie theory. See *conformity, rebellion, retreatism*, and *ritualism.*

Inner controls (*control theory*) – the thought processes such as morality or conscience reside within people and can prevent them from committing acts of deviance.

Innovators (*Robert Merton's theory of goals and means*) – those who accept cultural goals but reject the institutional means of achieving them.

Instinct – a genetically fixed pattern of complex behavior (i.e., behavior beyond reflexes) that appears in typical animals within a species. Genetically determined behavior triggered by specific conditions or events. The majority of human behavior is learned. Although humans have several reflexive behaviors, social scientists do not consider human behavior instinctual.

Institution – a set of norms surrounding the carrying out of a function necessary for the survival of a society. An established pattern of human social behavior in each society. *Examples include marriage, family, and government. The patterned and enduring roles, statuses, and norms formed around successful strategies for meeting basic social needs.*

Institution of science – the social communities that share specific theories and methods to understand the physical and social worlds.

Institutional capitalism – when large institutions such as pension plans, banks, and insurance companies hold significant shares of capitalistic enterprises.

Institutional discrimination – accepted social arrangements that place minority groups at a disadvantage.

Institutional racism – accepted social arrangements that discriminate based on race.

Institutionalization – 1. the embodiment of widespread norms, beliefs, and values into social structures, laws, and formal codes of conduct. 2. committing a person to an institution such as a nursing home or asylum.

Institutionalization of science – establishing careers for practicing scientists in major social institutions.

Institutionalized – social practices established, patterned, predictable, and supported by custom, tradition, or law.

Institutionalized means – legitimate, socially approved ways societies offer their members to achieve culturally approved goals.

Instrumental – a role involving problem-solving or task-oriented behavior in group or interpersonal relationships.

Instrumental leader – a group leader directing the group's attention to the task.

Instrumental role (*Parsons*) – a specialized role in groups, primarily concerned with completing group tasks and procuring resources. In family groups, the instrumental role is oriented toward the family's basic needs and providing financial support.

Insurrection – an organized revolt against civil authority to replace that authority with another.

Integration – the incorporation of disparate parts into a whole, bringing people of different ethnic groups into equal association.

Intelligence – 1. the level of intellectual ability in an individual. 2. gathering information (defensive, offensive, and industrial capabilities) about one nation by another.

Intelligence quotient (IQ) test – a standardized set of questions or problems designed to measure verbal and numerical knowledge and reasoning. A score attained on tests of symbolic or reasoning abilities. Most social scientists (excluding psychologists) put little stock in the validity of IQ tests.

Intensification – 1. applying ever-expanding technology and labor techniques to increase productivity. 2. the growth in the complexity of the mode of production (greater energy expenditures as well as energy produced and consumed) and population throughout social evolution. See *bureaucratization* and *rationalization*.

Interactionist theories – analyze social phenomena by examining how individuals create and make sense of their social world through communication.

Internalized racism – the unconscious acceptance, among racially marginalized groups, of ideas and stereotypes portraying them as inferior.

Interpretative sociology – several approaches to studying society, including symbolic interactionism and phenomenology, investigate the meaningful character of social life for its participants.

Intersectionality – different social categorizations (e.g., race, gender, and class) intersect and overlap, forming new and complex forms of inequality. Interconnections between gender inequality and racism, as well as others (e.g., homophobia, transphobia, ableism, and class stratification). Popular culture often confuses this term as one describing a multiplicity of identities (e.g., working-class lesbian), and *White feminism* dilutes meaning by disconnecting this term from race. Women of color simultaneously experience multiple forms of discrimination, so the exclusion, inequity, and harm become compounded.

Interest group – people organized to pursue specific interests in the political arena. The interests of these groups are often economic, but many are organized around moral concerns. People working to influence political decisions affecting them. The significant activities of interest groups are lobbying the members of legislative bodies, contributing vast sums to political campaigns, and, increasingly, running their propaganda campaigns to affect the legislative process.

Intergenerational mobility – a vertical social status change from generation to generation. *Movement up or down social hierarchy between generations.*

Interlocking directorates – linkages between boards of directors of different companies. These linkages occur because the same people (often of the same class) sit on several boards. The practice of overlapping memberships on corporate boards of directors.

Intermediate organization (*Robert Nisbet*) – a primary group based on religion, family, or community that, historically, stood between the individual and the state.

Intermittent reinforcement (*learning theory*) – a reward sometimes but not always when a desired behavior is shown.

Internal colonialism – the economic exploitation of a group within a society whereby the labor of group members is sold cheaply, and they are made to pay dearly for products and services.

Internalization – the process by which group members make the group's ideas, values, and norms their own. *Taking social norms, roles, and values into one's mind.*

International division of labor – the specialization of work tasks and occupations among nation-states; the interdependence of countries that trade on global markets. When there is an international division of labor, products are produced globally, but profits go only to a few.

Interpersonal violence – the use of force between individuals to kill, injure, or abuse.

Interpretive approach – a central theoretical perspective in sociology; focuses on how individuals make sense of the world and react to symbolic meanings attached to social life.

Intersocietal selection – the evolution of the global system of societies by which larger, more technologically advanced societies have prevailed in conflicts over territory and resources with more traditional sociocultural systems.

Interview (*research methods*) – questions a researcher administers personally to respondents. One-to-one conversations aimed at eliciting information about some aspects of social life. Interviews usually involve a predetermined schedule of questions and can be structured, semi-structured, or open-ended, depending on the information required.

Intragenerational mobility – a vertical change of social status experienced by an individual within their lifetime.

Intragenerational social mobility – a change in social position occurring during a lifetime.

Invention – an innovation in material or nonmaterial culture, often produced by combining existing cultural elements in new ways, a source of cultural change.

Invisible knapsack (*Peggy McIntosh*) – a metaphor for the privilege as an invisible collection of unearned assets people use to obtain success. Individuals who possess these assets are typically unaware that members of other groups (e.g., marginalized racial groups) do not possess them and are *invisible*.

IQ (intelligence quotient) test – a standardized set of questions or problems designed to measure verbal and numerical knowledge and reasoning.

Iron cage of rationality – when individuals are increasingly compelled to act following dictates of efficiency, calculation, and rationality.

Iron cage (*Weber*) – a rationalized society that subordinates individual thought and behavior to bureaucratic control.

Iron law of oligarchy (*Robert Michels*) – power in an organization tends to become concentrated by a small group of leaders. Robert Michels (1915) posited a generalization: "*Who says organization, says oligarchy.*" As bureaucracy enlarges and centralizes, more and more authority is placed at the top of these massive organizations. *Elites eventually control democratic organizations.*

Ironic spectator (*Chouliaraki*) – the detached, uninvested way people respond to human suffering with current media. Ironic spectatorship involves outward gestures of solidarity and compassion that are more about benefiting one's identity than genuinely helping others.

Irrationality factor – the paradox of supremely rational organizations. Bureaucracies act irrationally for the well-being of society. Because bureaucracies are designed for the efficient attainment of goals set by those at the top of the organization, and because those individuals often have goals antithetical to society's goals (say, profit versus welfare), the irrationality factor is very much a part of modern life.

Islamophobia – an irrational fear or hatred of or aversion to Islam, Muslims, or Islamic culture. *Discrimination or prejudice against members of the Islamic faith.*

J

Jeremiad – writings characterized by long lists of complaints, laments, or prophecies of doom.

Job displacement – the permanent loss of jobs due to shifts in employment patterns. With the transition from agrarian to industrial societies, many agricultural jobs were lost while new manufacturing and service jobs were created. The shifts continue.

Job insecurity – apprehension experienced by employees about both the stability of their work position and their role within the workplace.

K

Kaupapa Māori Theory – the vision, aspirations, and values of the Māori community.

Keynesian economics (*John Maynard Keynes*) – the economic theory that government intervention, through deficit spending, may be necessary to maintain high employment levels.

Kinesics communication – using body language.

Kinsey scale – measuring sexuality on a gradation between homosexuality or heterosexuality.

Kinship – socially defined family relationships based on common parentage, marriage, or adoption. *Network of social relationships linking individuals through common ancestry (i.e., blood ties), marriage, or adoption.*

Knowledge economy – a society no longer based primarily on producing material goods but on producing knowledge.

L

Labeling effect – the impact of labeling on an individual. *For example, tracking students in different reading groups may produce poor reading not because of the student's ability but because the student was placed in a poor reading group and, therefore, internalized the label.*

Labeling theory (or *societal reaction theory*) (*Howard Becker*) – an approach to studying deviance suggesting that people become 'deviant' because specific labels are attached to their behavior by political authorities and others. A social theory holds that society's reaction to specific behaviors significantly defines the self as deviant. People may become "deviant" because specific labels (e.g., thief, prostitute, homosexual) are attached to their behavior by criminal justice authorities and others.

Labor – physical or mental work as the primary production factor.

Labor-market segmentation – the existence of two or more distinct labor markets, one of which is open only to individuals of a gender or ethnicity.

Labor power (*Karl Marx*) – abstract human labor used in exchange for money.

Labor unions – organizations of workers seeking to improve wages and working conditions through various strategies, including negotiations and strikes.

Laissez-faire **economics** (*Adam Smith*) – the economic theory that the economic system develops and functions best when left to market forces, without government intervention. *The government should not interfere with commerce. This is one of the central doctrines of capitalism that, while part of the ideal, is rarely practiced.*

Language – a system of symbols that allows members of a society to communicate with one another. Symbols and a system of grammar for communication of complex ideas. *Spoken or written symbols are combined into a system and governed by rules.*

Latent functions – consequences of any social pattern unrecognized and unintended. An unintended consequence of one part of a sociocultural system overall or on other parts of that system. Latent functions are often indirect and not always obvious. *For example, in the United States, the reform of big-city political machines had many unintended consequences for the governability of American cities.* See *manifest function. Functional consequences that are not intended or recognized by the members of a social system in which they occur. Unrecognized or unintended consequences of a social process.*

Law – formalized rules established by political authorities and backed by state power to control or regulate social behavior. Written rules established by a political authority and backed by the government. *A written norm enforced by an official agency.*

Learning theory (*psychology*) – specific human behaviors are acquired or forgotten due to the associated rewards or punishments.

Least industrialized nations – primarily agricultural nations that account for half of the land on Earth.

Legal protection – the protection of minority-group members through the official policy of a governing unit.

Legitimacy – a particular political order gains legitimacy if most of those governed by it recognize it as just and valid. *The generally held belief that a particular social institution is just and valid.*

Legitimate – about power, the sense by people that those exercising power have the right.

Legitimation – how an institution engenders acceptance, validity, or commitment from individuals and other institutions.

Legitimation crisis – a situation that results when the commitment on the part of members to a particular social institution is not sufficient for that organization to function effectively. Governments that lack legitimation often rely on repression to continue their rules (which is very inefficient).

Legitimizing identities (*Castells)* – the dominant institutions of society promote collective identity to protect and reproduce the current social hierarchy.

Lesbian – a woman emotionally, erotically, and physically attracted to other women.

Lesbianism – same-gender activities or emotional attachments between women.

Liberal democracy – a system of democracy based on parliamentary institutions coupled with the free market system in economic production.

Liberal feminism – gender inequality is produced by reduced access for women and girls to civil rights and specific social resources, such as education and employment. *Liberal feminists tend to seek solutions through legislation changes that ensure individuals' rights are protected.*

Life chances – opportunities available to individuals because of their position in the class system. The probability of an individual having access to or failing to access opportunities or difficulties in society.

Life course – the biological and social birth sequence, growth, maturity, aging, and death.

Life-course analysis – examines how stages of life influence socialization and behavior.

Life expectancy – 1. the number of years a newborn in society can expect to live. 2. the number of additional years people of any age can, on average, expect to live. *The time people can, on average, expect to live when born.*

Life histories – studies the overall lives of individuals, often based both on self-reporting and on documents such as letters.

Life span – the maximum length of life biologically possible for a species member.

Life table – a statistical table with the death rate and life expectancy of each age-sex category for a particular population.

Lifelong learning – the idea that learning and acquiring skills should occur at all stages of an individual's life, not simply in the formal educational system early in life.

Lifestyle – the family, childbearing, educational attitudes and practices; personal values; type of residence; consumer, political, and civic behavior; religion.

Lifestyle changes – often requested when treating chronic disease. Rather than curing the disease, the patient makes changes in lifestyle (better nutrition, more exercise, smoking cessation, weight reduction, stress alleviation) that help to control the disease process.

Lifestyle movement – concerned with recognizing or accepting new kinds of identity. In contrast to emancipatory movements, lifestyle movements are typically concerned with self-actualization.

Limited war – warfare fought principally by a small number of soldiers to reach specific and politically limited objectives. See *total war*.

Line job – work as part of the central operations of an organization rather than providing support services for the operating structure.

Liquid modernity (*Bauman*) – modernity associated with the contemporary area. *It is a condition of constant change, instability, and mobility, affecting all areas of human life.*

Literacy – the ability of individuals to read and write.

Lobbying – influencing political decisions so they will be favorable to one's interests and goals.

Local knowledge – knowledge of a local community possessed by individuals who have lived long in that community.

Location (*Kanter*) – a person's position in an organization for control over decision-making.

Longevity – a duration of life or tenure in an organization.

Looking-glass self (*Charles Horton Cooley's theory of socialization*) – self-image based on how they believe others perceive them. *Our understanding of how others perceive us or our sense of how we appear to others. A social psychological concept states that an individual's self-concept is derived from interactions with others and from that individual's perception of how others perceive them. People form self-images based on what they perceive to be others' views of them.*

Low-income countries – nations with little industrialization and severe poverty are typical.

Low-trust system – a work setting in which individuals have little autonomy and control.

Luddite – a person who is against increased industrialization or modern technology. *The term, often used derogatorily, referred initially to early-nineteenth-century British textile artisans who rioted and destroyed textile machinery, believing that this innovative technology contributed to their replacement by less skilled low-wage workers.*

M

Macro level – an analysis focusing on large-scale institutions, structures, and processes. *A wide-scale view of the role of social structures within a society*

Macro-sociology – the study of large-scale society. *Sociological analysis focused on large-scale social forces. Studying large-scale organizations, sociocultural systems, or the world-system of societies.*

Magic (*Malinowski*) – "a practical art consisting of acts which are only meant to a definite end expected to follow." *Rituals influence supernatural beings to help achieve human ends.*

Majority World (or *Third World*) – countries outside the West, primarily in the Southern Hemisphere, where most of the world's population resides.

Making do (*De Certeau*) – tactic by which everyday people adapt to the strategies of control used by the powerful, often in innovative and resisting ways.

Male inexpressiveness – men's difficulties in talking about their feelings to others.

Malthusianism (*Thomas Robert Malthus*) – theory of population dynamics that population increase inevitably comes up against the "natural limits" of food supply because population grows geometrically (1, 2, 4, 8, 16, …) while food supply grows arithmetically (1, 2, 3, 4, 5, …). Because of this dynamic, Malthus asserted that population growth must be constantly limited through preventive and positive checks, significantly affecting the rest of the sociocultural system. See *positive checks* and *preventive checks*. The idea, first advanced by Thomas Malthus two centuries ago, is that population growth tends to outstrip the resources available to support it. Malthus argued that people must limit their frequency of sexual intercourse to avoid excessive population growth and a future of misery and starvation.

Managed care – health care reorganization along corporate lines. See *fee-for-service medicine* and *Health Maintenance Organization*.

Management – the coordination, supervision, or control of people and processes; the people who make decisions regarding an institution's operations.

Managerial capitalism – a change in the control of capitalist enterprises, from owners (who predominated in Marx's day) to very well-salaried managers.

Managerial demiurge (*C. Wright Mills*) – the increased proportion of managers at the top of government and business bureaucracies, an interlocking of these two bureaucracies, and the idea that increased areas are becoming the object of management and manipulation.

Manifest function – an intended and known consequence of one part of a sociocultural system or other parts. The intended function (or consequence) of something in a social system. The recognized and intended consequences of any social pattern. *The consequences of a social process. For example, the reform of big city political machines had the intended consequence of reducing corruption by city officials.* See *latent function*.

Manipulation – skillful or devious management.

Manner of interaction (Goffman) – the attitudes conveyed to get others to form certain impressions about us. *According to Goffman, it is one of the sign vehicles we use to present ourselves to others, along with the setting and our appearance.*

Manufactured consensus (*Marcuse*) – commonly shared norms, ideas, and values do not result from genuine agreement or free debate but instead arise through efforts to manipulate and control the population.

Manufacturing division of labor (or *detailed division of labor*) – the breakdown of product manufacturing into simple discrete steps, with each task assigned to an individual worker. Because it leads to greater productivity, the detailed division of labor is also increasingly applied to service, administrative, and professional occupations. See *division of labor*.

Manufactured risk – dangers created by human knowledge and technology's impact on the natural world. *Examples include genetically modified foods.*

Market economy – an economic system in which private individuals and businesses make decisions about exchanging goods and services rather than a central authority. An economic system in which the economic forces of supply and demand determine investment, supply, prices, and the distribution of goods. *Rational behavior typically makes economic decisions in market economies of supply and demand.*

Market research – social research explicitly aimed at determining the sales potential of a product or service.

Market situation (*Weber*) – the possibilities for engaging in exchange. *A shared market situation is like a shared class position.*

Marriage – a legally sanctioned relationship involving economic cooperation as well as normative sexual activity and childbearing, which people expect to be enduring. A socially approved sexual and economic relationship between two or more individuals. *A social institution recognizes and approves the sexual union of two or more individuals and includes a set of mutual rights and obligations.*

Marriage rate – number of marriages in a year per 1,000 single women (e.g., 15 to 44 years).

Marriage squeeze – when the eligible individuals of one sex outnumber the supply of potential marriage partners.

Marxism (*Karl Marx*) – contemporary social theory derives its main elements from Karl Marx's ideas. Marxist theory strongly emphasizes class struggle and material causation.

Marxian approach (*Karl Marx*) – a theory of ideas stressing the importance of class struggle centered around the social relations of economic production.

Masculinity – the characteristic behavior expected of men in a culture. *Attributes or behaviors characteristically associated with men.*

Mass hysteria – widely felt fear and anxiety.

Mass media – 1. any social or technological devices used to select, transmit, or receive information. 2. forms of communication, such as newspapers, magazines, radio, and television, designed to reach mass audiences. *Communications designed to reach a vast audience without personal contact between the senders and receivers. For example, newspapers, magazines, radio, and television. Widely disseminated forms of communication, such as books, magazines, radio, television, and movies.*

Mass production – the production of long runs of goods using machine power. Mass production was one outcome of the Industrial Revolution.

Mass society – a society in which industry and expanding bureaucracy have eroded traditional social ties. *A sizeable impersonal society in which individual achievement is valued over kinship ties and where people often feel isolated.*

Master status – central to the individual's identity and overshadows other statuses. *A status that overrides other statuses and becomes the one a person is known to others.*

Material (*Marxism*) – includes all that is independent of thought and ideas, often used in references to production.

Material culture – the physical objects of a sociocultural system. Material culture usually includes products, art, tools, and other tangibles. The tangible things created by members of a society and items of a culture. See *culture*.

Materialism – 1. material conditions (usually economic and technological factors) are central to social stability and change. 2. the philosophical view that matter is the only thing that can indeed be said to exist; fundamentally, things are composed of material, and phenomena result from material interactions.

Materialist – believing that material conditions are the foundation of sociocultural systems.

Materialist conception of history (*Marx*) – the view developed by Marx according to which 'material' or economic factors have a prime role in determining historical change.

Materialist strategy – a sociological perspective that humans are primarily motivated by material goods and living conditions.

Matriarchy – a sociocultural system in which females play a significant role in economics, government, or other major institutions. Most anthropologists insist that there are no true matriarchies in the sense of female dominance; however, there are societies such as the Iroquois in which females, particularly mothers, exercise equal, if not dominant, political power. *Social organization in which females dominate males.*

Matrilocality – a social custom in which married couples live in the wife's family's home.

Matrilineal – relating to, based on, or tracing ancestral descent through the maternal line.

Matrilineal descent – the practice of tracing kinship through only the female line. A system tracing kinship through women. See *patrilineal descent*.

Matrilocal – family systems in which the husband is expected to live near the wife's parents.

Matrilocality – a residential pattern in which a married couple lives with or near the wife's family. A family residential pattern in which the husband is expected to live near the wife's parents. See *neo-locality* and *patrilocality*.

Matthew effect – the social process whereby one advantage likely leads to additional advantages.

McDonaldization (*George Ritzer*) – refers to a process extensively described by Max Weber, who called it *rationalization*. A process by which society adopts the characteristics or principles of a fast-food restaurant, namely, standardization, homogenization, and scientific management. *A process by which the principles of the fast-food industry come to be applied to increased features of social life.*

"Me" portion of self (*George Herbert Mead*) – the portion of self that brings the influence of others into the individual's consciousness.

Mean (*statistics*) – a statistical measure of central tendency, or average, based on dividing a total by the number of individual cases. A measure of central tendency or average based on dividing a total by the number of individual cases involved. The mean is overly sensitive to extreme scores. *For example, the average life expectancy for people in a society with high infant mortality would be a misleading measure.* The sum of a set of mathematical values divided by the number of values is a measure of central tendency in a data series. *The arithmetic average of a series of numbers.* See *median*.

Means of consumption (*George Ritzer*) – goods and services consumed in a society. The means of consumption consist of such institutions as malls, superstores, Internet stores, warehouse stores, theme parks, cruise lines, mega malls, and casinos.

Means of production (*Karl Marx*) – producing material goods in society. Marx included in this concept both the "forces of production" and the social relations among the producers ("relations of production," which he based on the ownership of the technology). The means whereby material goods are produced in a society, including technology and the social relations between producers. See *forces of production* and *relations of production*.

Measures of central tendency (*statistics*) – ways of calculating averages, the three most common being the mean, the median, and the mode.

Mechanical solidarity (*Durkheim*) – a designation of social bonds based on shared morality that unites members of pre-industrial societies. The bond between an individual and a group based on shared interests, activities, beliefs, values, etc. When there is mechanical solidarity, one's conscience is enveloped by the collective conscience. *Group integration through shared values, norms, ideas, and behaviors.* See *organic solidarity*.

Mechanization – the use of machinery to replace human labor.

Median (*statistics*) – the number that falls halfway in a range of numbers. A way of calculating central tendency that is sometimes more useful than calculating a mean. The scores below the median are half the scores, and those above are the other half. The median calculates "central tendency," which is more useful than a calculated mean (mainly when the distribution includes many extreme scores). *The value occurs midway in a series of numbers arranged in order of magnitude or the middle case.*

Medicaid – a US government program (federal and state) providing medical care to the poor. *Federal-state matching program providing medical assistance to certain low-income persons.*

Medicalization – the tendency in the West to define deviance and social problems in terms of disease, genetic predisposition, or other personal pathologies.

Medical model – applying a medical perspective in explaining and treating troublesome human behavior.

Medicare (in the U.S.) – government health insurance for those over sixty-five. *Canada's tax-funded national health care program is available to every resident. Individuals are eligible if they receive Social Security benefits, federal disability benefits, or if they have end-stage kidney disease.*

Medicine – the institution responsible for defining and treating mental and physical problems among its members.

Megalopolis – a vast urban region containing several cities and their surrounding suburbs. *A vast, unbroken urban region consisting of two or more central cities connected by their surrounding suburbs.*

Melting pot – the idea that ethnic differences can be combined to create new patterns of behavior drawing on diverse cultural sources. *A pluralistic society in which people who originally come from different societies blend to form a new society.*

Mental disorder – the psychological inability to cope effectively with the demands of day-to-day life. Psychiatrists recognize two general mental disorders: *neurosis* (milder forms of illness, such as anxiety states) and *psychosis* (severe forms of disturbance, in which individuals lose touch with reality). The organic and sociocultural bases of various mental disorders are disputed matters.

Mental superstructure (*Weber*) – in sociocultural materialism, Max Weber's typology of motivations for human behavior. According to Weber, there are four such motivations: value-oriented rational action (*Wertrational*), affective action (action motivated by emotions), traditional action (action motivated by what Weber calls the "eternal yesterday"), and goal-oriented rational action (*Zweckrational*). See *cultural superstructure* and *superstructure*.

Meritocracy – a system in which social positions are filled based on individual merit and achievement rather than ascribed criteria such as inherited wealth, sex, or social background.

Metanarratives – broad, overarching theories or beliefs about the operation of society and the nature of social change. *Marxism and functionalism are examples of metanarratives that sociologists have employed to explain how the world works.*

Method of comparison – comparing one subgroup or society with another to understand social differences.

Methodological cosmopolitanism – an approach to social science that sees social phenomena occurring in an increasingly globalized context. *Methodological cosmopolitanism involves attention to processes transcending national borders.*

Methodological nationalism is an approach to social science that sees the nation-state as the primary object of analysis or primarily focuses on processes within a single nation-state.

Methodology – the rules, principles, and practices guiding evidence collection and conclusions.

Methods (*sociology*) – procedures to gather reliable and accurate *data* about the social world.

Metropolitan Statistical Area (MSA) – a geographical area containing either one city with 50,000 or more residents or an urban area of at least 50,000 inhabitants and a total population of at least 100,000 (except in New England, where the required total is 75,000). *There were 387 MSA as of July 2022.*

Metropolis – a large city that socially and economically dominates an urban area.

Micro level – an analysis of societies focusing on small-scale processes, such as how individuals interact and how they attach meanings to the social actions of others.

Microaggressions – subtle words, behaviors, and ideas expressed in interactions when a person from a majority or dominant group evokes a stereotype or judges minority groups. Microaggressions may be informed by overt prejudice or unconscious bias. *Regardless of intent, microaggressions operate through ideologies of power and privilege.*

Microculture – culture shared by a small group of people.

Microlevel phenomena – events that occur on a micro-sociological scale.

Micro-aggressions – small, commonplace behaviors or environmental features projecting prejudicial attitudes towards members of marginalized groups.

Micro-level theories – the study of specific relationships between individuals or small groups

Micropolitics – small-scale political actions.

Micro-sociology – the study of everyday life in social interactions. Sociological analysis focused on social interaction between individuals. *Studying small-scale patterns of human interaction and behavior within specific settings.*

Middle class – broadly defined occupationally as those working in white-collar and lower managerial occupations. In research, the middle class is sometimes defined according to income levels or subjective identification of the participants. Earning money by working professional (or *white-collar*) jobs. See *Bourgeoisie.*

Migration – the movement of people into and out of a particular territory. People move from one country or region to another to settle permanently. *The relatively permanent movement of people from one area to another.*

Militarism – a policy that emphasizes military preparedness, threats, and action in addressing the problems of the state. *A glorification of military ideals and capabilities.*

Military-industrial complex – an alliance among a nation's military establishment and defense industries that exchange personnel and share a common interest in furthering defense spending and weapons production. In some nation-states, the military-industrial complex influences government policy through contributions to political campaigns, lobbying, and spending defense dollars in electoral districts.

Military power (*Mann*) – derived from the necessity of defense and the social organization of military force.

Military rule – government by military leaders.

Millenarianism – the belief held by members of some religious movements that cataclysmic changes will occur soon (the second coming of Christ), heralding the arrival of a new epoch in human affairs.

Millenarian movements – based on the expectation that society will be suddenly transformed through supernatural intervention.

Minority – a category of people, distinguished by physical or cultural traits, who are socially disadvantaged.

Mini systems (*Immanuel Wallerstein*) – small, homogeneous, and simple societies in structure. Such societies are self-contained sociocultural systems. *Examples include hunting-and-gathering societies and simple horticultural, herding, and fishing societies.*

Minority group – people who are defined based on their ethnicity or race. They are often targeted for unequal treatment because of distinct physical or cultural characteristics. Any recognizable racial, religious, ethnic, or social group experiencing some disadvantage resulting from the action of a dominant group with higher social status and greater privileges. People in lower numbers who, because of distinct physical or cultural characteristics, experience inequality (e.g., *ethnic minorities*).

Minority World (or *First World* and *Developed World*) – the wealthy countries of the West, which include a minority of the world's population but are responsible for most of the consumption and have substantial influence over global politics.

Miscegenation – biological reproduction by partners of different racial categories. *The mixing of the races through marriage or sexual relationships.*

Misogyny – a strong contempt for women or femininity.

Mixed economy – significant elements of both capitalism and socialism. Many European countries have mixed economies, as, to some extent, does Canada.

Mixed methods (*research methods*) – using quantitative and qualitative research methods as part of a single research study.

Mobilities (*Urry*) – a research paradigm in contemporary sociology focused on studying movement. Mobilities scholars such as Urry study the movement of people, ideas, cultures, and things and are interested in topics like transportation, migration, and tourism.

Mobilization – the process of arousing people and resources to press for social change.

Mode (*statistics*) – the value that appears most often in each data set. The mode can sometimes be a helpful way of portraying central tendency. The number that appears most often in each data set. This can sometimes be a helpful way of portraying central tendency. *The value occurs most often in a series of mathematical values.* See *mean* and *median*.

Mode of production – the technology and the practices employed for expanding or limiting primary subsistence production, especially the production of food and other forms of energy. *Examples include the technology of subsistence, the relationships between technologies and the environment, and work patterns.* See *infrastructure* and *mode of reproduction*.

Mode of reproduction – the technology and practices employed for expanding, limiting, and maintaining population size. *Examples of variables included in the mode of reproduction are demography, mating patterns, fertility, mortality, nurturance of infants, contraception, abortion, and infanticide.* See *demography*, *infrastructure*, *mode of production*, and *population*.

Modeling – copying the behavior of admired people.

Modernity – the state of being modern, usually associated with industrial and hyper-industrial societies.

Modernization – the process of general social change brought about by transitioning from an agrarian to an industrial mode of production. *The economic and social transformation occurs when a traditional agricultural society becomes highly industrialized.*

Modernization theory – a version of market-oriented development theory that argues that low-income societies develop economically only if they give up their traditional ways and adopt modern economic institutions, technologies, and cultural values that emphasize savings and productive investment. *Explains patterns of social development. Modernization theories focus on relationships between internal factors in societies (such as the relationship between economic development and democratic institutions) and argue that poor countries should emulate the structural patterns of wealthy countries.*

Monarchies – political systems headed by a single person whose power is passed down through their family across generations.

Monarchy – a hereditary form of government in which a king, queen, or similar member of the nobility rules. A political system in which a representative from one family controls the government, and power is passed on through that family from generation to generation.

Monogamy – a marriage in which each partner is allowed only one spouse at any time. A bond that restricts the individuals involved in an exclusive sexual partnership for the duration of the relationship. See *serial monogamy.*

Monopoly – exclusive control of an industry, market, service, or commodity by a single organization. Single producers dominate each industry or market. See *oligopoly.*

Monopoly capitalism – when vast amounts of accumulated capital within corporations give these organizations enormous social, political, and economic power. Operating control of these organizations is vested in specialized management.

Monotheism – belief in a single divine being. Christianity, Islam, and Judaism are monotheistic religions.

Moral panic – widespread alarm in response to behaviors threatening moral standards.

Moral reasoning – why people think the way they do about right and wrong.

Mortality rate – the number of deaths that occur in a particular population in a specified period (usually a year).

Mores – a norm based on notions of morality. Norms that have strong moral significance, violations of which cause strong social reactions. *Examples include prohibitions against murder and sexual molestation of children. Strongly held social norms, a violation of which causes a sense of moral outrage.*

Mortality rate – the annual number of deaths per thousand in a population.

Most industrialized nations – highly industrialized, capitalistic countries, including America, Canada, Great Britain, France, Germany, and Japan.

Motive – a personal drive, intentional reason, or impulse that causes a person to act in a certain way.

Multicultural drift – the gradual move towards acceptance of multicultural societies, created by everyday interactions and experiences rather than academic theorists.

Multiculturalism (or *melting pot*) – 1. a sensitivity to the diverse cultural backgrounds and experiences within a society. 2. describe policies and ideologies promoting sensitivity. Ethnic groups exist separately and share economic and political life. *A pluralistic society in which the original cultural heritages of its citizens are recognized and respected.*

Multimedia – the combination of what used to be different media requiring different technologies (e.g., visuals and sound) on a single medium.

Multinational corporations – large corporations that do business in different countries.

Multi-linear evolution – an interpretation of social evolution that not all societies pass through predetermined stages of evolutionary development and that different societies follow varying paths of evolutionary change.

Multinational corporation (or *transnational corporation*) – a business corporation that operates in two or more countries.

Multiple-nuclei theory – urban development holds that cities develop around several different centers, each with activities.

N

Nation – a group as a cohesive unit based on various cultural, ancestral, or historical criteria. Members of a nation are typically similar regarding their language, religious beliefs, cultural practices, and ethnic identities. An autonomous political grouping that usually shares a common language and geography. *A group bound by a keen sense of shared values, cultural characteristics such as language and religion, and a perceived common history.*

Nation-state – a political apparatus over a specific territory with its citizens backed up by military force and a nationalistic, sovereign creed. A modern state in which a government has sovereign power within a defined territorial area and the mass of the population are citizens. Social organization in which political authority overlaps a cultural and geographical community. A *state* in which most citizens belong to the same *nation*.

Nationalism – an individual's internalization of beliefs and values expressing love, pride, and identification with a nation-state. Rituals and symbols are essential tools in fostering nationalism among the citizens. A set of beliefs, political ideas, and movements expressing identification with a given national community and pursuing the interests of that community.

Natural environment – the Earth's surface and atmosphere, including all living organisms and the air, water, soil, and other resources necessary to sustain life.

Nature *vs.* nurture debate – whether our behavior is primarily determined by biological factors (or *nature*) or by the influence of our social environment (or *nurture*). *Many approaches focus on how these factors interact.*

Necropolitics (*Mbembe*) – power to dictate who will live and who will die.

Negative sanctions – socially constructed expressions of disapproval. *Actions intended to deter or punish unwanted social behaviors.*

Negotiation – social interaction in which two or more parties in conflict or competition arrive at a mutually satisfactory agreement.

Neocolonialism (*Michael Harrington*) – the tendency of the most industrialized nations to exploit less developed countries politically and economically. The informal dominance of some nations over others uses unequal economic exchange conditions (as between industrialized countries of the Global North and countries of the Global South). *A recent global power relationship involves not direct political control but economic exploitation by multinational corporations.*

Neoliberalism – the economic belief that free market forces, achieved by minimizing government restrictions on business, provide the only route to economic growth.

Neo-locality – a residential pattern in which a married couple lives apart from the parents of both spouses. *A social custom in which married couples move together to a new home.* A family residential pattern in which the couple lives apart from the place of residence of both partners' parents. See *matrilocality* and *patrilocality*.

Network – a set of informal and formal social ties that link people to each other. *A series of social ties as essential sources of information, contacts, and assistance for its members.*

Network capital (*Urry*) – an individual resource needed for success in a network society. *Network capital involves technical and social skills, access to documents, technologies, and transportation, and ties with other individuals.*

Networked selves – social networking and digital technologies affect our sense of self.

New materialism – a theoretical perspective that scholars should consider how material objects and other non-human elements shape social life.

New racism – based on a belief in the superiority or value of (or even need for protection of) the *culture* of a particular race or ethnic group rather than superiority in *biological* traits.

New social movements – social movements emerging in Western societies from the mid–1960s. *New social movements are considered fundamentally different from conventional social movements in the issues they pursue and how they do so.*

Newly industrializing countries (NIC) – lower-income countries are fast becoming higher-income countries. Nation-states (e.g., South Korea) that recently became industrialized.

New money – the class of people whose wealth has been around only for a generation or two.

News values – the values and assumptions held by editors and journalists that guide them in choosing what is "*newsworthy*," what to report, what to leave out, and how they choose to report should be presented.

Nobility – the highest stratum of the estate system of stratification. Members had significant inherited wealth and did little or no discernible work.

Nomadic – societies moving residences from place to place.

Nomothetic – characterized by a tendency to generalize or search for universal laws or principles. *Sociology is a nomothetic enterprise.* See *idiographic*.

Non-human agency – non-humans have the agency (or capacity) to influence events.

Non-material culture – the intangible world of ideas created by members of a society. *The intangible, invisible parts of a culture, such as values. The norms, customs, beliefs, and ideologies of social groups.* See *material culture*.

Non-profit organization (*voluntary organization*) – an association or organization formed to further a purpose of importance to its members rather than primarily to earn a profit.

Non-state actors – international agencies such as the United Nations or the World Health Organization play a part in the world system.

Non-verbal communication – uses body movements, gestures, and facial expressions rather than speech. *Visual and other meaningful symbols without language.*

Normal science (*Kuhn*) – research based on past scientific achievements accepted as a valuable foundation for further study.

Norm – a rule or expectation of conduct that prescribes or forbids a behavior.

Normative consensus – shared agreement among the vast majority in a group or society about what behaviors are appropriate and expected of its members.

Normative structure – long-standing patterns of norms and expectations of behavior within a society or an organization.

Norms – rules and expectations by which a society guides its members' behavior. *Guidelines or expectations for behavior. S*hared rules about acceptable or unacceptable social behavior.

Northern Theory – produced from the perspective of the Global North.

Nuclear family – consists of a mother, father (one or both), and dependent children living separately from other relatives. *One or both parents and their children.*

O

Objective knowledge – how much an individual actually knows versus *subjective knowledge* (i.e., how much an individual thinks he/she knows about something). *Objective knowledge can be produced through careful observation, comparison, and experimentation.*

Objectivity – a perspective striving to reduce or eliminate bias in conducting or interpreting research and scholarship. Procedures researchers follow to minimize distortions in observation or interpretation due to personal or social values. *State of personal neutrality in conducting research.*

Occupation – a person's principal job or profession, the activity by which they earn subsistence. *A position in the work world involving specialized knowledge and activities. Paid employment in which an individual works regularly.*

Occupational distribution – the number of workers in each occupational classification.

Occupational prestige – social respect accorded to individuals or groups because of the status of their occupation.

Occupational segregation – the concentration of workers by gender (or ethnicity) into specific jobs but not others.

Offshoring (or *outsourcing*) – contracting services or manufacturing to another organization to reduce costs. Contracting of a company's tasks that were previously performed internally. *When the organization is in another country, the process is outsourcing.*

Oligarchy – rule by a few within an organization or in society. *Rule of the many by the few.*

Oligopoly – when a small number of firms dominate an industry or market. When four or fewer firms supply 50 percent or more of a given market, the effects of oligopoly become apparent. *These effects are reputed to be a rise in price and a lowering of quality because of the decline of competition. Control of an industry, market, service, or commodity by a few large organizations.* See *monopoly*.

Ontology – a theory and study of what exists, types of humans, and how they emerge, change, and are related.

Open-lineage family – a system in pre-industrial Europe in which family relationships are closely intertwined with the local community.

Open system (*organizational theory*) – the degree to which an organization is open to and dependent on its environment.

Operationalization (*research*) – the procedures or operations conducted to measure a variable.

Operatives and laborers – unskilled and semi-skilled - usually in manufacturing or construction.

Opportunity (*organizations*) – the potential of a position for expanding work responsibilities and rewards.

Oral history (*research methods*) – interviews with people about events they witnessed or experienced earlier.

Ordinary cosmopolitanism – single community behavior or ideas evident every day.

Organic solidarity (*Emile Durkheim*) – the social cohesion resulting from various parts of a society functioning as an integrated whole. *Social cohesion based on the interdependence of the division of labor rather than on similarity between individuals. Integration of a group by mutual interdependence.* See *mechanical solidarity*.

Organization – a large group of individuals involving a definite set of authority relations. *A social group deliberately formed to pursue specific values and goals.*

Organizational ritualism – behavior in organizations, particularly in bureaucracies, in which people follow the rules and regulations so closely that they forget the purpose of those rules and regulations.

Organizational waste – the inefficient use of ideas, expertise, money, or material.

Organized crime – criminal activities carried out by organizations established as businesses.

Orientalism – a perspective on Eastern culture cultivated by Western academics, artists, and intellectuals. *Orientalism depicts Eastern culture as exotic, alien, irrational, or backward compared to the superior West.*

Other – an oppositional group against which self-image is constructed. The characteristics of the self are defined in opposition to the characteristics of the other.

Otherness – groups defined as being different from the norm, marginalized, fetishized, or rendered invisible from mainstream society.

Out-group – does not belong and does not feel loyalty.

Outer controls (*control theory*) – individuals who encourage people not to deviate.

Outsiders – Individuals who are thought to violate the established norms of a social group.

Outsourcing (or *offshoring*) – contracting services or manufacturing to another organization to reduce costs. Contracting of a company's tasks that were previously performed internally. When the organization in question is in another country, the process is *offshoring*.

Ownership – the legal right to the possession of an object or thing. For Marx, ownership of the means of production was a crucial factor in understanding a sociocultural system.

Ozone depletion – a decline in the total ozone volume in Earth's stratosphere. This depletion of the ozone layer, which protects plant and animal life from harmful ultraviolet radiation, is believed to have been caused by the production of chlorofluorocarbons and other gases. See *environment* and *pollution*.

P

Panic – a frightened response by an aggregate of people to an immediate threat.

Panopticon (*Foucault et al.*) – a metaphor for modern surveillance and self-formation. It is a type of prison designed by philosopher Jeremy Bentham and his brother in the 19th century, in which cells are built around a central but not visible (for the inmates) guard tower, such that prisoners come to assume they are being watched continuously, even if they are not.

Paradigm (*sociology of science*) – a coherent tradition of scientific law, theory, and assumptions that forms a distinct approach to problems. A theoretical framework or worldview within which middle-range theories and generalizations regarding social reality are formulated and evaluated. *Philosophical and theoretical frameworks used within a discipline to formulate theories, generalizations, and the experiments performed in support of them.*

Parallel marriage – when husband and wife both work and share household tasks.

Paranoid nationalism (*Hage*) – compared to an earlier form of *defensive nationalism* that viewed the threat to nations as external, paranoid nationalism is built on the newly vulnerable working and middle-class members projecting this vulnerability onto things deemed culturally alien, particularly within the nation's borders.

Participant observation (*research methods*) – researchers systematically observe people while they join their routine activities. Research method in which the researcher observes while participating in the activities of the studied social group. A method widely used in sociology and anthropology in which the researcher participates in the activities of a group or community being studied.

Participatory democracy – a system of democracy in which all members of a group or community participate collectively in making significant decisions. *Most nation-states today are too large and complex for participatory democracy to be a feasible form of government.*

Party (*Weber*) – group-oriented to the acquisition of power. *Parties are directed toward the accomplishment of a particular goal.*

Passing – when others see a member of one group as a member of a different group (e.g., a light-skinned Black person *passing* as Caucasian).

Pastoral societies (or *herding societies*) – when raising and herding animals such as sheep, goats, and cows are the primary means of subsistence; there is often a need to migrate between different areas according to seasonal changes or seek fresh grazing. *Relies on the domestication and breeding of animals for food.*

Pastoralism – technology based on the domestication of animals.

Patient dumping – treating only patients who can pay, leaving people with low incomes to governmental or charitable organizations.

Patriarchal family – an organization in which the father is the formal head of the family.

Patriarchy – a social organization with power primarily monopolized or held by men, to the exclusion of women. *A social organization in which men dominate women.*

Patrilineal descent – a system tracing kinship through men. See *matrilineal descent.*

Patrilocality – a residential pattern in which a married couple lives with or near the husband's family. A family residential pattern in which the wife is expected to live near the husband's parents. *A social custom in which married couples live in the husband's family home.* See *matrilocality* and *neo-locality.*

Pauperization – the act or process of impoverishing someone. *Marx theorized that capital must ultimately lead to the pauperization of the masses.*

Pay equity (or *comparable worth*) – the principle that jobs dominated by women and jobs dominated by men should be evaluated based on training, skills, and experience to equalize wages. *People should be paid equally for jobs of comparable worth. A policy of equal pay for men and women doing similar work, even if the jobs are labeled differently by sex.*

Peak oil – the year when oil production reaches its maximum and begins to decline. Peak oil can refer to a particular oil field, a nation-state, or the world.

Peasants – people in agrarian societies who produce food from the land using traditional farming methods of plowing and animal power, farm workers in agrarian societies.

Peer group – a social group whose members have interests, social position, and age in common. *Members are usually the same age with interests and social positions in common.*

Performativity (*Butler*) – the process by which gender identities are created and reinforced through behaviors, gestures, and elocutions.

Peripheral country – has a marginal role in the world economy and is dependent on core countries in its trading relationships. *Countries have a marginal role in the world economy and thus depend on the core-producing societies for their trading relationships.* See *core country* and *semi-peripheral country.*

Personal crime – directed against individuals.

Personal space – the area immediately around one's body that one can claim as one's own.

Personality – consistent patterns of attitudes and beliefs projected to the social world.

Petty Bourgeoisie (*Marxism*) – a bourgeoisie sub-class comprised of small-scale merchants, businesspeople, and professionals.

Physician assistant – a trained medical assistant who handles many routine medical problems, allowing the physician to deal with the more complex cases.

Pilot studies (*research design*) – trial runs in survey research.

Planned economy (or *command economy*) – an economic system in which government agencies plan investment, supply, prices, and the distribution of goods. *Examples include the former Soviet Union and contemporary North Korea.* See *market economy*.

Platform capitalism – the widespread use of digital platforms.

Play – spontaneous activity undertaken freely for its own sake yet governed by rules and often characterized by an element of make-believe.

Play stage (*George Herbert Mead*) – second of three stages of childhood socialization. In the play stage, the child begins to take on the role of significant others, such as pretending to be his or her mother. Through this behavior, the child begins to see himself or herself as others do. See *game stage* and *imitation stage*.

Plea bargain – an agreement between the prosecution and the accused offender where the accused will plead guilty in return for a reduced charge.

Pluralism – 1. in ethnic relations exists when majority and minority groups value their distinct cultural identities and simultaneously seek economic and political unity. 2. in political sociology, the view that society is composed of competing interest groups, with power diffused among them. *A political theory that power resources are distributed throughout society and used by various groups to compete for influence.*

Pluralist – one who subscribes to pluralist theory.

Pluralistic society – composed of many kinds of people.

Pluralist theory – an analysis of politics emphasizes the role of diverse and competing interest groups in preventing too much power from being accumulated by political and economic elites.

Polarization effect – An aspect of moral panics in which a split is created between two groups, typically the 'deviant' group and the 'correct' group.

Policy research – social research aimed at clarifying issues and problems that changes in social policy can then address. *Assesses alternative possibilities for public or social action regarding their costs or consequences.*

Political action committee (PAC) – an interest group organization that raises and contributes money to politicians who support the group's interests.

Political economy – in Marvin Harris's definition, the structural components of sociocultural systems are organized around production, exchange, and consumption within and between large-scale political units (e.g., bands, villages, states, and empires).

Political economy model – a land use theory emphasizing political and economic interests.

Political order – the institutionalized system of acquiring and exercising power.

Political party – 1. an organized group sharing similar political positions who field candidates for elections and attempt access to institutional political power. 2. (*Mann*) power held by a centralized, institutionalized, regulative body controlling an associated territory. *An organized group seeking control or influence in political decisions through legal means. An organization of people with similar interests and attitudes established to achieve legitimate government control and use that power to pursue specific programs.*

Political revolution – a substantial change in political governance based on a revolt against the existing order that is often violent, including the American and French revolutions of the late 18th century that are seen as constitutive of modernity.

Politics – attempts to influence governmental activities.

Pollution – the contamination of soil, water, or air by noxious substances. Pollution is one of the principal constraints of the environment. See *depletion*, *environment*, and *intensification*.

Polyandry – marriage in which a woman may have more than one husband.

Polygamy – marriage between one man and more than one woman.

Polygyny – a marriage in which a man may simultaneously have more than one wife.

Polytheism – belief in two or more gods. Belief in two or more divine beings. See *monotheism*.

Popular culture – prevalent in a particular social group. Beliefs, norms, material objects, and artistic expressions are part of the everyday life of a people. *Often defined in opposition to high or elite culture.*

Population – 1. (*demography*) all people living in a geographic area. 2. (*social research*) the researcher studies the entire group. For large groups, sampling is usually undertaken.

Population (*research*) – the total number of cases with a particular characteristic.

Population (*social research*) – 1. the people who are the focus of a study or survey. 2. people sharing one or more attributes, typically geographic location.

Population density (or *density*) – the number of people living in each area. This is usually measured by the number of people per square kilometer or square mile.

Population exclusion – efforts of society to prevent ethnically diverse groups from joining.

Population replacement level – when the birth and death rates in a particular area are about equal, leading to zero population growth.

Positive checks (*Malthus*) – measures and activities by which the life span of an existing human is shortened. "Positive" (a misapplied term) is used not in the usual sense of good or desirable but in contrast to "*preventive.*" *Rather than preventing births from occurring, positive checks are actions that directly terminate life—that actively cut down the existing population by reducing the human life span.* See i*nfanticide, Malthusianism,* and *preventive checks.*

Positive sanction – a socially constructed expression of approval.

Population transfer – the efforts of a dominant ethnic group to move or remove members of a minority ethnic group from an area.

Positive sanctions – rewards for socially desired behavior.

Positivism (*sociology*) – the view that the study of the social world should be conducted according to the principles of natural science. A philosophical position with close ties between the social and natural sciences, which share a common logical framework. Accurate observation, description, and measurement are considered critical in this perspective.

Positivist – explaining human action without considering the individual's interpretation.

Post-colonial feminism – focuses on the experiences of non-white, non-Western women.

Post-colonial melancholy – a feeling of sadness, regret, and longing associated with a growing recognition of the negative aspects of colonization. *Typically associated with nostalgia for the time of empire, especially in Britain.*

Post-colonial studies – an academic discipline studying the ongoing social, cultural, and economic effects of colonialism and imperialism.

Post-colonial theories – analyze social phenomena by examining their role in creating or maintaining Western / European dominance.

Post-feminism – feminism is no longer necessary as a political movement and gender equality has been achieved.

Post-Fordism – the dominant production system in most contemporary industrialized economies, associated with a decline in mass production. The transition from mass industrial production, characterized by Fordist methods, to more flexible forms of production favoring innovation and aimed at meeting market demands for customized products. *Post-Fordism is typically thought to involve the rise of service professions, an emphasis on information and communication technologies, and a shift to small-batch production.*

Post-industrial economy – providing services and information has higher relative importance than manufacturing goods.

Post-industrial society (*Daniel Bell*) – organized by knowledge and planning rather than industrial production. A post-industrial society is based on producing information rather than material goods. *Based on producing services and information rather than material goods. This notion is advocated by those who believe that the industrial order is passing. An economy based on services and technology, not production.* See *hyper industrialism.*

Postmodernism – a theoretical perspective widespread in cultural studies and anthropology based on the idea that there is no objective social reality but that different realities are constructed in the minds of individuals from the words and images (or discourse) exchanged between people.

Post-modernity – cultural patterns or social structures seeming to depart from, or otherwise break with, those characteristics of 'modern' societies.

Post-structuralism – a school of thought emerging in 1960s France, which developed in reaction to the structuralist movement that preceded it.

Postmodern society – pluralistic and diverse, with no 'grand narrative' guiding its development.

Postmodernism – the belief that society is no longer governed by history or progress.

Poststructuralism (*Michel Foucault*) – an approach to social science derived from linguistics and popularized in sociology in the work of Michel Foucault.

Poststructuralists reject the idea that absolute truths about the world can be discovered, arguing instead that plural interpretations of reality are inevitable.

Poverty level – an estimate set by the federal government of the minimum income a family of four needs to survive.

Poverty line. – the income needed to maintain a family at a basic level, often determined by the government.

Power (*Weber*) – the ability of an entity or individual to control, direct, or otherwise influence another entity or individual. The ability to achieve aims or further the interests that one holds even when opposed by others. *Achieve ends despite resistance. The capacity of an individual group to control or influence the behavior of others, even in the face of opposition.*

Power elite (*C. Wright Mills*) – people in the highest positions of government, corporations, and the military who hold enormous power in modern industrial societies. *Describes the leaders of military, corporate, and political groups, each of which is thought to share similar political interests and social networks. An intricately connected group of the corporate rich, political leaders, and military commanders who decide the most critical social and political issues. The United States is run by a small group representing the most wealthy, powerful, and influential people in business, government, and the military.*

Power structures – organization of power that dictates behavior and norms within a society, such as a government or corporation.

Practices (*Bourdieu et al.*) – an action providing a foundation for broader social patterns.

Precariat – a social class comprised of people in precarious forms of employment.

Pre-industrial society – a broad classification of modes of production before industrialism. *The most common are hunting-and-gathering, horticultural, pastoral, and agrarian societies.*

Prejudice – pre-emptive judging of a group or individual based on assumed characteristics. *A "prejudged" unfavorable attitude toward the members of a particular group assumed to possess negative traits. Harboring preconceived ideas about an individual or group that are resistant to change even with added information. Prejudice may be either positive or negative. A generalization about a group applied indiscriminately and inflexibly with little regard for facts, leading to mental prejudgments based on stereotypes. Prejudices can lead to hostility and discrimination.*

Prestige – social recognition, respect, and deference accorded to individuals or groups based on social status. *Social respect accorded to individuals or groups because of position status.*

Preventive checks (*Malthus*) – the various measures and activities by which people attempt to prevent conception and birth. See *infanticide*, *Malthusianism*, and *positive checks*.

Primacy of the infrastructure (*Marvin Harris*) – efforts to understand or explain a widespread social practice or belief must begin with examining the relationship between infrastructure and the environment. Harris initially labeled this the principle of *infrastructural determinism*, an unfortunate choice since Harris explicitly recognizes the probabilistic nature of the relationship. Due to misunderstandings and misinterpretations, he later renamed this principle the *primacy of the infrastructure*.

Primary deviance (*Lemert*) – a deviant act that elicits little or no reaction from others. *Behavior invisible to others, short-lived, or unimportant, and, therefore, does not contribute to the public labeling of an individual as deviant.*

Primary economic sector – the sector of an economy in which natural resources are gathered or extracted.

Primary group – a social group characterized by frequent face-to-face interaction, commitment, emotional ties members feel for one another, and relative permanence. *With frequent face-to-face contact, little task orientation, and emotional intimacy among members.*

Primary labor market – the economic position of individuals engaged in occupations providing secure jobs, good benefits, and working conditions. See *secondary labor market*.

Primary group – a typically small group who have an enduring personal relationship with one another and interact intimately. *Examples include families, clans, local communities, voluntary organizations (e.g., churches or clubs), and close friends. These groups can perform many functions, including socialization, education, enforcing social discipline, regulating reproduction, and producing food and material goods. The distinction between primary and secondary groups is fundamental to analyzing social structure provided by sociocultural materialism; together, the two forms of social organization encompass all human groups.* See *secondary group*.

Primary needs (*Karl Marx*) – the natural needs we are born with, including food, water, and shelter. See *secondary needs*.

Primary sector – part of a modern economy based on extracting resources directly from the natural environment, including mining and agricultural production.

Primary socialization – the process by which children learn the cultural norms of the society into which they are born. *Learning experiences from the people who raised them.*

Primogeniture – a law stipulating that only a first-born son could inherit his father's wealth.

Principle of cumulative advantage – when some institutions' positive features generate further benefits.

Private health care – fee-for-service- is available only to those who pay the complete costs of services.

Privatization (*administration*) – transfer of public services from government administration to private enterprise. *In Canada, widespread privatization occurred in the 1980s and 1990s in the mining, fisheries, oil and natural gas, transportation (e.g., shipping, rail, air, and trucking), and telecommunications industries. Privatization has extended to military and security services, education, and prisons in the United States.*

Privatization (*sociology*) – the tendency of families in industrial societies to turn away from the community and workplace toward a primary focus on privacy, domesticity, and intimacy.

Privilege – specific individuals or groups have advantages based on various characteristics, such as race, gender, sexuality, etc.

Processes of socialization – those interactions convey to persons being socialized how they are to speak, behave, think, and feel.

Production – providing goods or services.

Profane – elements of society that belong to the ordinary everyday world rather than the realm of the supernatural. *Belongs to the mundane, everyday world.* See *sacred*.

Profession – an occupation that requires extensive educational qualifications, has high social prestige, and is subject to codes of conduct laid down by central bodies (or professional associations). *An occupation rests on a theoretical body of knowledge and thus requires specialized training usually recognized by granting a degree or credential.*

Project identities (*Castells*) – collective identity allows individuals to redefine their social positions and to seek a transformation of the overall social structure.

Projection (*psychological process*) – attributing one's unacceptable feelings or desires to others to avoid guilt and self-blame.

Proletariat (*Marxism*) – the class not owning or controlling the means of production within the capitalist system. *Industrial workers with nothing to sell in the free market except labor. To subsist, members of the proletariat must sell their labor power to the bourgeoisie for a wage. The working masses, the working class under capitalism.*

Propaganda – information systematically spread by an organization to further its agenda.

Property – the rights and obligations for an object, resource, or activity.

Property crime – theft that does not physically harm an individual.

Proposition – a statement about how variables are related to each other.

Props (*Goffman's impression management theory*) – the things used to decorate a setting and include manner of dress.

Prostitution – the selling of sexual favors for economic gain.

Protestant ethic (*Weber*) – a belief in hard work, thrift, and personal discipline, common to the values of the Protestant faith. The belief of certain Protestants, especially Calvinists, that arduous work is a Christian duty that builds moral character. Weber theorized that these Protestant values of hard work and thrift, combined with predestination beliefs, prompted Calvinists (and, to a lesser extent, other Protestant sects) to view worldly success as evidence that a person was saved—that he or she was among the elect. This led them to value profit and facilitated the transition to capitalism. *For Weber, this was a cultural spark that had an elective affinity with capitalism and allowed it to grow in influence.*

Pseudo-individualization (*Adorno*) – elements of mass culture, such as products or popular songs, appear to be unique and different when highly standardized. *For Adorno, this creates an illusion of choice.*

Psychoanalytic theory – the unconscious shapes much of human behavior.

Psychopath (or *sociopath*) – an anti-social personality disorder in which the individual lacks a conscience, engages in behavior with little consideration of the harm done to others, and experiences no feelings of guilt or remorse for the harm that he or she causes. While psychopaths can mimic human emotions, they do not experience any genuine sense of a social bond with others.

Psychosis – a severe mental disorder that fails to distinguish between internal and external reality. The affected person cannot function effectively in their social life.

Public health care – government-funded health care services available to all population members.

Public sphere (*Jürgen Habermas*) – the public debate and discussion arena in societies.

Public sociology – engaging non-academic audiences to address social problems.

Push and pull factors – in the early study of global migration, internal and external forces were believed to influence migration patterns. *Push factors* are the dynamics within the country of origin (e.g., unemployment, war, famine, or political persecution). *Pull factors* describe features of destination countries (e.g., labor markets, lower population density, and a high standard of living).

Q

Qualitative research methods (*research methods*) – gathering detailed data to understand better the studied social phenomena. An investigation by which a researcher gathers impressionistic, not numerical, data. *Researching social life from the perspective that not everything can be counted and understanding people's experiences and perspectives is a key aim of sociological research. Methods include participant observation, ethnography, interviews, and focus groups.*

Qualitative sociology – in-depth interviews, focus groups, or analysis of content sources as the source of its data.

Quantified self (*Lupton*) – self-identities increasingly expressed or understood through numbers and measures.

Quantitative research methods (*research methods*) – sociological methods allowing social phenomena to be measured and analyzed using mathematical and statistical techniques. Aim to quantify elements of social life, often to compare groups. *These approaches, which include survey research and statistical analysis of the results, often aim to identify general patterns in society or within a group.*

Quantitative sociology – statistical methods such as surveys with large numbers of participants.

Queer Theory – emerging primarily in the 1990s, focuses on the social construction of gender and sexual identities and how dominant forms can be transgressed.

Questionnaire (*research methods*) – a series of written questions a researcher supplies to subjects requesting responses.

Quality circle (QC) – industrialized group production where workers use their expertise to participate in decision-making.

Queer theory – prejudiced towards heterosexuals and non-heterosexual voices must challenge heterosexual assumptions that underlie contemporary thinking.

R

Race – a largely informal rank in biological taxonomy, typically referring to genetically distinct populations of individuals within the same species. A socially defined category of people with genetically transmitted physical characteristics. *Social relationships applicable to individuals and groups with attributes or competencies assigned based on biologically grounded features. Classification of humans into groups based on distinguishable physical characteristics forms the basis for significant social identities.*

Racial profiling – using race by agents of social control, such as police or airport security, as the primary criterion for deciding whether to subject an individual to more intensive scrutiny.

Race–conflict theory (*Marx's conflict theory*) – focuses on perpetual conflict and inequality between racial and ethnic groups.

Racialization – when an individual becomes categorized as part of a racial group.

Raciology (or *scientific racism*) (*Gilroy*) – the continued use of racial thinking, especially attempts to reassert essential or biological differences between human races.

Racism – prejudice or discrimination based on perceived race. The institutional processes by which racial inequality is sustained. Racism is driven by the belief that one racial group is superior. It is more than just an insult or an individual act of violence; it is about historical and cultural patterns, unconscious bias that affects social relations, and structural discrimination. The attribution of inferiority to a particular racial category; a specific form of prejudice focused on race. *Attributing characteristics of superiority or inferiority to a population sharing specific physically inherited characteristics.*

Racist ableism – the cumulative impact when ableism intersects with racial discrimination.

Racial discrimination – the unfair treatment and lack of opportunities due to ascribed racial markers such as skin color or other perceived physical features, ancestry, national or ethnic origin, or immigrant status.

Radical feminism – gender inequality results from male domination in all aspects of social and economic life.

Radical movement – seeks fundamental change in the sociocultural system.

Random sampling (*experimental design*) – a sampling method in which a sample is chosen so every member of the population has the same probability of being included. *A sample of units drawn from a larger population, so each has a known and equal chance of being selected.*

Range – the spread of values in a set of figures.

Rank – the place in a social hierarchy.

Rank differentiation – see *differentiation* and *rank*.

Rape – a completed sexual assault by a person, usually upon another. The use of force to compel one individual to engage in a sexual act with another.

Rate of natural increase – the difference between birth and death rates, excluding immigration.

Rational action (*Weber*) – social action guided by conscious ideas and decisions. Contrast *traditional action* (i.e., guided by habit) or *affective action* (i.e., guided by emotion).

Rational choice theory – humans make cost-benefit analyses before engaging in significant social actions such as having children or attending college.

Rational–legal authority (*Weber's power theory*) (*bureaucratic authority*) – power legitimized by legally enacted rules and regulations. Authority based on law, rules, or regulations. See *charismatic authority* and *traditional authority.*

Rationalism – the reliance on logic, observation, and reason to guide one's behavior and beliefs.

Rationality – a mental state characterized by coherent thought processes that are goal-oriented and based on a cost-benefit evaluation. *Deliberate, matter-of-fact calculation of the most efficient means to accomplish a particular goal.*

Rationalization (*Max Weber*) – modern society exchanges emotional traditions and moral values for rational qualities, such as workplace efficiency and increased productivity. *Subjecting social relationships to calculation and administration. Process by which modes of precise calculation and organization involving abstract rules and procedures increasingly dominate the social world. Rationalization is a habit of thought that replaces tradition, emotion, and values as motivators of human conduct. Bureaucracy is the result of rationalization applied to human social organization.* See *bureaucratization* and *intensification.*

Rationalization of society (*Weber*) – the historical change from tradition to rationality as the dominant mode of human thought. *Bureaucracies would gain increasing power over modern life, eventually governing most aspect of society.*

Reactionary movement. – focuses on resisting change or advocating for the return to an earlier order.

Real culture (*opposed to ideal culture*) – social patterns approximating cultural expectations.

Real values – what people consider truly important, as evident in their behavior and spending time and money.

Realist approach – social problems are objective challenges regardless of whether they are recognized.

Realm of freedom (*Marxism*) – when individuals may act as they please, unconstrained by material necessities.

Realm of necessity – constraint by the necessity of working to meet material needs.

Rebellion – 1. In *anomie theory*, deviance occurs when individuals reject culturally valued means and goals and substitute new ones. 2. in political sociology, opposition to an established authority is expressed. Social actions aimed to remove rulers or regimes rather than bring about significant structural changes. *In Robert K. Merton's anomie theory, rebellion is one of the five modes of adaptation, characterized by a rejection of both normative goals and the socially sanctioned means of achieving them and the substitution of new goals and means in their stead.* See *coup d'état, Revolution, conformity, innovation, retreatism*, and *ritualism.*

Rebels (*Robert Merton's theory of goals and means*) – those who reject cultural goals and the institutionalized means of achieving them but replace them with goals and means of their own.

Recidivism – the tendency of convicted criminals to repeat offenses.

Recidivism rate. – percentage of ex-convicts convicted of new offenses after release.

Reciprocity – a system of the exchange of goods based on social ties.

Redlining – the systematic denial of service (e.g., loan or insurance) to groups, ostensibly based on the neighborhood but practically and in its impact based on perceived race.

Reference group – a social group serving as a reference for evaluations or decisions. Standards and opinions to evaluate beliefs, values, and behaviors. *Comparisons for purposes of self-evaluation. People identify with and provide standards of behavior, values, beliefs, attitudes, or other metrics.*

Reflexive / Reflexivity – the capacity to reflect on their behavior and recognize the structural factors that shape, constrain, or otherwise inform it. Reflexivity is linked with sociological *imagination. Reflexivity is also the capacity of a group or academic discipline to reflect on its assumptions or apply its methods to itself. Connections between knowledge and social life. Knowledge gained about society affects actions. For example, reading a survey about a political party's high level of support might also lead an individual to express support.*

Reform movement – concerned with implementing a limited program of social change. Accepting the *status quo* but seeking specific social reforms. *Examples include changing the health care system to provide universal access to care or reasserting government regulation over the actions of corporations.*

Refugees – people who flee their country for political or economic reasons or to avoid war and oppression.

Regressive movement – aims to move the social world back to where members believe it was earlier.

Regulatory capture – an industry's domination of a regulatory agency by lobbying or staffing the agency with people drawn from the regulated industries.

Rehabilitation – a program for reforming an offender to preclude subsequent offenses.

Reification – an error of treating an abstract concept as having a natural, material existence.

373

Reincarnation – rebirth of the soul in another body or form. *This belief is most often associated with Hindus and Buddhists. The belief that while the physical body dies, a person's soul is immortal and goes on to be reborn into another body.*

Relations of production (*Karl Marx*) – the social relations people enter due to their participation in economic life. Relations of production are socially patterned and independent of the wills and purposes of the individuals involved. The primary distinction between these individuals is whether they own the forces of production or have only their labor to sell.

Relative deprivation – the thesis that people's subjective feelings of deprivation are not absolute but related to their assessment of themselves compared to others. *A perceived disadvantage arising from a specific comparison (e.g., social or economic standing based on a comparison to others in a society).*

Relative poverty – the condition of having much less income than the average person in society, even if one can afford the necessities of life. The average standard of living in a society. *The deprivation of some people in relation to those with more. Refers to the overall standard of living in any given society.*

Reliability (*statistics*) – the probability that a given measure would be the same if measured again. Not all measures are reliable. *The quality of consistent measurement.*

Religion – a social institution involving beliefs and practices based upon a conception of the sacred. *Institutions responsible for answering people's larger questions and explaining the seemingly inexplicable. A social institution with shared beliefs reinforcing social values through ritual. Beliefs adhered to by community members involving symbols regarded with a sense of awe or wonder, together with ritual practices in which community members engage. Organized cultural practices and worldviews linking us to the supernatural.*

Religious movement – an organized religious group aiming to change religious institutions.

Religiosity – a measure of religious faith's intensity and importance to an individual.

Replication – reproducibility of research by others.

Replication study (*experimental design*) – experiment repeated on another sample of subjects at a different time. Such studies are checks on the validity and reliability of research.

Representative democracy – a political system in which decisions affecting a community are made, not by its members but by the people they have elected for this purpose.

Representative sample (*experimental design*) – a representation from a larger population that is statistically typical of that population.

Reproductive technology – techniques of influencing the human reproductive process.

Research and development (R&D) – investments in basic research and the practical application of fundamental discoveries.

Research design (*experimental design*) – the overall logic and strategy of the research methods for a particular study. *The specific research study plan includes sampling, measurement, and data analysis.*

Research methods (*experimental design*) – the diverse methods of investigation used to systematically gather empirical (i.e., verifiable observations) material. *A systematic plan for conducting research.*

Research tool (*experimental design*) – a systematic technique for conducting research.

Reserve army of labor (*Marxism*) – the unemployed population, whose presence is thought to depress working conditions and wages.

Resistance – a refusal to accept or comply with the power of another.

Resistance identities (*Castells*) – collective identity emerges when social changes disenfranchise or marginalize people. *Resistance identities entrench against social change.*

Resocialization – radically altering an inmate's personality through deliberately manipulating the environment. Relearning cultural norms and values by mature individuals, usually in the context of a total institution. The process of socializing with people away from a group or activity in which they are involved. *Learning new norms and values.* See *total institution.*

Resource mobilization theory – social movements are affected by their ability to marshal vital resources.

Retirement center – a city or town where many people move when they retire.

Retreatism (*Robert Merton's theory of goals and means*) – 1. those who reject cultural goals and the institutionalized means of achieving them. 2. (*anomie theory*) deviance when individuals abandon culturally valued means and goals. The escape from society's demands by rejecting culturally prescribed goals and methods of achieving them. *Retreatism is one of the five modes of adaptation in Robert K. Merton's anomie theory. Those who adapt through retreatism are society's dropouts: psychotics, tramps, and substance abusers.* See *conformity, innovation, rebellion*, and *ritualism.*

Reverse racism – describes minorities who discriminate against majority members. Racism is perpetuated by a social system favoring a dominant group. All groups hold positive and negative prejudice towards outsiders, but this is not racism. A dominant member acting out prejudice against a minority is backed by institutional power and historical violence that minorities do not have.

Revolt – an uprising in which subordinate groups challenge established authority.

Revolting subjects (*Tyler*) – subjectivities positioned by those with cultural power as disgusting or revolting, a type of symbolic violence. *The label can be used by those to which it is applied to resist (or revolt) against this violence.*

Revolution – 1. the overthrow of a government by the governed; a process of change involving the mobilization of a mass social movement toward radically transforming society. 2. any drastic and far-reaching political, economic, social, or technological change, such as the Agricultural, Industrial, or Digital Revolutions.

A forcible overthrow of an existing government or social organization. In Marxism, revolution refers explicitly to the overthrow of a ruling class by a ruled class. A large-scale change in the political leadership of a society and the restructuring of noteworthy features of that society. A violent overthrow of the government by its citizens.

Revolutionary movement – aims to reorganize existing society completely.

Riot – a destructive and sometimes violent collective outburst. An outbreak of collective violence directed against persons, property, or both.

Rising expectations – when people feel that past hardships should not have to be suffered in the future.

Risk society (*Ulrich Beck*) – industrial society has created many new dangers and risks unknown in previous ages. *Societies are increasingly dominated by concern over risk and a desire to regulate and control risk, the central of which are risks ironically caused by science and technology and a culture that believes risks can be fundamentally mitigated. For example, the risks associated with global warming.*

Rite of passage – a communal ritual that marks the transition from one status to another. *Examples include a confirmation or bar mitzvah, a graduation, or a wedding ceremony.*

Ritual (*sociology of religion*) – the rules of conduct concerning behavior in the presence of the sacred. *It is intended to produce feelings of reverence, awe, and group identity. Formalized modes of behavior in which the group or community members regularly engage. Religion represents one of the primary contexts in which rituals are practiced, but the scope of ritual behavior extends well beyond this sphere. Most groups have ritual practices.*

Ritualism (*anomie theory*) – deviance in which individuals lose sight of socially valued goals but conform closely to socially prescribed means. The adherence to legitimate means of achieving success even when one is blocked from reaching goals and going through the motions. Ritualism is one of the five modes of adaptation in Robert K. Merton's anomie theory. See *conformity, innovation, rebellion,* and *retreatism.*

Ritualists (*Robert Merton's theory of goals and means*) – reject cultural goals but accept the institutionalized means of achieving them.

Rival hypothesis – an explanation competing with the original hypothesis in a study.

Role – 1. to functionalists, the culturally prescribed and socially patterned behaviors associated with particular social positions. 2. for interactionists, it is the effort to mesh the demands of a social position with one's own identity. *A set of norms, values, and personality characteristics expected of a person based on the setting he or she is in.*

Role accumulation – adding more statuses and roles to the ones an individual already has.

Role conflict – develops when the demands of two or more roles are incompatible. *Results from the competing demands of two or more roles. When two or more social roles make incompatible demands on a person.*

Role exit – the process of leaving a role central to one's identity and building an identity in a new role while considering one's prior role.

Role expectations – commonly shared norms about how a person should behave in a particular role.

Role model – an admired person who is an example to emulate.

Role performance – the behaviors of a person performing a specific social role.

Role set – the cluster of roles that accompanies a particular status.

Roles – commonly held expectations about how people should behave in social positions. Individuals are thought to 'play' roles when conforming to these expectations. All roles a person occupies at a given time. *For example, a woman might be a doctor, daughter, wife, mother, and sister.*

Role strain – results from conflicting expectations within a given role.

Rowdyism – generalized interpersonal violence or property destruction occurring at spectator events.

Ruling class – a small group controlling the means of economic production and dominating political decisions. *People who exercise overwhelming power and control within a society.*

Rumor – a report passed informally from one person to another without firm evidence.

S

Sanction – a socially constructed expression of approval or disapproval.

Sacred – inspires attitudes of awe or reverence among believers in each set of religious ideas. *Something set apart from the everyday world that inspires attitudes of awe or reverence among believers.* See *profane.*

Sample survey – a systematic method of collecting information from respondents using personal interviews or written questionnaires.

Sampling (*experimental design*) – studying a proportion of individuals or cases from a larger population as representative of that population. *Taking a small part of a population to draw inferences from the analysis of the sample characteristics of the population.*

Sanction – a mode of reward or punishment that reinforces socially expected behavior. *A social reward or punishment for approved or disapproved behavior can be positive or negative, formal or informal. A reward for conformity or a punishment for nonconformity that reinforces socially approved behavior.*

Sapir-Whorf hypothesis – people perceive their world through the framework of language. Thus, language determines (or, according to the weak version of the theory, influences) other aspects of culture because it provides the categories through which reality is defined.

Scapegoating – blaming, punishing, or stigmatizing a powerless individual or group for wrongs that were not of their doing. When a particular group is blamed for outcomes, they are not responsible for it. *Blaming a convenient but innocent person or group for trouble or guilt.*

Schizophrenia – a severe mental disorder in which an individual typically has delusions or hallucinations and a distorted view of reality.

Schooling – formal education.

Science – 1. applying systematic methods of observation and careful logical analysis. 2. the body of knowledge produced using the scientific method. An approach used to obtain reliable knowledge about the physical and social worlds based on systematic empirical observations; the knowledge so obtained.

Scientific management (or *Taylorism*) (*Frederick Winslow Taylor*) – a set of ideas (i.e., *scientific management*) when productivity could be immensely increased by separating industrial tasks into a series of simple operations precisely timed and optimally coordinated.

Scientific method – the research process to assure the validity, reliability, and generalization of results. These steps include observation (or gathering the data), hypothesis testing, and data analysis.

Scientific productivity – making discoveries, confirming, or disconfirming theoretical hypotheses through experimentation and other types of research, and publishing the research results.

Scientific racism (or *raciology*) (*Gilroy*) – the continued use of racial thinking, especially attempts to reassert essential or biological differences between human races.

Scientific revolution – changes in scientific inquiry, beginning in the mid-16th century. The dramatic overthrow of one intellectual paradigm by another. Key features include the emergence of science as a *distinct discipline*, the *separation of science from religion*, and the development of the *scientific method*.

Science – a logical system that bases knowledge on direct, systematic observation.

Scientism – an ideology claiming that science and the scientific method alone can provide factual knowledge and understanding of the world. Scientism rejects any alleged truths that cannot be explained by that method.

Script (*role theory*) – the learned performance of a social role.

Second shift – labor performed by women at home in addition to paid work performed in formal employment.

Second-wave feminism (1960s to the 1980s) – focusing on gender equality and discrimination against women. *Second-wave feminism was concerned with inequalities in the workplace and the family.*

Secondary analysis (*research methods*) – using primary data from others.

Secondary deviance (*Lemert*) – repeated deviant behavior brought on by other people's adverse reactions to the original act of deviance. *Behavior discovered by others and publicly labeled as deviant.*

Secondary economic sector – the sector of an economy in which raw materials are turned into manufactured goods.

Secondary group (or *secondary organization* and *formal organization*) – members organized around a specific task or goal and tend to interact based on roles defined in relation to that task or goal, with little emotional commitment to one another. A large and impersonal social group whose members pursue a specific interest or activity. Secondary organizations, typically larger than primary groups, are coordinated through bureaucracies. *With infrequent or short-term contact, little task orientation, and no emotional intimacy among members. Examples include governments, political parties, the military, corporations, educational institutions, media organizations, service and welfare organizations, and professional and labor organizations. Secondary groups perform many of the same functions primary groups can perform (such as socialization, education, enforcing social discipline, and regulating production and reproduction). However, the allocation of these functions among groups varies by society and as a society evolves from simple to more complex.* See *primary group.*

Secondary labor market – the economic position of individuals engaged in occupations that provide insecure jobs and poor benefits and conditions of work. *Jobs provide minimal benefits to workers.* See *primary labor market.*

Secondary literature (*social sciences*) – a scholar's work on another scientist's theory or writings. Textbooks and encyclopedias are secondary rather than primary literature.

Secondary needs – desires and wants become important when primary needs are satisfied. *Many secondary needs are learned.*

Secondary sector – an economy that transforms raw materials into manufactured goods.

Secondary source – all sources that discuss, interpret, or represent material that originated earlier (contrast with primary source).

Second World – refers to the former Soviet Union and communist industrial societies of Eastern Europe. See *First World, Third World, Global North*, and *Global South.*

Sect – a group that has broken off from an established religion. A sub-group (typically religious) that branched or separated from the leading group. An exclusive, highly cohesive group of ascetic religious believers. *Sects usually last longer and are more institutionalized than cults. A religious movement that breaks away from orthodoxy. A religious group that sets itself apart from society.*

Sector theory – urban development explains that cities develop in wedge-shaped patterns following transportation systems.

Secular – temporal beliefs (i.e., *of this world*) rather than spiritual.

Secularization – a process of decline in the influence of religion. Decline in the social influence of religion. The historical decline in the importance of the supernatural and the sacred. Erosion of belief in the supernatural. *Includes a growing respect for rationality, cultural and religious pluralism, tolerance of moral ambiguity, faith in education, and belief in civil rights, the rule of law, and due process. The historical decline in the importance of the supernatural and sacred. Modern societies have become increasingly secular, and tracing the extent of secularization is complex. Secularization can refer to levels of involvement with religious organizations (e.g., rates of church attendance), the social and material influence wielded by religious organizations, and the degree to which people hold religious beliefs.* See *rationalization.*

Segregation – the physical and social separation of categories of people. *For example, people's spatial and social separation based on ethnicity or race.*

Self (*George Herbert Mead*) – the capacity to be reflexive and take the role of others. *Part of a person's personality consists of self-awareness and self-image. A person's understanding and perception of their individuality.*

Self-consciousness – the individual's awareness of having a distinct social identity, a person separates from others. *Humans are not born with self-consciousness but acquire an awareness of self through early socialization.*

Self-employment – earning a living without working for a large organization.

Self-fulfilling prophecy – a belief or prediction about a person or situation that influences that person or situation, so the belief or prediction comes true. *The mere application of a label changes behavior and thus justifies that label. An expectation about an outcome helps bring it about.*

Self-identity – the ongoing process of self-development and definition of our identity through which we formulate a unique sense of ourselves and our relationship to the world around us.

Semi-peripheral country – often in the initial stages of industrialization that occupies an intermediate zone between core and peripheral countries. Semi-peripheral countries provide labor and raw materials to core countries, and they often manufacture and export goods that core countries no longer find profitable to produce themselves. *They may engage in some exploitation of peripheral countries. Countries that supply sources of labor and raw materials to the core industrial countries and the world economy but are not themselves fully industrialized.* See *core country* and *peripheral country.*

Semi-profession – an occupation that did not accord the status of a total profession. Semi-professionals lack highly specialized knowledge and skills, such as those needed to practice law or medicine, as well as the power, latitude on the job, and prestige of complete professionals; they lack compensation. *They are overwhelmingly employed by bureaucracies (although increasing numbers of professionals work in such organizations as well). Examples include teachers, social workers, nurses, and other occupations dominated by females, and this latter characteristic determines their status as semi-professions.*

Semiotics – studying signs and symbols, especially their meaning.

Serial monogamy – the process of contracting several exclusive sexual relationships in succession. *Rather than lifetime marriages, the dominant pattern in the West is serial monogamy: marriage, divorce, and remarriage.* See *monogamy*.

Service workers – a census classification of employees who provide labor related to cleaning, sales, daycare, entertainment, and other personal services.

Setting (*Goffman*) – where interaction takes place; one of the sign vehicles people use to present themselves to others, along with manner of interacting and appearance.

Settler colonization – a distinct type of colonization in which a new society of settlers replaces the current inhabitants of a colonized territory.

Sex – the biological distinction between females and males. *A classification by which individuals are defined as male or female (or intersex) based on genetics or physiological characteristics, increasingly seen as more complex.*

Sex ratio – the number of males for every hundred females in each population.

Sex role – gender-specific role behavior people learn from society.

Sex stratification – the ranking and differential reward system of the sexes.

Sexism – the view that one sex (typically men) is superior to the other, thereby justifying an unequal distribution of power between the two sexes. *Discrimination or prejudice against one sex based on perceived differences. The belief that one sex is innately superior.*

Sexual harassment – comments, gestures, or physical contact of a sexual nature that are deliberate, repeated, and unwelcome. *Making persistent unwanted sexual advances (physical or verbal) by one individual toward another within a relationship where the individuals have unequal power (such as an employer and employee). Unwanted sexual advances, remarks, or behavior by one person towards another persist even after apparent resistance.*

Sexual orientation – an individual's preference for sexual partners (e.g., same-sex, other sex, either sex, neither sex). *An individual's physical or romantic attraction to the opposite sex (heterosexual), to their sex (homosexual), or both sexes (bisexual). Research suggests that, regardless of sexual orientation, humans possess some degree of bisexuality. One's sexual or romantic attraction.*

Sexual revolution – the widespread change in sexual behavior and attitudes among men and women in the Western world during the twentieth century. The sexual revolution is most associated with the 1960s, although some claim it began in the 1920s.

Sexuality – an individual's gender identity, including sexual preferences, desires, and tastes. *A broad term referring to the sexual characteristics and behavior of humans.*

Sharing economy – an economic model in which private individuals rent out assets to others, typically on a peer-to-peer basis.

Sibling – a brother or sister.

Sick role – the patterns of behavior expected of one who is frequently sick. The assumption of this role often exempts a person from his or her usual role obligations. *This role's assignment to someone can disempower someone viewed as incapable of executing ordinary tasks and responsibilities.*

Sign vehicles (*Goffman*) – the mechanisms we use to present ourselves to others. Sign vehicles consist of setting, appearance, and manner of interacting. (*George Herbert Mead*) – individuals vital to developing our sense of self. *Significant others are those who have an essential influence or play a formative role in shaping the behavior of another.*

Significant other (*Charles Horton Cooley*) – a person whose opinions matter and who can influence another's thinking. *A person with whom one has an intimate relationship. Specific individuals that impact a person's life.*

Situational deviance – acts only defined as deviant in particular contexts.

Skilled worker – someone who is literate and has experience and expertise in specific production areas or on specific machines.

Slavery – social stratification in which others claim individuals as property. A stratification system in which one person owns another, usually for economic gain.

Snowball sampling (*research methods*) – a method of gathering a sample for research studies based on research participants recruiting acquaintances and friends.

Social action – behavior meaningful to the actor or to the observer.

Social action theory (*Max Weber*) – human behavior has a primary or advanced social action impacting communities. *Considers or is influenced by the actions of others.*

Social agency – an individual's ability to operate under free will and make their own choices; larger structures and norms often limit social agency.

Social behavior – expected, accepted behavior of individuals in a community that serves as functional communication.

Social capital (*Bourdieu*, 1985) – resources arising from social networks and relationships. *Social knowledge and connections enable people to accomplish goals and extend influence.*

Social categories – groups who may not interact but share social characteristics or statuses.

Social change – a modification or transformation in the way society is organized. *Alteration in the fundamental structures of a social group or society.*

Social class – a group's position in a social hierarchy based on prestige or property ownership. A socioeconomic category based on differences between groups of individuals that create differences in their life chances and power. *Dividing people into classes based on social and economic factors.*

Social construction – a theoretical perspective that explains most social behaviors as created and learned within a cultural, social, and historical context.

Social construction of reality – the process of socially creating definitions of situations to appear natural. *Theory suggests that life experiences and interactions with others shape how people present themselves.*

Social constructivist approach – focuses on how problems are '*constructed*' by society or how problems come to be recognized and thought of as problems.

Social contract – a theory of society and political authority founded on the consent of those governed or subordinated to the rules and laws of that society.

Social control – the patterned and systematic ways society guide and restrains individual behaviors so that people act in predictable and desirable ways. *The set of positive and negative sanctions that a group uses to bring individual members into compliance with its norms and values. How societies enforce social norms and reduce expressions of deviance. The ways a society devises to encourage conformity to norms.* See *sanction*.

Social control agents – regulate and enforce social control within an organization or sociocultural system. In society at large, this includes criminal justice and mental health systems.

Social Darwinism – an early and now largely discredited view of social evolution emphasizing the importance of "survival of the fittest" or the struggle between individuals, groups, or societies as the force driving development. *Social Darwinism became widely popular in the latter half of the nineteenth century and was often used to justify existing inequalities, especially those based on race.*

Social differentiation – the process through which different statuses develop within a group or a society.

Social disintegration – the process of a society losing coherence and declining over time. Durkheim attributed this to the weakening of the collective conscience caused by the increasing division of labor.

Social disorganization – the structural condition of society caused by rapid change in social institutions, norms, and values.

Social dynamics – analyses concerned with patterns and processes of social change. Contrast *social statics*.

Social dysfunction – disruptions of typical social life and expectations; remedying social dysfunction can positively reinforce social norms.

Social environment – the relationships of a sociocultural system with other societies.

Social evolution – theories of cumulative sociocultural change hold that human societies move from simple to complex forms of organization. *This theory was originally used by nineteenth-century scholars who sought to use evolutionary theory from biology to study the long-term development of societies.*

Social exclusion – the outcome of multiple deprivations that prevent individuals or groups from participating fully in the economic, social, and political life of the society in which they are located.

Social facts (*Emile Durkheim*) – 1. the aspects of social life that shape our actions. *Durkheim believed that social facts could be studied scientifically.* 2. the laws, morals, values, religious beliefs, customs, fashions, rituals, and all the cultural rules that govern social life. *Aspects of social structure, such as values or norms, exercise control over individual behavior, typically by influencing or eliciting specific actions.*

Social forces – the social structures and culture individuals face in a society. *The elements of society and social organizations influence individual human behavior.*

Social functions (*Bronislaw Malinowski and Robert K. Merton*) – theory that social systems have two functions: manifest functions are deliberate and planned, while latent functions are unplanned and incidental. *The consequences of any social pattern for the operation of society.*

Social group – a collection of individuals who interact systematically with one another. Two or more individuals who interact systematically with one another and share a high degree of common identity. *Social groups may range in size from dyads to large-scale societies. Groups may range from tiny associations to large-scale organizations or societies.*

Social identity – expectations and opinions others hold based on the groups or the characteristics ascribed. Has a complex interactive relationship with a person's self-identity. *Our understanding of who we are, who other people are, and, reciprocally, other people's understanding of themselves and others.*

Social inequality – unequal opportunities or rewards for people in different social positions.

Social institution – a central structural entity in a sociocultural system that addresses a basic need of the system. Social institutions involve fixed modes of behavior backed by strong norms and sanctions that tend to be followed by most members of society. *A major sphere of social life, or societal subsystem, organized to meet a basic human need. Patterns of beliefs and behaviors focused on meeting social needs. Building blocks of social structure that set and regulate social behavior; the central social institutions are family, government, education, religion, and economy.*

Social integration – the degree to which an individual feels connected to the other people in his or her group or community.

Social interaction – any form of social encounter between individuals. *How people behave concerning one another using language, gestures, and symbols. The process by which people act and react to others. Positive or negative exchanges between individuals reinforce the rules and systems of a society.*

Social issue – a problem produced by a society's institutional structure. Social issues affect many people but are often experienced and interpreted as individual problems. *Examples in modern Western society include divorce, poverty, and racial and ethnic discrimination.*

Social justice – the fair administration of laws without regard to ethnicity, sexual orientation, gender, religion, class, or characteristics.

Social learning theory – suggests that people learn through observation and imitation, even though they are not rewarded or punished for certain behaviors.

Social mobility – the movement from one status to another within a stratified society. Change in people's position in a social hierarchy. *Movement of individuals or groups between different socio-economic positions. Movement within the social hierarchy.*

Social movement – a group organized (often loosely) to achieve some social aim – typically to create or prevent social change. Collective attempts to further a common interest or secure a common goal through action outside established political institutions. *Social movements seek to bring about or block social change and typically exist in relations of conflict with organizations whose objectives and outlooks they frequently oppose. However, movements that successfully challenge power, once they become institutionalized, can develop into formal organizations.*

Social network – a set of interdependent relations between individuals. A web of social ties linking people who identify with one another.

Social order – a situation of social stability in which the norms or structures of a society are supported and maintained by its members. Contrast state of *disorder* or *chaos*.

Social organization – the pattern of relationships within a group or society.

Social patterns – repeated behaviors among members of the same society across time.

Social psychology – the scientific study of how individual behavior is socially influenced.

Social relations of production – the organization of economic life based on owning or not owning the means of production, purchasing, or selling labor power, and controlling or not controlling other people's labor power.

Social reproduction – the process that perpetuates characteristics of social structure over periods. See *agency of socialization.*

Social role – the expected behavior occupying a particular social position. *One's place in society includes that role's behavioral expectations, privileges, duties, and rights.*

Social self (*G. H. Mead*) – the basis of self-consciousness in individuals. The social self is the identity conferred upon an individual by the reactions of others. A person achieves self-consciousness by becoming aware of this social identity.

Social sciences – disciplines related to sociology that study human activity and communication, including psychology, anthropology, economics, and political science.

Social solidarity – the social ties that bind a group of people, such as kinship, shared location, and religion.

Social statics – analyses concerned with the present structure of societies or understanding the stability of current social orders. Contrast *social dynamics.*

Social stratification (or *stratification*) – structured inequalities between social groups regarding their access to material or symbolic rewards. The relatively permanent ranking of societal positions regarding unequal power, prestige, or privilege. *Structured inequalities in life chances between groups in society. These inequalities are fixed; individuals within each broad group have similar attitudes, beliefs, and backgrounds. While all societies involve some forms of stratification, vast differences in wealth and power arise only with the development of state-based systems. The most distinctive form of stratification in modern societies involves class divisions.*

Social structure – 1. recurrent and patterned relationships among individuals, organizations, nations, or other social units. 2. arrangement of institutions that define a society; social structures often undergo social change. *The pattern of human relationships formed by human groups and institutions within a society.*

Social systems – relationship networks of individuals in a society

Social trends – short-lived behavior shared by a larger society.

Socialism – a system under which resources and means of production are owned by society, rights to private property are limited, the good of the whole society is stressed more than individual profit, and the government maintains control of the economy.

Socialist feminism – the belief that women are treated as second-class citizens in patriarchal capitalist societies and that both the ownership of the means of production and women's social experience need to be transformed because the roots of women's oppression lie in the total economic system of capitalism. *Socialist feminists have criticized some socialists' gender-blind understanding of class.*

Socialist societies – when productive resources are owned and controlled by the state rather than by individuals.

Socialization – the process by which the individual learns the norms, values, and practices common to a particular social group. *The social processes through which children develop an awareness of social norms and values and achieve a distinct sense of self. The lifelong process through which humans develop an awareness of social norms and values and achieve a distinct sense of self. Preparing newcomers to become members of an existing social group by helping them learn appropriate attitudes and behaviors. The process whereby people learn to become competent group members.*

Societal reaction theory (or *labeling theory*) (*Howard Becker*) – an approach to studying deviance suggesting that people become 'deviant' because specific labels are attached to their behavior by political authorities and others. A social theory holds that society's reaction to specific behaviors significantly defines the self as deviant. People may become "deviant" because specific labels (e.g., thief, prostitute, gay person) are attached to their behavior by criminal justice authorities and others. The resulting treatment of the individual pushes them into performing the deviant role. *Deviance focuses on the process by which some people are labeled deviant by others (and thus take on deviant identities) rather than the nature of the behavior. Identity and behavior are influenced by how individuals are labeled or specific terms describing or categorizing them. Deviance and conformity result not so much from what people do but from how others respond to those actions; it highlights social responses to crime and deviance. Deviance is that which is so labeled.*

Society – a system of structured social relationships connecting people to a shared culture. Some societies, like *hunters and gatherers*, are tiny, numbering no more than a few dozen people. Others are vast, involving many millions (e.g., Chinese society has a population of more than a billion). *A collection of people with territory, interaction, and culture. People with a shared and distinct culture living in a defined territory feel unity and see themselves as distinct from other people. People share a sense of culture or interact within a shared space, and institutions bind them. Society is the complex patterns that shape social relationships.*

Society's rewards – the things a society holds in high esteem, such as wealth, power, and prestige.

Socio-economic status (SES) – a calculation based on a complex formula considering education, occupation, and income. *The combination of wealth, education, occupation, and living conditions define a person's or group's standing in society.*

Socio-economic stratification – social organization describing the degree to which people are organized into categories (or classes) based on economics (e.g., wealth or occupation).

Sociobiology – the scientific study of the biological basis for human behavior. *An approach that attempts to explain the social behavior of humans in terms of biological principles.*

Sociocultural materialism – a variant of cultural materialism that emphasizes the relationship between intensification, bureaucratization, and rationalization as well as feedback loops from structural and cultural elements to the material infrastructure of society. See *cultural materialism.*

Sociocultural system – material, structural, and cultural elements that make up the total system.

Socioeconomic status (SES) – a frequently used measure of class determined by a combination of income, occupational prestige, and education. *An index of social status considering a person's occupation, education, and income.*

Sociological imagination (*C. Wright Mills*) – 1. applying imaginative thought to asking and answering sociological questions. 2. the ability to anticipate the effects of social patterns and history on human behavior. An ability to see relationships or draw links between personal experience and the broader social context. Applying creative thought to asking and answering sociological questions. *Sociological imagination involves 'thinking oneself away' from the familiar routines of day-to-day life. The ability to understand how your own past relates to that of other people, as well as to history in general and societal structures in particular.*

Sociology – the study of human groups and societies, emphasizing the analysis of the industrialized world. Sociology is a group of social sciences, including anthropology, economics, political science, and human geography. *The divisions between the social sciences are unclear, and all share a specific range of common interests, concepts, and methods. The study of companionship; in other words, what makes up society, including culture, and its impact on social membership in different societies.*

Sociology of the body – focuses on how our bodies are affected by social influences. Health and illness, for instance, are determined by social and cultural influences.

Sociology of deviance – the branch of sociology concerned with the study of deviant behavior and with understanding why some behavior is identified as deviant.

Sociopath (or *psychopath*) – an anti-social personality disorder in which the individual lacks a conscience, engages in behavior with little consideration of the harm done to others, and experiences no feelings of guilt or remorse for the harm that he or she causes. *While psychopaths can mimic human emotions, they do not experience any genuine sense of a social bond with others.*

Solid waste – the accumulation of noxious material substances. See *depletion*, *environment*, and *intensification*.

Solidarity (*Durkheim*) – the internal forces of social cohesion. More generally, the left often uses a term to describe the political consciousness of an emerging class struggling against oppression - e.g., working-class solidarity.

Southern Theory (*Connell*) – social science theories with the perspective of the Global South. *Connell argues that Northern and urban perspectives have dominated sociology.*

Sovereign power (*Foucault*) – power characteristic of medieval and feudal societies in which a political leader attempts to maintain social control via public displays of force and authority.

Sovereignty – the authority a state claims to maintain a legal system, use coercive power to secure obedience, and maintain its independence from other states.

Specialization – the process by which people concentrate on a small part of the whole enterprise and define their occupations accordingly. *For example, more than thirty areas of specialization can be identified in sociology.*

Species – a distinct population of individuals with definitive biological characteristics capable of interbreeding with each other but not with other populations.

Split labor market. – when one group of laborers (usually defined by race, sex, or ethnicity) is routinely paid less than others.

Spoiled identity (*Goffman*) – an identity permanently ruined because of a severe stigma.

Sponsored mobility – a pattern in which certain children are selected at an early age for academic and university education and are thus helped to achieve higher social status.

Sport – a game in which the outcome is affected by physical skill.

Staff job (*organizations*) – an advisory or administrative job that supports the organization's manufacturing, production, selling, or other primary activities.

Stage theory – suggests that nations go through various systematic stages of development.

Standing army – a full-time professional army.

Standpoint theory – marginalized groups have a unique, valuable perspective on social phenomena, particularly marginalization and oppression. *Standpoint theorists argue that groups have fundamentally different experiences and perspectives of the world, and excluding certain groups creates biased knowledge.*

State – a political community with clearly defined borders and a single governing body that has the power to police, defend and create laws over that territory. *The institutionalized, legal organization of power within territorial limits. A political apparatus (government institutions, plus civil service officials) ruling over a given territory, with authority backed by law and the ability to use force.*

State capitalism – a system under which resources and means of production are privately owned but closely monitored and regulated by the government.

State sector – the economic sector controlled by local, state, or federal governments supplying goods and services directly to that state.

State society – possesses a formal apparatus of government.

State terrorism – the use of torture, death squads, and disappearances by political states to intimidate citizens.

Stateless society – lacks formal institutions of government.

Statics – social equilibrium or the absence of change.

Status (*Weber*) – social position within society. Status may refer to the social honor or prestige that other members of a society accord a particular individual or group. *Positive or negative estimations of honor determine social ranks. A socially defined position with prescribed rights, obligations, and expected behaviors. The social honor or prestige accorded to a person or a particular group by other members of a society. The position that a person occupies in a particular setting.*

Status attainment – the process through which people arrive at a given position within a stratified system.

Status-attainment model – a view of social mobility suggests the importance of the father's education, the father's occupation, the son's education, and the son's first job for a man's adult status. (Early research was based only on men.)

Status group – people sharing a social identity based on similar values and lifestyles.

Status inconsistency (*Gerhard Lenski*) – when an individual holds two status positions of different prestige. *Any inconsistency between various statuses.*

Status offense – an act illegal for juveniles but not for adults (such as running away from home or engaging in sexual activities).

Status quo – the existing state: the way things currently exist.

Status set – all statuses held by an individual at a given time. A group's social status.

Status symbol – a sign or symbol we wear or carry that represents a particular status.

Stepfamily (or *blended family*) – consisting of two adults, both with children from previous relationships, plus their children.

Stereotype – a rigid and inflexible image of the characteristics of a group. Stereotypes attribute these characteristics to all individuals belonging to that group. A generalized belief about a group, indiscriminately applied to group members. A fixed and inflexible characterization of a group. *An assumption made about a person or a group, often based on incorrect or incomplete information. Attitudes exaggerate generalized ideas and feelings about specific social groups, both positive and negative.*

Stigma (*Goffman*) – any physical or social characteristic believed to be demeaning. A symbol (or a negative social label) of disgrace that affects a person's social identity. *An attribute or behavior that is socially undesirable or causing social rejection. A trait that causes a loss of prestige in the eyes of others.*

Stigmatization – the process of spoiling a person's identity by labeling him or her negatively.

Strain theory (*Robert Merton, criminology*) – crime occurs when individuals use illegitimate means to obtain socially valued goals or ends. People experience strain and frustration when prevented from achieving culturally approved goals through institutionalized means.

Stratification (or *social stratification*) – a societal system in which there is an unequal distribution of society's rewards, and people are arranged hierarchically into layers according to how many of society's rewards they possess. *Structured inequalities in life chances between groups in society. These inequalities are fixed; individuals within each broad group have similar attitudes, beliefs, and backgrounds. While all societies involve stratification, vast differences in wealth and power arise only with the development of state-based systems. The most distinctive form of stratification in modern societies involves class divisions.*

Straw man – an argument based on misrepresentation of an opponent's position. To "attack a straw man" is to create the illusion of having refuted a proposition by replacing it with a superficially similar proposition (the "straw man") and then refuting it without ever having dealt with the original position.

Strength of weak ties (*Granovetter*) – the importance of social networks between acquaintances.

Strike – a stoppage of work/withdrawal of labor by a group of workers for specific ends. A temporary work stoppage by a group of employees.

Structural change – society's demographic, economic, and rank-order changes.

Structural-functional perspective (*Talcott Parsons*) – a central theoretical perspective focusing on how parts of society fit or adjust to maintain the equilibrium of the whole.

Structural functionalism (or *functionalism, Talcott Parsons*) – analyses societies as social systems in which various social institutions perform specific functions, ensuring the system's smooth operation. *Theory that society moves as a large, interconnected machine and that if the society is functioning, everyone benefits (conversely, if part of society is dysfunctional, the rest of society cannot function correctly)*

Structural functionalist theory – a sociological view of society as a complex unit of interrelated parts. Sociologists who apply this theory study social structure and social function.

Structural strain theory (or *anomie theory, Robert Merton's theory of deviance*) – forms of deviance are caused by a disjunction between society's goals and the approved means to achieve those goals. Deviance and crime occur when there is an acute gap between cultural norms and goals and socially structured opportunities for individuals to achieve those goals.

Structural unemployment – related to changes in the composition of the industries that make up an economy. This results in workers whose skills and training have become obsolete and who have little chance of finding employment in a comparably paying job.

Structure (*sociology*) – all human institutions, groups, and organizations.

Structuration – the two-way process by which we shape our social world through our actions but are reshaped by society.

Structure – social factors, recurring patterns, and institutional forms constraining and enabling our actions (or agency).

Subaltern – the subjected or oppressed groups in societies; those subordinate to dominant or elite groups.

Subaltern studies group – South Asian scholars, formed at the University of Sussex in 1970–80, studied post-colonial societies and the representation of *subaltern* groups (i.e., subordination based on class, caste, gender, race, language, or culture).

Subculture – a distinguishable group that shares several features with the dominant culture within which it exists and has unique features such as language, customs, or values. *A cultural group within a larger culture typically adopts values, ideas, and cultural practices at odds with those of the larger culture. Any population segment distinguishable from the broader society by its cultural pattern. A group that espouses a way of living different from the dominant culture.*

Subjective knowledge – how much an individual thinks he/she knows about something versus how much they actually know (i.e., *objective knowledge*). Also known as perceived or self-assessed knowledge.

Subjective meanings – the values and interpretations individuals place on their life situations and experiences; may vary from person to person.

Subjective social class – a person's perception of his or her class position.

Substantive rationality (*Weber*) – rationality exercised within a context of human values, traditions, and emotions. See *formal rationality*.

Suburb – a small community within an urban area, including a central city.

Suburbanization – the development of housing areas outside cities' political boundaries.

Suffrage – the right to vote. Members of women's organizations, formed around the turn of the 20th century in many countries, campaigned for this right from women, some using militant action. *These groups are central to First-wave feminism.*

Sui generis [Latin, *in a class by itself*] – of its kind, unique, or in a class of its own.

Sunbelt – the area south of the 37th parallel in the U.S., including Clark County in Nevada.

Super diverse world – cultural diversity is increasing in societies, both in the number of ethnic groups within societies but also in the form of diversity in ethnic groups themselves.

Superego (or *conscience*) (*Freudian theory*) – the part of the mind that encourages conformity to societal norms and values. The part of the self that reflects moral and social standards internalized by the individual. *Human personality upholding societal norms.*

Superstructure (*sociocultural materialism*) (*Marxism*) – the general ideals, norms, and values of a society. Marxist thought holds that the base determines the superstructure. *The symbolic universe (i.e., shared meanings, ideas, beliefs, values, and ideologies) that people associate with the physical and social world. Superstructure can be divided into cultural and mental components.* See *cultural superstructure* and *mental superstructure*.

Surplus value (*Marxism*) – the value of an individual's labor power is 'left over' when an employer has repaid the cost involved in hiring a worker. The difference between the amount of money a product is sold for and the amount the product costs to make. Surplus value is considered 'created' by the worker and 'appropriated' or taken by the capitalist. The value of an individual's labor power (calculated by the value the labor contributes to the product minus the amount of money paid to the worker by the capitalist). The conventional name for this difference is *profit*. Thus, the capitalist system is based on "expropriating" surplus value (or stealing labor) from workers.

Surveillance – the monitoring of people's activities to ensure compliant behavior. Modern surveillance techniques include video cameras, microphones, and a broad range of electronic surveillance methods whereby information about people can be stored, retrieved, and shared.

Survey (*research methods*) – a method of sociological research that usually involves the administration of questionnaires to a population being studied and the statistical analysis of their replies to find patterns or regularities. *A collection of data carried out systematically, often using a questionnaire or a series of interviews.*

Survival circuits – dynamic networks of people and money supporting the economies of Majority World countries. Survival circuits often involve women, who, as low-wage migrant workers, send remittances back to their home countries.

Sustainable development – the notion that economic growth should proceed only as far as natural resources are recycled rather than depleted, biodiversity is maintained, and clean air, water, and land are protected.

Sweatshop – a derogatory term for a factory or shop where employees work long hours for low pay under poor conditions. A workplace that violates safety standards, labor laws, or worker compensation. Such shops now thrive in many peripheral countries.

Symbol – any object or sign that evokes a shared social response. *An item meaningfully representing another (e.g., a flag representing a nation).*

Symbolic interaction (*sociology*) – a theoretical approach that focuses on social reality as constructed through the daily interaction of individuals and strongly emphasizes the role of symbols (gestures, signs, and language) as core elements of this interaction. Using symbols to exchange meaning with others (communication) seen by some sociologists as the foundation of society. *Relies on shared symbols such as language.*

Symbolic interactionism (*George Herbert Mead*) – an interpretive perspective that individuals learn meanings through interaction with others and then organize their lives around these socially created meanings. Focuses on creating meaning through interpersonal communication as the foundation for social identity and social patterns. A theoretical approach in sociology developed by G. H. Mead strongly emphasizes the role of symbols and language as core elements of all human interaction. *A theoretical perspective through which scholars examine the relationship of individuals within their society by studying their communication (language and symbols). A sociological paradigm that dictates how members of a society interact with each other, specifically with mutually agreed–upon gestures and symbols (e.g., stopping at a stop sign, waving hello, smiling).*

Symbolic interactionist perspective – a sociological framework that views society as a product of the everyday social interactions of individuals.

Symbolic violence (*Bourdieu*) – the process through which dominated groups are excluded from social spaces and accept their lower social position as natural, legitimate, or deserved.

Synthesis – combining elements from separate sources to produce a coherent whole. *Much of macro social theory consists of the synthesis of the ideas and insights of many theorists.*

Systemic discrimination – when societal discrimination (e.g., racism, sexism, homophobia) permeates a society's social structure, making social behaviors inherently discriminatory.

T

Taboo – a sociocultural prohibition on a particular action, person, place, animal, or plant. A norm so firmly held by society that its violation brings extreme disgust. *Public knowledge of the violation of a taboo often results in severe sanctions. A strongly prohibited social practice, the most potent social norm.*

Taylorism (or *scientific management*) (*Frederick Winslow Taylor*) – a set of ideas (i.e., *scientific management*) when productivity could be immensely increased by separating industrial tasks into a series of simple operations precisely timed and optimally coordinated.

Technical specialist – an individual with specialized knowledge in demand in specific fields.

Technological determinism – the belief that technological development shapes social life in relatively fixed ways.

Technology – the application of logic, reason, and prior knowledge to the problem of how to exploit raw materials available in the natural environment and, by extension, how to use products manufactured from these raw materials to create more sophisticated products. *Social technologies employ the same thought processes in addressing problems of human organization. Technology involves creating material instruments (such as machines) used in human interaction with nature and social instruments (such as bureaucracy) used in human organization. The application of knowledge to production from the material world. The practical applications of scientific knowledge.* See *rationalization*.

Telecommunications – communication of information, sounds, or images at a distance through a technological medium.

Tension release theory – sports serve as a social safety valve, allowing individuals to vent seething aggressions.

Terrorism – the use of violence or the threat of violence to achieve political, social, or economic ends. Although many restrict the term to only those acts committed by non-governmental groups, state terrorism is a significant factor in the social world. *An attack on people designed to frighten society and force it to meet the terrorists' demands. Politically motivated violent attacks on civilians by individuals or groups.*

Tertiary economic sector – offering services to individuals and businesses.

Tertiary sector – part of an economy that provides services (e.g., nursing care, psychological counseling) engaged in by private and government entities.

Theism – a belief in a god or gods.

Theoretical approach – a set of guiding ideas.

Theory – a general principle summary statement explaining regularly observed events. *A system of orienting ideas, concepts, and relationships that organize the observable world.*

Theories – general ideas, hypotheses, or assumptions about the social world. Theories offer potential answers to questions we have about social phenomena. *An attempt to identify general properties that explain regularly observed events. A proposed explanation*

Theory X (*organizational behavior*) – people hate their jobs, want to avoid responsibility, resist change, and do not care about organizational needs.

Theory Y (*organizational behavior*) – people desire to work, be creative, and take responsibility for their jobs and the organization.

Theory Z (*organizational behavior*) – organizational culture valuing long-term employment, trust, and close personal relationships between workers and managers.

Third space (*Bhabha*) – abstract social spaces 'between' recognized groups or identities (i.e., between distinct cultures), where new practices, ideas, and identities can emerge.

Third-wave feminism – a social movement beginning in the 1990s as a reaction against second-wave feminism. Third-wave feminism criticized second-wave feminism for neglecting to address the relationship between gender inequality and other forms of inequality, such as race and class.

Third World – the less developed societies, in which industrial production is either virtually non-existent or only developed to a limited degree. *Most of the world's population lives in Third World countries. Formerly used to refer to countries that did not number among the industrialized nations of the First World and were not aligned with the Soviet bloc (or Second World). Because these countries were poor, relatively unindustrialized nations, the term "Third World" came to designate the worlds underprivileged.* See *Global South, First World*, and *Second World*.

Third-world feminism – focuses on women's experience in the Third World.

Thomas Theorem (*W. I. Thomas*) – "if a person perceives a situation as real, it is real in its consequences."

Tone policing – discursive practice when members of majority groups focus on the language and perceived emotion of marginalized or underrepresented groups during discussions of inequality rather than the content, lived experiences, and knowledge of minorities or disempowered groups.

Total fertility rate – an estimate of the average number of children born to each woman over her reproductive life if current age-specific birth rates remained constant.

Total institution (*Erving Goffman*) – an organization where individuals are isolated for extended periods as their lives are controlled and regulated by the organization's administration. A highly standardized institution where authority figures determine and monitor all the residents' actions. *A place where people spend 24 hours every day for an extended part of their lives, cut off from the rest of society and tightly controlled by the people in charge. A term popularized by Erving Goffman to refer to facilities such as asylums, prisons, and monasteries that impose on their residents a forcibly regulated system of existence in complete isolation from the outside world. Examples include prisons, mental hospitals, or army boot camps.* See *resocialization*.

Total war – warfare in which all the resources of the modern state are committed, including a large proportion of the population (both directly and indirectly), all the armed forces, and a large proportion of the industrial sector of society. See *industrialization of war*.

Totalitarianism – a form of government in which an authoritarian government attempts to regulate every aspect of socio-cultural life. A political system under which the government maintains tight control over citizens' lives. *Autocracy using state power to control and regulate all phases of life.*

Totem (*Durkheim*) – a symbol associated with a group given sacred significance and often used as an identifying insignia.

Totemism – a system of religious belief studied by attributes sacred qualities to a particular animal or plant. *Religious belief attributes divine properties to a particular animal or plant.*

Tournament selection – an educational pattern in which a continual selection process serves to weed out candidates; winners move on to the next selection round, and losers are eliminated from the competition.

Tracking – grouping students in educational institutions based on test scores predicting their abilities. *Grouping students by ability, curriculum, or both.*

Trading network – a pattern of economic exchange between companies or countries.

Traditional action (*Weber*) – one of four action types motivated by custom or tradition. See *affective action, Wertrational*, and *Zweckrational*.

Traditional authority (*Weber's power theory*) – based on long-established custom or tradition, rests on well-established cultural patterns. See *charismatic authority* and *rational-legal authority*.

Traditional state – a society in which the production base is agriculture or the herding of animals. See *agrarian society* and *herding society*.

Transformative movement – aims to produce significant social change in a society.

Transitional class (*Karl Marx*) – an economic class in which earlier relations of production linger in the beginning stages of new relations of production. *Examples include peasants or landowners in a feudal system that has become capitalist.*

Transnational capitalist class – a global social class controlling supranational corporations, organizations, and such institutions.

Transnational corporation – see *multinational corporation*.

Triad (*Georg Simmel*) – a group composed of three people. Such groups tend to separate into a dyad against one (i.e., *triadic separation*).

Tribe – a social group organized based on clan and kinship whose members share a common culture and language. *Today, tribal organizations typically function outside state structures (although the state may nominally recognize their existence).*

Tribute – a regular payment of money or goods from a subjugated nation-state to the conqueror nation. *Tribute can buy physical protection, or it can serve to guarantee some measure of freedom (as it prevents the subjugated from being enslaved).*

U

Unconscious (*Freud*) – desires, motives, and ideas unavailable to a person's conscious mind. Experiences that become too difficult to confront and so become hidden from the surface workings of life.

Underclass – individuals in mature industrial societies situated at the bottom of the class system who have been systematically excluded from participation in economic life. *The underclass is typically composed of people from ethnic or minority groups. A group under the class structure that is economically, politically, and socially marginalized and excluded.*

Underdevelopment – a concept used in social science to describe the economic state of societies that were exploited or previously colonized by Western countries. Underdevelopment suggests a process through which powerful, wealthy states actively exploit the poor and less powerful.

Underemployment – employment at a job below one's skill or educational level. Hiring people in jobs not customarily filled by individuals with relatively high experience or education levels.

Unemployment rate – a government measure for those not working but actively seeking work.

Underground economy – exchanges of goods and services that occur outside the arena of the ordinary, regulated economy and, therefore, escape official record keeping. *Economic activity generates unreported income to the government as required by law.*

Unemployment rates – measure the proportion of people who are 'economically active' and available for work but cannot get a paid job. *A person who is 'out of work' is not necessarily unemployed in the sense of having nothing to do. Homemakers, for instance, do not receive any pay, but they usually work very hard.*

Unilinear evolution – a discredited view of social evolution according to which all societies pass through the same stages of development. *It is often invoked as a straw man in arguments that seek to discredit newer, more sophisticated theories of social evolution.*

Unintended consequence – a significant effect of social action on the total sociocultural system (or other parts of that system) was neither intended nor foreseen by the participants. *Robert K. Merton developed the concepts of "latent function," "manifest function," and "dysfunction" to analyze these unintended consequences more precisely.*

Union – a social organization set up to represent the worker's interests in the workplace and broader society.

Unit of analysis – what is being studied in social research.

Upper class – a social class that encompasses the most affluent members of society, especially those immensely wealthy, have a high social standing and exert significant financial and political influence. *Broadly composed of the more affluent members of society, especially those who have inherited wealth, own large businesses, or hold stocks and bonds. Highest social group comprises people with inherited wealth and a recognizable family name.*

Urban ecology – studying links between cities' physical and social dimensions. *An urban life analysis examining the relationship between the city and its physical surroundings. Urban ecology is based on an analogy with adjusting plants and organisms to their physical environment.*

Urban renewal – governmental programs encouraging the renovation of deteriorating city neighborhoods through the renovation or destruction of old buildings and the construction of new ones. *Reviving deteriorating neighborhoods by recycling land and existing buildings, improving the urban environment, managing local areas better with the participation of local citizens, and using public funds to regenerate the area and attract further private investment.*

Urbanism (*Louis Wirth*) – 1. denotes distinctive characteristics of urban social life, such as impersonality. 2. the extent to which a community has the characteristics of city life.

Urbanization – the growth of cities. Increasing concentration of people from rural areas into cities. *The development of towns and cities, the concentration of humanity in cities. Process by which most of the population comes to live within commuting distance of a major city.*

Utilitarian organization –a group organized around a specific purpose, such as making money or giving charity.

V

Validity – the quality of measuring what one intends. The degree to which the measurement of a variable reflects the intended concept. *For example, the validity of IQ tests in measuring intelligence is questioned by many social scientists.*

Value-added theory – suggests that many instances of collective behavior represent efforts to change the social environment.

Values – firmly held general ideas that people share about what is good and evil, desirable, or undesirable; values provide yardsticks for judging specific acts and goals. *Culturally defined standards by which people assess desirability, goodness, and beauty and serve as broad guidelines for social living. Ideas or judgments about the kind of society in which people want to live or what constitutes a good society can guide action. A culturally approved belief about what is right or wrong, desirable, or undesirable.*

Values – culturally defined standards people or groups hold about what is desirable, proper, beautiful, exemplary, or bad. *Values serve as broad guidelines for social life.*

Variable – a characteristic that varies in magnitude along which an object, individual, or group may be categorized. Aa logical set of attributes with different degrees of magnitude or categories. *For example, age is a variable on which people can be classified according to the number of years they have lived. A concept whose value changes. A dimension along which an object, individual, or group may be categorized (e.g., income or height), allowing specific comparisons with others or over time. Examples include income and age.*

Verstehen [German, *deep understanding*] – understanding behavior on an emotional level. Understand social behavior in terms of the motives individuals bring to it. *German for perceiving and understanding the nature and significance of a phenomenon and grasping or comprehending the meaning intended or expressed by another. Weber used the term to refer to the social scientist's attempt to understand the intention and the context of human action.*

Vertical integration – a business organization to control the business environment by assuming control of one or more of its resources or business outlets.

Vertical mobility – the movement upward or downward in social status. *Movement up or down a hierarchy of positions in a social stratification.* See *stratification.*

Vested interest – an expectation of private gain that often underlies the expressed interest in a public issue.

Victimless crime – violation of law in which no person aside from the offender is directly victimized. Crimes in which laws are violated, but no identifiable victim exists. *Examples include using illegal drugs or gambling illegally.*

Virtual community – Internet-based groups rooted in long-lasting public discussions that contain sufficient human feeling to constitute personal relationships in cyberspace.

Vital statistics – statistical information about births, deaths, marriages, immigration, and other population characteristics.

Vocation (or *calling*) – employment or occupation someone is emotionally or morally drawn towards or to which they are exceptionally resolute, qualified, or well suited.

Voluntarism – believing people have free will to choose actions and behaviors. Contrast *determinism.*

Voluntaristic theories – emphasizes *voluntarism.*

Voluntary association – a group in which members are united by pursuing a common goal.

Voluntary organization (or *non-profit organization*) – an association or organization formed to further a purpose of importance to its members rather than primarily to earn a profit.

W

War – armed conflict between nations or societies.

Waves of globalization – globalization has progressed through several distinct periods of activity rather than one continuous process.

Wealth – income from investments, ownership of productive assets, salaries, bonuses, shares, and property. *Accumulated money and material possessions controlled by an individual, group, or organization. The total value (minus debts) of what is owned.*

Weberian approach (*Max Weber*) – the views held by conflict theorists stressing the significance of conflict in social life, especially conflict among status groups based on occupation, ethnic background, or religion.

Welfare – government aid (e.g., services and money) to people experiencing poverty. Government aid to the upper and middle classes. *This aid is often disguised as tax incentives (e.g., home mortgage interest deduction) or subsidized services (e.g., higher education).*

Welfare capitalism – a system that features a market-based economy coupled with an extensive social welfare system that includes free health care and education for all citizens.

Welfare state – a political system that provides a wide range of welfare benefits for citizens. *A government system providing human services for citizens.*

Wertrational – value-based action concerning a goal; one of Weber's four action types. The value may reflect an individual's ethical, religious, or philosophical convictions or be perceived because of a holistic or long-term way of thinking. *While the value-based goal is not rationally chosen, the means used to attain the goal are rational.* See *affective action, traditional action*, and *Zweckrational*.

White-collar –non-manual occupations such as administrative or professional jobs. The growth of bureaucracy has brought with it a proliferation of white-collar occupations. *C. Wright Mills wrote extensively about this class of worker, arguing that because those who hold white-collar jobs are dependent on bureaucratic organizations for their livelihood and because even relatively minor personal traits can help or hinder the smooth functioning of such organizations, these workers must sell not only their time and skills but their personalities. In this way, white-collar jobs profoundly impact the values, outlook, and social behavior of those who occupy these positions.*

White-collar crime (or *middle-class workers*) – illegal activities by those in white-collar (or professional) jobs. *Illegal acts committed by "respectable" individuals, often while practicing their occupations. A nonviolent crime the capitalist class commits during their occupations. Criminal activities carried out by white-collar or professional workers during their jobs. The tendency of middle-class men to wear white shirts to work. For example, embezzling money or stealing computer time.*

White ethnics – Caucasians that value and preserve aspects of their ethnic heritage.

Will – an *id*-like nature focused on the individual satisfaction of all wants and desires; the first and "lower" part of Durkheim's dual conception of human nature. *Centered on the body, these egoistic drives and desires recognize no interests but those of the individual actor, pushing the individual to satisfy all wants and desires even at the expense of the will of others. The will knows no boundaries and is a "tyranny of passions imposed by nature"; it is the root of all human evil and the source of immorality.*

Working class – a social class of industrial societies broadly composed of people involved in manual occupations. *These jobs are unskilled and poorly paid, providing few benefits and little job security. People who sell their labor to a higher class. They may have had vocational or technical training and have jobs such as electricians or factory workers.*

Working poor – people whose work leaves them vulnerable to falling below poverty.

World economy – a single division of labor that spans multiple cultures. Unlike a world empire, a world economy does not have a unified political system. *Capitalism, according to Immanuel Wallerstein, is a world economy.*

World-empire – in world-systems theory, multiple political units are brought to heel under a centralized political force that extracts surplus, or "tribute," from the subjugated using military domination. *Such systems are unstable, partly due to the expense of maintaining the necessary administrative apparatus and military force and partly due to resistance from the oppressed.*

World-systems (*Immanuel Wallerstein*) – theory emphasizes the interconnections among countries based on the expansion of a capitalist world economy. Examines patterns of inequality in the global economy. *Analyzes societies regarding their position within global economic systems. According to Wallerstein, the capitalist world system now determines the relationships among nation-states. The economy of core countries, semi-peripheral countries, and peripheral countries. As societies industrialized, capitalism became the dominant economic system, leading to the globalization of capitalism. World systems theory divides the world into core, semi-periphery, and periphery countries, arguing that the core countries exploit and dominate others for their gain.*

World systems analysis – stresses understanding national behavior regarding historical and contemporary relationships among nations and societies.

X

Xenophobia – the fear or hatred of foreigners.

Y

Youth culture – the specific cultural attributes many exhibit in any given period. *Youth culture involves behavioral norms, dress codes, language use, and other aspects, many of which tend to differ from the adult culture of the time.*

Zero population growth (ZPG) – occurs when the population of a nation or the world remains stable from one year to the next. *Population stability achieved when each woman has no more than two children.*

Zweckrational – rational action concerning a goal; one of Weber's four action types. The term refers to straightforward means-ends calculations. See *affective action, traditional action, rationalization,* and *Wertrational.*

CLEP study aids by Sterling Test Prep

Biology Review

Biology Practice Questions

Chemistry Review

Chemistry Practice Questions

Introductory Psychology

Introductory Sociology

American Government

History of the United States I

History of the United States II

Western Civilization I

Western Civilization II

Visit our Amazon store

Made in United States
Cleveland, OH
07 June 2025

17570043R00223